Crossing the Scriptures

A Starter Course for New Believers
A Dessert for Long-time Believers
A Buffet for All Christians

By Debra Chapoton

Copyright 2011 by Debra Chapoton
Available in print: ISBN-13:978-1461123972

All Bible quotations unless otherwise noted are from the New International Version (NIV) copyright 1973, 1978, 1984 and 2011 by Biblica.
All bold, underlined and italic prints are the author's.

This book is dedicated to the faithful members of our Bible Study group at Topinabee Community Church and especially to my husband, Paul Chapoton, who never missed a class.

Contents:

Chapter 1	Aleph	10
Chapter 2	Bet	24
Chapter 3	Gimel	33
Chapter 4	Dalet	41
Chapter 5	Hey	52
Chapter 6	Vav	61
Chapter 7	Zayin	69
Chapter 8	Het	79
Chapter 9	Tet	90
Chapter 10	Yod	100
Chapter 11	Kaph	110
Chapter 12	Lamed	122
Chapter 13	Mem	128
Chapter 14	Nun	136
Chapter 15	Samek	151
Chapter 16	Ayin	162
Chapter 17	Pey	174
Chapter 18	Tzaddi	187
Chapter 19	Quph	202
Chapter 20	Resh	214
Chapter 21	Shin	228
Chapter 22	Tav	245

Forward

I've heard many people say that the Old Testament is just a lot of bloodshed and that the picture of God that it presents is one of a vengeful tyrannical God. Many people think that the New Testament is a mixture of fact and fantasy. I believe that the whole Bible is the inspired Word of God. Everything in it is true. I think that some translations are better than others. I think that one must **study** the book the way you would study any other subject and always refer back to the original text. (Exactly why I decided to learn Hebrew.) God is not tyrannical and vengeful but rather loving and just.

As far as the Old Testament being blood and vengeance – I, too, was often repelled and confused by the stories and histories of the Israelites. I've read the Bible cover to cover a few times and I've read all of the books many times over out of order. Finally I had an "aha" moment when it all fell into place quite simply. The Old Testament is 39 books that tell of mankind vacillating between worshiping and obeying God and then turning away from Him and being idolatrous and immoral. Man's behavior requires judgment. The New Testament is 27 books declaring a message of hope: Christ has taken on our punishment (death) and paid for our sins. If we accept that he has done this, then hooray, we get out of the punishment, but if we don't accept it then we're on our own and the judgment is eternal separation from God, i.e. hell.

Back to the blood and idolatry – the Old Testament is made up of 39 books that can be categorized as follows:

5 books of the Law (Genesis, Exodus, Leviticus, Numbers, Deuteronomy)
12 books of Old Testament History (Joshua through Esther)
5 books of Wisdom (Job, Psalms, Proverbs, Ecclesiastes, Song of Songs)
5 books of Major Prophets (Isaiah, Jeremiah, Lamentations, Ezekiel, Daniel)
12 books of Minor Prophets (Hosea through Malachi)

Throughout these books God's plan unfolds. First we have the covenants He made with Adam and Noah and Abraham. We watch the Israelites follow God, turn to idols, turn back to God, fall away again, over and over. The miracles and love are abundant and yet they keep being "adulterous" so to speak. From the perspective of the Jews there are two kinds of people: Jews and Gentiles. And I think that this is also God's perspective. It's like you have two children, your firstborn and your second born. The Jews are God's firstborn, but the Gentiles are in the family, too, and the promises and inheritance are for the Gentiles as well.

The first 5 books give us the history of man from Adam on and the formation of Israel as God's chosen people (and yes, Adam and Eve were real, not myths, and the Jews recounted their genealogies and named names all the way back to them). These books tell us of all of the laws for living and how to make offerings to God, peace offerings, sin offerings, grain offerings, etc. We find the 10 commandments in Exodus and Deuteronomy. God **does** get angry with man when he disobeys and there **are** consequences. He is a firm and fair parent.

The 12 books of Old Testament History record the events after the Jews entered the Promised Land. We find the rise and fall of David's kingdom, the Babylonian exile and the return.

The 5 books of Wisdom are meditative and prayerful and poetic. There are several chapters in Psalms, Proverbs and Lamentations that were written as acrostics, that is, each verse (or series of verses) begins with the next consecutive letter of the Hebrew alphabet. There are 22 letters so it's easy to see the pattern when a chapter has 22 (or 66) verses. Of course the Bible wasn't written with the verse numbers, but you can see the poetry of verses in the original. Smack dab in the middle of the Bible you will find Psalm 119, the longest chapter of the Bible. There are 176 verses (8 x 22) so the first 8 verses each start with the first letter of the Hebrew alphabet, the next 8 with the second letter and so on. Some people think these are hidden codes. I think they are not hidden at all, but quite obvious. God in his infinite intelligence has woven his word together in an intricate pattern that is fascinating and awesome. (For further amazement and inspiration read *The Bible Wheel* by Richard Amiel McGough or go to biblewheel.com.) This is what really got me interested in learning Hebrew.

The 5 books of the Major Prophets are filled with prophecies, naturally. Isaiah is like a mini-bible in that it has 66 chapters divided in the same way as the Bible: 39 chapters of idolatry and disobedience, then 27 chapters of hope and redemption. The New Testament quotes Isaiah more than any other prophet, most likely because it has the greatest OT revelations of Christ (read chapters 40 and 53 especially). Lamentations is not prophetical, but it is the eyewitness account of the destruction of the Temple by Jeremiah who prophesied that it would happen and that they would be exiled 70 years (exactly right on).

The 12 books of the Minor Prophets continue the old, old story: prophets say repent but people turn away and God judges, people return to worship for a time, they receive blessings then fall off again, time for another prophet . . .

There are hundreds of prophecies throughout that tell of a coming Messiah. Most of the Scriptural requirements for what he will do and what will happen during His reign can be found in Isaiah. Hundreds of prophecies were fulfilled with Jesus' first coming and the rest will be fulfilled at His second coming. Some prophecies are so precise that they are impossible to ignore.

Now let's look at the New Testament. These 27 books can be divided as 5 NT History books (the 4 Gospels about Christ and the Acts of the Apostles) and 22 Epistles (letters written by Paul, James, Peter, John and Jude).

Why are there 4 Gospel accounts and is there a reason for their differences? Four witnesses give us a deeper understanding of the events as well as individual perspectives. Different viewpoints would be expected. I especially liked learning how parallel accounts reveal specific key links to the alphabetic verses. For example: Matthew matches up to the 18th Hebrew letter (tzaddi) which is the root for righteous or righteousness. Compare Matthew 5:6 (Blessed are they which do hunger and thirst after **righteousness**, for they shall be filled) to Luke 6:21 (Blessed are ye that hunger now, for ye shall be filled). In 6 other comparisons between Matthew and Luke you find the same thing (Mt. 5:10 – Luke 6:22, Mt. 6:33 – Luke 12:31, Mt. 10:40 – Luke 9:48, Mt. 13:17 – Luke 10:24, Mt. 23:35 – Luke 11:50, and Mt. 23:29 – Luke 11:47). The Gospel of Mark matches up to the 19th Hebrew letter (quph) which starts the word for swift. In comparing Mark's accounts of the casting out of the demon, five thousand fed, healings at Gennesaret, the boy healed of being deaf and mute and the question asked of Jesus of how to inherit eternal life with the accounts in Matthew and Luke of the same events, Mark's accounts always include **running**. Luke's accounts include **wisdom**: Mt. 10:19, Mark 13:11 and Luke 21:12 all quote Jesus telling the disciples not to worry about what to say, but only Luke mentions wisdom. Luke also emphasizes **friends**: compare the same stories in Matthew about the Centurion's servant, the lost sheep, the warning of hellfire and being hated for Christ's sake – in every instance Luke inserts the word **friends**. (There are other examples with the word **see** in Luke, and by the way, "friends" and "see" start with the same Hebrew letter, the 20th letter, resh) If God designed the Bible then I expect to find the theme continuing in the book of John, i.e. the 21st Hebrew letter (shin) better be pretty prevalent. Guess what? It is. To send (shalach), peace (shalom), name (shem), hear / obey (shama) and keep / watch (shamar) are overly abundant and the really amazing thing is that the New Testament was written in Greek, but the Hebrew pattern remains. This is a sampling of the unique perspectives in this Bible study book.

    The 22 epistles are, to me, like discovering important personal documents. (What if you found your great-grandparents' love letters to one another? Wouldn't you be interested?) Before you read one of these short books I recommend that you first find out what was happening in the author's life and in the church that he's writing to. Of course these letters are meant for us today, too, but understanding first century culture and customs will clarify things. Go online and read Bible scholar commentaries. I have found that each verse can be like a treasure chest that as soon as you open it (begin to study it) it overflows with treasure. Most Bibles have footnotes and commentaries that should never be overlooked.

    Jesus lived. He died for our sins then rose from the dead to conquer death and live eternally. Every time I look at someone I must remember that Jesus died for that person, too. That tends to change my outlook quite a bit.

Alphabetic Verses:
Also called "acrostic verses" alphabetic verses are found in Psalms, Proverbs and Lamentations. Each verse starts with the next consecutive Hebrew letter making memorization an easier assignment. The most famous and longest is Psalm 119, right in the center of the Holy Scripture. This chapter takes each letter and starts eight verses in a row with it before moving on to the following letter. This interesting rhetorical feature is believed by some to be hidden codes; others think that this is possibly a poetic way of saying that the subject is being covered completely from end to end. Besides Psalm 119, acrostics appear in Psalms 111 and 112, where each letter begins a line; in Psalms 25, 34, and 145, where each letter begins a half-verse; in Psalm 37, Proverbs 31:10-31, and Lamentations 1, 2, and 4, where each letter begins a whole verse; and in Lamentations 3, where each letter begins three verses. Check your Bible now to see if your translation footnotes this aspect of the Holy Word.

Let's look at Psalm 119. It is the longest psalm as well as the longest chapter in the Bible. It is referred to in Hebrew by its opening words, "*Ashrei temimei derech*" ("happy are those whose way is perfect"). It is the prayer of one who delights in and lives by the Torah, the sacred law. There are 176 verses, 8 verses for each of the 22 Hebrew letters. The first 8 verses each start with the Hebrew letter Aleph (a), the next 8 with Bet (b) and so on through the alphabet (alephbet). We have lost the amazing beauty of the psalm in translation. However, one thing is very obvious: there is a repetition of the following words throughout all of the verses: law, statutes, ways, precepts, decrees, commands, and word. For example in the fourth stanza there are several words that start with Dalet (d), among them the word "derech" or "derek" which is translated "way," "commands" and "precepts" in the NIV Bible or "way," "testimonies," and "commandments" in the King James Bible. If you go through all 176 verses and note how often these words are used, it seems pretty obvious that the Lord is telling us to know his WORD. When all the alphabetic verses in Psalms, Proverbs and Lamentations are examined and the key words culled and applied to their corresponding books (the divine order right in front of us) then we have some awesome and intricate weavings of the Lord's magnificent tapestry.

As we look at each individual book in the Bible, we will see the bonds between these key words and themes, subjects, topics or the very words themselves to the corresponding book. We will see how the Hebrew alphabet, in its exact order, matches the order of the books in the Christian Bible, connecting acrostic verse words, individual letter meanings and each of the 66 books.

The Hebrew Alphabet:
On the next page are the Hebrew letters (5 of them have a second form used when they are at the end of a word), their names and their symbolic (and often literal) meanings (credit to www.biblewheel, www.inner.org, www.hebrew4christians):

א = aleph = ox, bull = leader, strength, first

ב = bet = house, tent = household, in, into

ג = gimel = camel = pride, to lift up

ד = dalet = door = pathway, to enter

ה = hey = window, fence = to reveal, behold

ו = vav = nail = and, add, secure, hook

ז = zayin = weapon = cut, to cut off

ח = het = fence, hedge, chamber = private, to separate

ט = tet = twist, serpent, snake = to surround

י = yod = hand (closed hand) = deed, work, to make

כ ך (2 forms) = kaph = palm of hand (open hand) = to cover, allow, strength

ל = lamed = staff, ox goad = prod, go toward, tongue

מ ם (2 forms) = mem = water = massive, overpower, chaos

נ ן (2 forms) = nun = fish, heir to the throne = activity, life

ס = samek = support = support, turn

ע = ayin = eye = see, know, experience

פ ף (2 forms) = pey = mouth = speak, open, word

צ ץ (2 forms) = tzaddi = fish hook = harvest, desire

ק = quph = back of the head = behind, the last, least

ר = resh = head = person, head, highest

ש = shin = teeth = consume, destroy

ת = tav = cross, mark, sign = covenant, to seal

Here's how we're going to go through the Bible. The books are listed below in order going down, but since there are 22 Hebrew letters and 66 books in the Old and New Testaments, we will take three books at a time going across – all three aleph books, then all three bet books, and so on. This is how we will discover amazing connections between books that are spaced equidistance apart. **Have your Bible open for reference.**

Chapter 1 Aleph

Aleph	*1. Genesis*	*23. Isaiah*	*45. Romans*
Bet	2. Exodus	24. Jeremiah	46. 1st Corinthians
Gimel	3. Leviticus	25. Lamentations	47. 2nd Corinthians
Dalet	4. Numbers	26. Ezekiel	48. Galatians
Hey	5. Deuteronomy	27. Daniel	49. Ephesians
Vav	6. Joshua	28. Hosea	50. Philippians
Zayin	7. Judges	29. Joel	51. Colossians
Het	8. Ruth	30. Amos	52. 1st Thessalonians
Tet	9. 1st Samuel	31. Obadiah	53. 2nd Thessalonians
Yod	10. 2nd Samuel	32. Jonah	54. 1st Timothy
Kaph	11. 1st Kings	33. Micah	55. 2nd Timothy
Lamed	12. 2nd Kings	34. Nahum	56. Titus
Mem	13. 1st Chronicles	35. Habakkuk	57. Philemon
Nun	14. 2nd Chronicles	36. Zephaniah	58. Hebrews
Samek	15. Ezra	37. Haggai	59. James
Ayin	16. Nehemiah	38. Zechariah	60. 1st Peter
Pey	17. Esther	39. Malachi	61. 2nd Peter
Tzaddi	18. Job	40. Matthew	62. 1st John
Quph	19. Psalms	41. Mark	63. 2nd John
Resh	20. Proverbs	42. Luke	64. 3rd John
Shin	21. Ecclesiastes	43. John	65. Jude
Tav	22. Song of Songs	44. Acts	66. Revelation

Aleph + Genesis

א

The word Genesis has become synonymous with beginnings. In Hebrew this book is called "Bereshith" (בְּרֵאשִׁית) meaning "in the beginning" because that's how this book starts. It is generally believed that it was written by Moses, inspired by God, of course. The major themes of Genesis are beginnings and the self-revelation of God. This is the book you read to find the stories of the creation, the fall and redemption of man, the story of Cain and Abel and then Cain and Seth, the great flood, the tower of Babel and the call of Abram (Abraham). There is the story of Lot and Sodom & Gomorrah, the lives of Isaac, Jacob and Esau and, finally, the story of Joseph. God makes several covenants with man: the Edenic Covenant (1:28), the Adamic Covenant (3:14), the Noahic Covenant (9:1), and the Abrahamic Covenant (15:18).

Let's look at the first letter of the Hebrew alphabet: Aleph

א

Verse 1 of Genesis says: "In the beginning God (Elohim) created the heaven and the earth." Elohim starts with aleph, in fact many of God's names start with aleph: El (God, Mighty One), El Shaddai (God Almighty), El Olam (God Everlasting), El Elyon (God Most High). Also many facets of God's nature begin with this letter as well: love, light, truth, faith, Sovereign Lord. These are all Hebrew words that start with aleph.

When you write the three letters in Hebrew that spell "aleph" you get 3 different words - <u>eleph</u> which mean "ox" or "thousand", <u>alaph</u> which means "teach", "learn" or "tame", and <u>aluph</u> which means "prince", "chief", "leader", "master", "ruler", "guide" and "teacher". The first one, eleph, may seem weird at first if you're trying to relate the letters to Biblical symbolism. What has an ox to do with anything Biblical? An ox signified strength. It was the chief domesticated animal of the time and had to be "tamed". That brings us to the second word, alaph, which means "tame" as well as "teach" and "learn" with the idea of learning by association. The last word, aluph (prince, leader, etc.), appears in Genesis 52 times, that's 64% of all the times it appears in the entire Bible. I think Genesis is showing us very clearly **who** our leader, master and guide is: **God**.

There are many words that begin with aleph besides God's names, such as "one", "love", "light", "truth" and "faith". These are such important words to our beliefs that I suggest you pause a moment and think about why they would all begin with this first Hebrew letter.

Now think of the Ten Commandments (Exodus 20 or Deuteronomy 5). What's the first one? **No other gods before me!** God is Number 1, the One and Only, the Eternal Omnipotent God. His first initial is the first Hebrew letter. Throughout Genesis we get a good picture of God as our Father: He keeps reaching out to man, provides new covenants, never gives up on us and blesses us. He is the Sovereign Ruler over all of His creation. By the way, the Hebrew word for "created" and the Greek equivalent are prominent not only in Genesis, but in Isaiah and Romans (the other two aleph books) to the tune of 10 times above average.

Let's start at the beginning. Read Genesis 1:

¹ In the beginning God created the heavens and the earth. ² Now the earth was formless and empty, darkness was over the surface of the deep, and the Spirit of God was hovering over the waters. (*New International Version (**NIV**) Copyright © 1973, 1978, 1984, 2011 by Biblica, all subsequent Bible quotes will be from the **NIV** unless otherwise noted*)

Now, what can you argue with there? We've got a beginning. We've got a Creator and we've got the creation. Science can (and does) present a number of "theories" and not one is in conflict with this first verse. (These theories do keep changing or getting updated, but the Bible stays constant.)

There are 5 major views about the 6 days of creation. One view, that there was a gap between verses 1 and 2, seeks to explain where to put the fall of Satan as well as how to fit in the time spans of dinosaurs. Thus, those who subscribe to this view believe that there was an original creation in verse one and then a re-creation in verse 2.

However, Exodus 20:11 states clearly that God created the heavens, earth, sea and all within in 6 days. Does this negate the "gap" view?

³ And God said, "Let there be light," and there was light. ⁴ God saw that the light was good, and he separated the light from the darkness. ⁵ God called the light "day," and the darkness he called "night." And there was evening, and there was morning—the first day.

The Talmud (a collection of ancient Jewish writings) says that the darkness was the absence of light. This is an important and deep understanding. Science can measure light, but can only measure darkness in terms of light, that is, the absence of light. Next God named day and night, then there was evening followed by morning and thus the first day. Day One. Time was created on Day One. The Hebrew words here for evening and morning are *erev* (disorder) and *boker* (orderly). I'm going to look at the original Hebrew words a lot in this book as I'm extremely aware of how things get lost, missed or misunderstood in translation. I think it's important to see that here, with the creation of light, God brought order from disorder. Or, to "coordinate" with the scientists, cosmos from chaos.

Also note that God saw that the light was good.

⁶ And God said, "Let there be a vault [an expanse] between the waters to separate water from water." ⁷ So God made the vault and separated the water under the vault from the water above it. And it was so. ⁸ God called the vault "sky." And there was evening, and there was morning—the second day.

I once heard a sermon explaining in very scientific terms how there was no rain on earth at first. Much like a moist terrarium the earth produced its flora naturally. The first mention of rain in the Bible is, of course, the great flood.

⁹ And God said, "Let the water under the sky be gathered to one place, and let dry ground appear." And it was so. ¹⁰ God called the dry ground "land," and the gathered waters he called "seas." And God saw that it was good.

Again God saw that it was good.
¹¹ Then God said, "Let the land produce vegetation: seed-bearing plants and trees on the land that bear fruit with seed in it, according to their various kinds." And it was so. ¹² The land produced vegetation: plants bearing seed according to their kinds and trees bearing fruit with seed in it according to their kinds. And God saw that it was good. ¹³ And there was evening, and there was morning—the third day.

Again God saw that it was good. Plants and trees and vegetation are good.

¹⁴ And God said, "Let there be lights in the vault of the sky [the heavens] to separate the day from the night, and let them serve as signs to mark sacred times, and days and years, ¹⁵ and let them be lights in the vault of the sky to give light on the earth." And it was so. ¹⁶ God made two great lights—the greater light to govern the day and the lesser light to govern the night. He also made the stars. ¹⁷ God set them in the vault of the sky to give light on the earth, ¹⁸ to govern the day and the night, and to separate light from darkness. And God saw that it was good. ¹⁹ And there was evening, and there was morning—the fourth day.

Finally, the sun and the moon and the stars. And God saw that it was good.

²⁰ And God said, "Let the water teem with living creatures, and let birds fly above the earth across the vault of the sky." ²¹ So God created the great creatures of the sea and every living thing with which the water teems and that moves about in it, according to their kinds, and every winged bird according to its kind. And God saw that it was good. ²² God blessed them and said, "Be fruitful and increase in number and fill the water in the seas, and let the birds increase on the earth." ²³ And there was evening, and there was morning—the fifth day.

Day 1 – light and dark, day and night
Day 2 – the sky between the waters above and below
Day 3 – dry land and vegetation
Day 4 – the sun, moon and stars
Day 5 – the sky and waters fill with birds and fish. And God saw that it was good.

²⁴ And God said, "Let the land produce living creatures according to their kinds: the livestock, the creatures that move along the ground, and the wild animals, each according to its kind." And it was so. ²⁵ God made the wild animals according to their kinds, the livestock according to their kinds, and all the creatures that move along the ground according to their kinds. And God saw that it was good.
²⁶ Then God said, "Let us make mankind in our image, in our likeness, so that they may rule over the fish in the sea and the birds in the sky, over the livestock and all the wild animals, and over all the creatures that move along the ground."

27 So God created mankind in his own image,
in the image of God he created them;
male and female he created them.
28 God blessed them and said to them, "Be fruitful and increase in number; fill the earth and subdue it. Rule over the fish in the sea and the birds in the sky and over every living creature that moves on the ground."
29 Then God said, "I give you every seed-bearing plant on the face of the whole earth and every tree that has fruit with seed in it. They will be yours for food. **30** And to all the beasts of the earth and all the birds in the sky and all the creatures that move along the ground—everything that has the breath of life in it—I give every green plant for food." And it was so.
31 God saw all that he had made, and it was very good. And there was evening, and there was morning—the sixth day.

Day 6 – Wow, that was a big day. Animals first (and they were good) and finally man. And God gives man a job – to rule over all the other living creatures.

Man is created in God's image. The Hebrew word here is *tselem* meaning shade, phantom, illusion, resemblance, representative figure. Think about that. This little word's most celebrated use is right here in this first chapter of Genesis.

God created male and female. Later, in chapter 2, the account backtracks and gives the specifics of Adam and Eve's creation, Adam from dust and Eve from his rib. But in chapter 1 we see that God blesses mankind and gives him food, animal and plant. Thus ends the sixth day of creation. But wait. This time God says, as he looks at all that he has created, that it was **very** good. Big day, big week.

1 Thus the heavens and the earth were completed in all their vast array.
2 By the seventh day God had finished the work he had been doing; so on the seventh day he rested from all his work.

And there you have the creation account. As I said before there are 5 views about the length of the days. I mentioned the "gap" view. There is also the intermittent day view which allows for eons of time between literal days. The pictorial day theory asserts that there were 6 days during which God told Moses about each part of creation. The day-age theory declares that each day was of indeterminate length, thus allowing for the age of the dinosaurs. The literal day premise maintains that each day was a literal 24 hour period. I believe God created the heavens and the earth. Done deal. And here's how I accept the Big Bang Theory:

According to the Big Bang Theory everything was small as a pea and then blew up. The universe expanded at a rate of expansion so that it is now 1,000,000,000,000 times larger (one million squared). Science says that the Big Bang was 15 ¾ billion years ago.

Fine. That theory coordinates with Scripture in the following way: God created things on the 6 days described in Genesis in 24 hour days, but at the scientific rate of expansion of the universe that first day is now seen from our perspective as 8 billion years long. (Think of concentric circles radiating out from the middle, each one successively smaller by half as they slow down.) The second day would be seen as 4 billion years long, 3rd day as 2 billion, 4th day as 1 billion, 5th day as ½ billion and 6th day as ¼ billion (totaling 15 ¾ billion years). The scientific community ascribes the appearance of the Milky Way, water, life, transparent atmosphere, animal and aquatic life, and human life to time periods of those durations. That matches the Biblical story right in order! Go look.

Furthermore, per science's numbers, if you divide the 15 ¾ billion years by the current expansion (million squared) that equals .015. We have 365 days in a year. Multiply 365 by .015 and you get 5.74 which is almost a completed sixth day. In other words, we are living in the late "afternoon" of the 6th day of creation.

א

Aleph + Isaiah

We are continuing with the first Hebrew letter, aleph, which has the symbolic meaning of **leader** or ox.

The book of Isaiah was written by the prophet Isaiah whose name means "God is my salvation." This book is often considered a miniature replica of the Bible because of its format. It is comprised of 66 chapters (as the Bible has 66 books) which are divided into two distinct halves. Amazingly the first half is 39 chapters of Israel's problems with idolatry – matching perfectly with the Old Testament's 39 books requiring judgment on immoral, idolatrous mankind. As the New Testament embraces 27 books of hope and redemption through Christ, Isaiah's final 27 chapters paint a picture of the Messiah coming as king and savior. Amazing!

The major themes in this book are that, first, Israel is in exile and there is divine judgment upon their oppressors. Next we have the return from Babylon followed by the manifestation of the Messiah in humiliation. Then there is the blessing of the Gentiles, the manifestation of the Messiah in judgment, the reign of David's righteous branch in the kingdom age and finally, the new heavens and the new earth. Isaiah looks toward the captivities and then beyond the captivities.

This book has a very clear vision of grace. We see the Messiah in His Person and in His sufferings and then we see the blessing of the Gentiles through Him.

Whereas our first aleph book, Genesis, was the 1st book of the Law, Isaiah is the 1st book of the Prophets. The third aleph book, Romans, is the 1st book of the Epistles. What unique connections does Isaiah have with these two books? First of all it is in only these three books that God is named "El Olam" meaning "Everlasting God" or "Eternal God." In Genesis 21: 33 we find:

> 33 Abraham planted a tamarisk tree in Beersheba, and there he called on the name of the LORD, the **Eternal God**.

In Isaiah 40:28 it is written:
> 28 Do you not know?
> Have you not heard?
> The LORD is the **everlasting God**,
>   the Creator of the ends of the earth.
> He will not grow tired or weary,
>   and his understanding no one can fathom.

We find the Greek equivalent in Romans 16:26:

> 26 but now revealed and made known through the prophetic writings by the command of the **eternal God**, so that all the Gentiles might come to the obedience that comes from faith—

NO WHERE ELSE in the entire Bible do we find this particular name for God. It occurs only in the books that match up to aleph, which, since God is the "Alpha and the Omega," the beginning and the end, makes perfect sense to me.

Another interesting connection is with the Hebrew word for "create". When we think of Genesis we usually think of the Creation story. The word for create is used only with God as the subject in Genesis chapter 1. Compare the following 3 charts which graph the number of occurrences of the word "create":

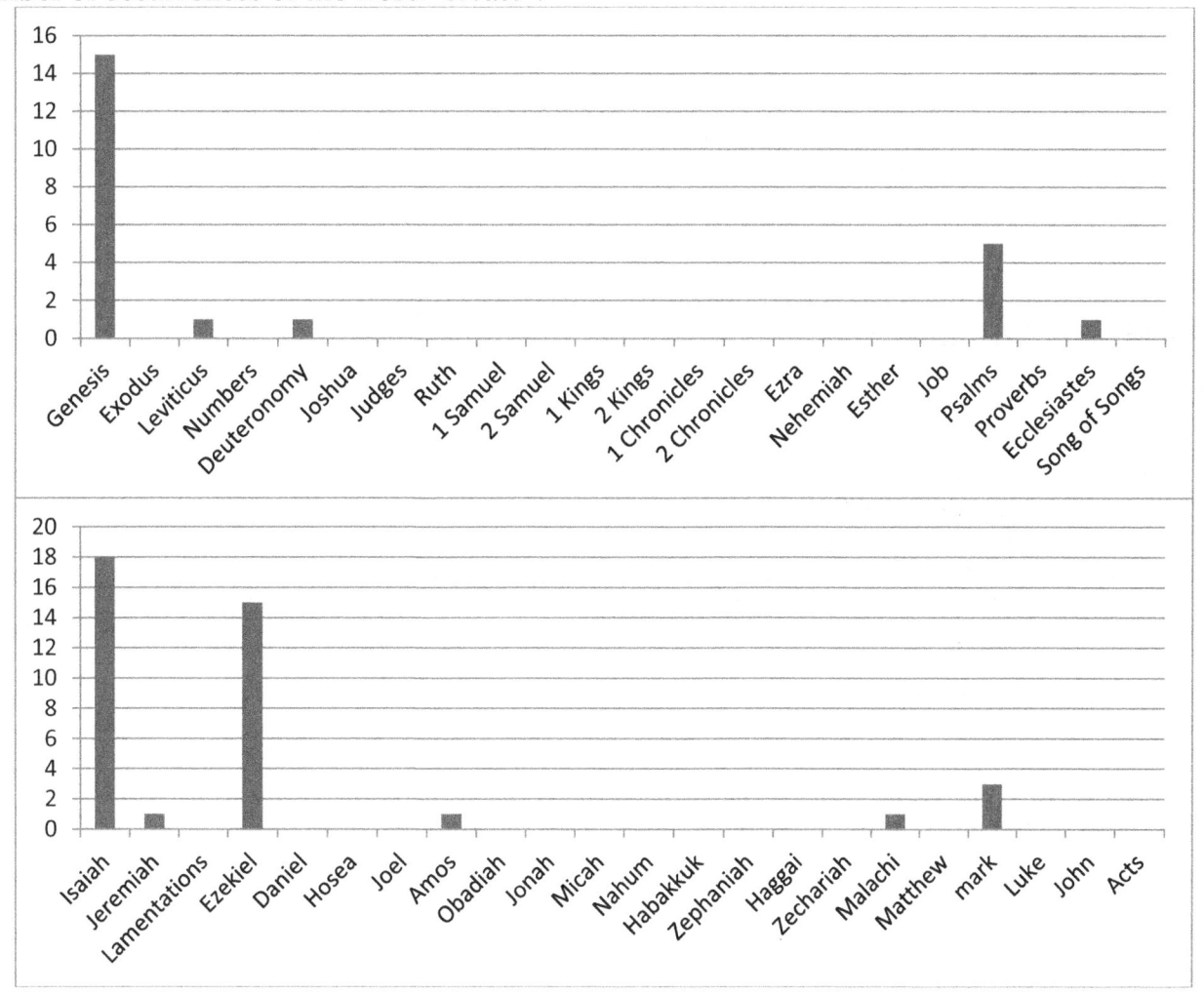

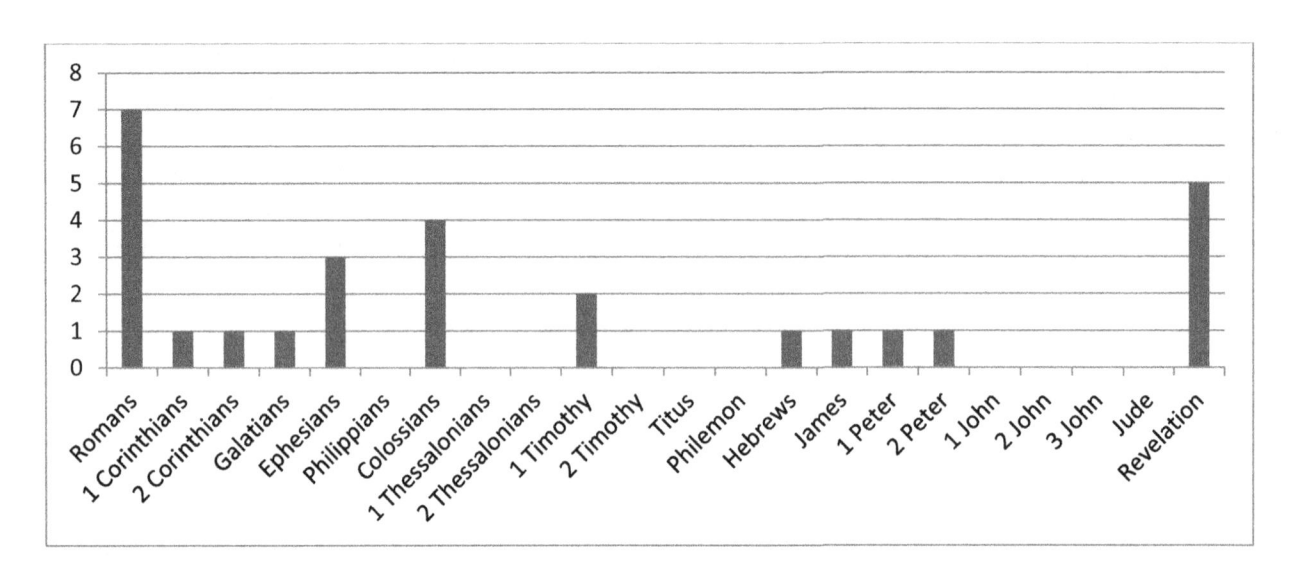

[Bar chart showing frequency counts by New Testament book: Romans 7, 1 Corinthians 1, 2 Corinthians 1, Galatians 1, Ephesians 3, Philippians 0, Colossians 4, 1 Thessalonians 0, 2 Thessalonians 0, 1 Timothy 2, 2 Timothy 0, Titus 0, Philemon 0, Hebrews 1, James 1, 1 Peter 1, 2 Peter 1, 1 John 0, 2 John 0, 3 John 0, Jude 0, Revelation 5]

These three aleph books have the amazingly highest frequency of the creation word in each of the 22 book sets.

But wait, there's more. Look at Isaiah 64:8; 29:16; and 45:9:

> **8** Yet you, LORD, are our Father.
> We are the clay, you are the potter;
> we are all the work of your hand.
> **16** You turn things upside down,
> as if the potter were thought to be like the clay!
> Shall what is formed say to the one who formed it,
> "You did not make me"?
> Can the pot say to the potter,
> "You know nothing"?
> **9** "Woe to those who quarrel with their Maker,
> those who are nothing but potsherds
> among the potsherds on the ground.
> Does the clay say to the potter,
> 'What are you making?'
> Does your work say,
> 'The potter has no hands'?

So, God created us in Genesis and here in Isaiah we have the beautiful imagery of our Lord as the Potter. We are the clay that He molds and forms. Take a guess now, which other book in the entire Bible aligns with this creation/potter/clay metaphor? Did you guess Romans? Here is Romans 9:20-21:

> **20** But who are you, a human being, to talk back to God? "Shall what is formed say to the one who formed it, 'Why did you make me like this?'" **21** Does not the potter have the right to

make out of the same lump of clay some pottery for special purposes and some for common use?

How absolutely marvelous this is! I'll save some other miraculous links for when we get to Romans. In my research I found that several scholars referred to the book of Isaiah as "the Romans of the Old Testament." Interesting.

א

Aleph + Romans

The first Hebrew letter is God's first initial. This letter starts the word for father (av) which is made up of the first two Hebrew letters that symbolize leader and house (you'll learn about house in the next section) – the father is the leader of the house. Aleph represents leader or ox, so for a little humor, perhaps some fathers are the ox of the house.

Just as the first aleph book, Genesis, was the 1st book of the Law, Isaiah, the second aleph book, was the 1st book of the Prophets, and Romans is the 1st book of the 22 Christian Epistles. Romans was written by the Apostle Paul. Its major themes are the gospel of God, the redemption truth and reconciling the promises to Israel with the promises concerning the Gentiles. Its greatest teaching is the doctrine of grace. This book shows us that all are guilty before God but can receive justification through the righteousness of God by faith.

Let's look first at Romans 3:25, 26:

²⁵ God presented Christ as a sacrifice of atonement, through the shedding of his blood— to be received by faith. He did this to demonstrate his righteousness, because in his forbearance he had left the sins committed beforehand unpunished— ²⁶ he did it to demonstrate his righteousness at the present time, so as to be just and the one who justifies those who have faith in Jesus.

Now compare that to Isaiah 53:11:

¹¹ After he has suffered,
  he will see the light of life and be satisfied;
by his knowledge my righteous servant will justify many,
  and he will bear their iniquities.

As promised in Isaiah, Christ bore our iniquities. Now compare Romans 11:25-27 with Isaiah 45:17:

²⁵ I do not want you to be ignorant of this mystery, brothers and sisters, so that you may not be conceited: Israel has experienced a hardening in part until the full number of the Gentiles has come in, ²⁶ and in this way all Israel will be saved. As it is written:
    "The deliverer will come from Zion;
  he will turn godlessness away from Jacob.
²⁷ And this is my covenant with them
  when I take away their sins."

¹⁷ But Israel will be saved by the LORD
with an everlasting salvation;

you will never be put to shame or disgraced,
to ages everlasting.

When we looked at the 2nd aleph a book we saw the connective verses about the potter (God) and the clay (man) that were in Isaiah and then reappeared in Romans, now we'll look at the story that started in Genesis, the first aleph a book, and finished in Romans. Watch.

Genesis 17: 1 – 5:

¹ When Abram was ninety-nine years old, the LORD appeared to him and said, "I am God Almighty; walk before me faithfully and be blameless. ² Then I will make my covenant between me and you and will greatly increase your numbers."
³ Abram fell facedown, and God said to him, ⁴ "As for me, this is my covenant with you: You will be the father of many nations. ⁵ No longer will you be called Abram; your name will be Abraham, for I have made you a father of many nations.

Romans 4: 16 – 18:

¹⁶ Therefore, the promise comes by faith, so that it may be by grace and may be guaranteed to all Abraham's offspring—not only to those who are of the law but also to those who have the faith of Abraham. He is the father of us all. ¹⁷ As it is written: "I have made you a father of many nations." He is our father in the sight of God, in whom he believed—the God who gives life to the dead and calls into being things that were not.
¹⁸ Against all hope, Abraham in hope believed and so became the father of many nations, just as it had been said to him, "So shall your offspring be."

Wow. What are the odds that this obvious link would show up in Romans rather than any other of the Epistles or Gospels? Well, I guess the odds are really good when you realize that God designed the Holy Bible. You can find even more of these connections by comparing for yourself how the Bible talks about Abraham's seed in Genesis 15:5 and Romans 4:18. Sarah has a son – Genesis 18:14 & Romans 9:9. The seed is called Isaac – Genesis 21:12 & Romans 9:7. Rebecca conceives – Genesis 25:11 & Romans 9:10. The elder brother serves the younger – Genesis 25:23 & Romans 9:12. Satan is crushed – Genesis 3:15 & Romans 16:20.

Here are some other really cool things about Romans. In chapter 5, verses 12 – 21 we find the explanation of the perfect contrast between Adam and Christ. Read this slowly and thoughtfully because it is really deep:

¹² Therefore, just as sin entered the world through one man, and death through sin, and in this way death came to all people, because all sinned—
¹³ To be sure, sin was in the world before the law was given, but sin is not charged against anyone's account where there is no law. ¹⁴ Nevertheless, death reigned from the time of Adam to the time of Moses, even over those who did not sin by breaking a command, as did Adam, who is a pattern of the one to come.

15 But the gift is not like the trespass. For if the many died by the trespass of the one man, how much more did God's grace and the gift that came by the grace of the one man, Jesus Christ, overflow to the many! **16** Nor can the gift of God be compared with the result of one man's sin: The judgment followed one sin and brought condemnation, but the gift followed many trespasses and brought justification. **17** For if, by the trespass of the one man, death reigned through that one man, how much more will those who receive God's abundant provision of grace and of the gift of righteousness reign in life through the one man, Jesus Christ!

18 Consequently, just as one trespass resulted in condemnation for all people, so also one righteous act resulted in justification and life for all people. **19** For just as through the disobedience of the one man the many were made sinners, so also through the obedience of the one man the many will be made righteous.

20 The law was brought in so that the trespass might increase. But where sin increased, grace increased all the more, **21** so that, just as sin reigned in death, so also grace might reign through righteousness to bring eternal life through Jesus Christ our Lord.

Do you understand the perfect symmetry between Adam's sin and Christ's sacrifice?

In Paul's letter to the Romans, chapter 8, we find the ONLY place in all the Scriptures where we learn an intimate fact about the Holy Spirit – that the Spirit prays for the believer:

26 In the same way, the Spirit helps us in our weakness. We do not know what we ought to pray for, but the Spirit himself intercedes for us through wordless groans. **27** And he who searches our hearts knows the mind of the Spirit, because the Spirit intercedes for God's people in accordance with the will of God.

The Holy Spirit intercedes for us! This is very comforting, as is another verse in Romans – 8:28:

28 And we know that in all things God works for the good of those who love him, who have been called according to his purpose.

How is this comforting? Whatever happens, good, bad or tragic, God can bring good from it. I know of a young man whose suicide devastated his family. Yet at the funeral the brave mother begged everyone to refrain from blaming themselves for ignoring the signs or failing to do something to prevent this horrible death. She trusted God and gave a marvelous testimony to her Lord and Savior and because of that thirteen people came forward and were saved. Glory to God! I'm sure there is very little that could comfort a grieving mother, but I am also sure that the Lord did comfort her with the knowledge that so many came to Christ through that tragedy.

Another distinctive passage in Romans is the most severe condemnation of sexual immorality found in the Bible. It comes early on in chapter 1: 24 – 32:

24 Therefore God gave them over in the sinful desires of their hearts to sexual impurity for the degrading of their bodies with one another. **25** They exchanged the truth about God for

a lie, and worshiped and served created things rather than the Creator—who is forever praised. Amen.
26 Because of this, God gave them over to shameful lusts. Even their women exchanged natural sexual relations for unnatural ones. **27** In the same way the men also abandoned natural relations with women and were inflamed with lust for one another. Men committed shameful acts with other men, and received in themselves the due penalty for their error.
28 Furthermore, just as they did not think it worthwhile to retain the knowledge of God, so God gave them over to a depraved mind, so that they do what ought not to be done. **29** They have become filled with every kind of wickedness, evil, greed and depravity. They are full of envy, murder, strife, deceit and malice. They are gossips, **30** slanderers, God-haters, insolent, arrogant and boastful; they invent ways of doing evil; they disobey their parents; **31** they have no understanding, no fidelity, no love, no mercy. **32** Although they know God's righteous decree that those who do such things deserve death, they not only continue to do these very things but also approve of those who practice them.

Do you approve of those who practice these things? It is pretty clear here that you should not. Do not hide behind the "political correctness" of "tolerance". God does not tolerate these things. You can love the sinner, but hate the sin.
Finally, Romans includes more benedictions than any other book. Here they are. Romans 11:33-36; 15:13; 15:30-33; 16:20; and 16:25-27:

33 Oh, the depth of the riches of the wisdom and knowledge of God!
How unsearchable his judgments,
and his paths beyond tracing out!
34 "Who has known the mind of the Lord?
Or who has been his counselor?"
35 "Who has ever given to God,
that God should repay them?"
36 For from him and through him and for him are all things.
To him be the glory forever! Amen.
13 May the God of hope fill you with all joy and peace as you trust in him, so that you may overflow with hope by the power of the Holy Spirit.
30 I urge you, brothers and sisters, by our Lord Jesus Christ and by the love of the Spirit, to join me in my struggle by praying to God for me. **31** Pray that I may be kept safe from the unbelievers in Judea and that the contribution I take to Jerusalem may be favorably received by the Lord's people there, **32** so that I may come to you with joy, by God's will, and in your company be refreshed. **33** The God of peace be with you all. Amen.
20 The God of peace will soon crush Satan under your feet.
The grace of our Lord Jesus be with you.
25 Now to him who is able to establish you in accordance with my gospel, the message I proclaim about Jesus Christ, in keeping with the revelation of the mystery hidden for long ages past, **26** but now revealed and made known through the prophetic writings by the command of the eternal God, so that all the Gentiles might come to the obedience that comes from faith— **27** to the only wise God be glory forever through Jesus Christ! Amen.

Chapter 2 Bet

Aleph	1. Genesis	23. Isaiah	45. Romans
Bet	*2. Exodus*	*24. Jeremiah*	*46. 1st Corinthians*
Gimel	3. Leviticus	25. Lamentations	47. 2nd Corinthians
Dalet	4. Numbers	26. Ezekiel	48. Galatians
Hey	5. Deuteronomy	27. Daniel	49. Ephesians
Vav	6. Joshua	28. Hosea	50. Philippians
Zayin	7. Judges	29. Joel	51. Colossians
Het	8. Ruth	30. Amos	52. 1st Thessalonians
Tet	9. 1st Samuel	31. Obadiah	53. 2nd Thessalonians
Yod	10. 2nd Samuel	32. Jonah	54. 1st Timothy
Kaph	11. 1st Kings	33. Micah	55. 2nd Timothy
Lamed	12. 2nd Kings	34. Nahum	56. Titus
Mem	13. 1st Chronicles	35. Habakkuk	57. Philemon
Nun	14. 2nd Chronicles	36. Zephaniah	58. Hebrews
Samek	15. Ezra	37. Haggai	59. James
Ayin	16. Nehemiah	38. Zechariah	60. 1st Peter
Pey	17. Esther	39. Malachi	61. 2nd Peter
Tzaddi	18. Job	40. Matthew	62. 1st John
Quph	19. Psalms	41. Mark	63. 2nd John
Resh	20. Proverbs	42. Luke	64. 3rd John
Shin	21. Ecclesiastes	43. John	65. Jude
Tav	22. Song of Songs	44. Acts	66. Revelation

ב

Bet + Exodus

The name of the second letter is based on the word for **house**, found in over 2000 verses. Its shape in the ancient script represented a **tent** – △ – the typical **house** of the Hebrews as they wandered in the wilderness. It looks a lot like our letter b if you tip it up. The Hebrew word for father is made up of the aleph (leader) and the bet (house): symbolically and literally the father is the leader of the house.

The Midrash (Rabbinic literature commentating and clarifying biblical texts) asks the question: Why does the Bible begin with the letter *Bet?* The answer is that since bet is closed in all directions except forward (reading right to left), it implies that there was nothing before. We can know only what comes from that point on.

The book of Exodus gets its name from the exodus that occurred, but the Hebrew name is based on the first word of this book, Sh'mot, which means names. Look at your Bible and see how the book starts with the names of the sons of Israel. This book was written by Moses and records the redemption out of Egyptian bondage. Other major themes are the giving of the Law and the provisions of sacrifice and priesthood. You could divide the book into three sections: 1st, Israel in Egypt and under bondage for 400 years; 2nd, moving from the Red Sea to Sinai and God making the covenant with Israel through the Ten Commandments; 3rd, Israel at Sinai and the construction and consecration of the Tabernacle, the **house** of the Lord. Three bet words are evident in each section – son (ben), covenant (brit) and house (bet).

Exodus teaches that redemption is essential to a relationship with the most Holy God. Even a redeemed people cannot have fellowship with Him unless they are constantly cleansed and purified from corruption, defilement, and transgressions (sin).

Let's look specifically at The Plagues. Read chapters 7 through 11. There are nine plagues before the horrible 10th plague that culminated in the Passover. The plagues were 1) Blood in the Nile, 2) Frogs, 3) Gnats, 4) Flies, 5) Death of Livestock, 6) Boils, 7) Hail, 8) Locusts and 9) Darkness. Let's take them in groups of three since they seem to cluster nicely that way. The first three were distressing and uncomfortable, but relatively minor compared to what was next. The second set of three were a bit more painful for the Egyptians and very destructive. The last three were dreadful. The plagues are an answer to Pharaoh's question. Look at Exodus 5: 1-2:

¹ Afterward Moses and Aaron went to Pharaoh and said, "This is what the LORD, the God of Israel, says: 'Let my people go, so that they may hold a festival to me in the wilderness.'"
² Pharaoh said, "Who is the LORD, that I should obey him and let Israel go? I do not know the LORD and I will not let Israel go."

"Who is the LORD?" he asks. Well, the Lord God Almighty is going to make the answer pretty clear. The plagues answer the question. There are definite relationships between the plagues and the Egyptian gods, Pharaoh's gods. Remember, the number one commandment is "no other gods". The first plague on the river Nile turns it to blood. The Egyptians had three gods of the Nile: Hapi, the bull god of the Nile, Isis, the goddess of the Nile and Khnua, the ram god, guardian of the Nile. By messing with their river God is proving that He is greater than they. Some of the Israelites had been worshipping these gods, so this was a big indictment and judgment on these false gods that must have shaken things up for both nations.

The second plague was a horrible infestation of frogs ("croakers" in the original). Frogs, according to Egyptian belief, were regarded as having divine power and they were not to be killed. Now when you read that they infiltrated everywhere you should also imagine the Egyptians' reluctance to kill them. The Egyptian goddess, Heqet, had the body of a woman and the head of a frog and was a fertility symbol. God seems to be showing that He, and only He, gives children.

Both the 1st and 2nd plagues were duplicated by Pharaoh's magicians, but the 3rd plague was different. Insects, probably gnats or maybe lice, came upon man and beast, but Pharaoh's magicians couldn't copy this feat and gave God the glory, saying "This is the finger of God." At least one scholar submits that the gnat plague was a challenge to Set, the god of the desert, since the plague began with Aaron smiting the dust of the earth (the desert) with his staff. Unlike the first two plagues, this plague had no warning for Pharaoh. Of course, his heart was still hardened and he would not listen.

The next three plagues get a little more severe. We have three destructive plagues. The land was ruined by flies. Then the livestock all died. Then men and animals alike were struck with festering boils. Yuck. The Egyptian gods that the Lord was opposing in this way were Uatchit, represented by a fly, Apis and Hathor, the bull god and the goddess with the head of a cow, and Sekhmet, goddess over disease and Sunu, god of pestilence.

Plagues seven, eight and nine were dreadful and alarming. God showed his superiority over Nut, the sky goddess, Osiris, god of crops and fertility and Set, god of storms, by sending a plague of hail. Hail fell and lightning flashed and it was the worst storm ever. Take that. And if that wasn't enough for them it was followed with the plague of locusts which totally invaded the country, covering the ground until it was black. The ninth plague was a plague of darkness which challenged the Egyptian sun god, Re, as well as the sky goddess, Nut.

The final plague was the most horrible, but its result was that Moses and his people could finally leave Egypt. The plague on the firstborn meant that the Lord struck down all the firstborn in Egypt – from the firstborn of Pharaoh to the firstborn of the prisoner – and the firstborn of all the livestock as well. Can you imagine the crying, the grief, the horror? The Israelites, however, were saved from this plague by a Passover lamb. By putting some of the blood of the lamb on their doorframes the Lord would "pass over" their houses and not permit the destroyer to enter and strike them down. This whole sacrificial idea is a foreshadowing of Christ, the Lamb of God, as our ultimate stand-in. The Lord will "pass over" us on Judgment Day because Jesus has already paid our debt – His blood saves us.

We really need to look at the Passover celebration as revealed in the instructions given to Moses and Aaron in chapter 12 of Exodus because the symbolism is wonderfully woven into the Jewish and the Christian experience.

Each household needed a lamb, a perfect male, and they had to take it on the tenth day of the month and not sacrifice it until the fourteenth day. Compare: Jesus entered Jerusalem on the 10th day and was crucified on the 14th day.

Passover restrictions required that they had to eat the lamb and not break any of the bones. Compare: Jesus was crucified, but His legs were not broken (as was the custom in crucifixions).

In celebrating the Seder (Passover) dinner Jews still put three pieces of unleavened bread together (representing the Father, Son, and Holy Spirit) then take the middle piece, break it and wrap it in white cloth (symbolizing Christ's death) and hide it (the burial). If you've seen Matzah bread you know it is striped and pierced (as was Jesus – whipped and later pierced with a sword). Later the bread is found (resurrection). The third cup of wine is drunk; it is the cup of redemption.

As you're going to see Jesus is all over the Old Testament in symbols, prophecies and archetype.

You see Him even in the **10 Commandments**. Read Exodus chapter 20. The first commandment is basically "I am Adonai your God" (The word here is the tetragrammaton made up of 4 Hebrew letters that might be pronounced Yahweh or Jehovah, but Jews replace this sacred name with Adonai or HaShem). If you started reading at verse 1 of chapter 20 then you know that God "spoke" all these words: the commandments. He starts with this implicit fact that He is our God.

"You shall not have other gods before me." Literally, it says "before my face," implying forever and everywhere, since God is omnipresent and eternal.

"You shall not take the name of Adonai your God in vain." This commandment prohibits the voicing of the Lord's name in an empty or useless way. Did you read that? **Do not** say "oh my God." (!) It has become a habit for too many people and it breaks my heart when I hear anyone and especially small children repeating this phrase.

"Remember the Sabbath day and keep it holy." Set it apart. The Sabbath should be special. Heed God's word, after all He spends several verses on this one command explaining that you should not work on the Sabbath.

"Honor your father and your mother." Now the commands switch from being about our relationship with God to being about our relationship with others. Notice that this command to honor your parents continues with a blessing for you if you obey. Read verse 12 and see what you will get if you honor your father and your mother.

"You shall not murder." If your translation says "kill" it is wrong. That is too broad a word. The actual Hebrew implies illegal killing only, hence murder. This commandment does not prohibit justified killing or killing in war.

"You shall not commit adultery." Could that be any clearer?

"You shall not steal." Stealing implies a lack of trust that God will supply all of our needs.

"You shall not bear false witness against your neighbor." This commandment is implicit in our lives if we live by the truth.

"You shall not covet" and this goes on to list the things that you shall not covet: your neighbor's house, wife, servants, ox, donkey, or anything he owns. To covet is to have a selfish desire or even lust.

The commandments are given in Deuteronomy 5 as well. Now let's get back to our connection with the 2nd Hebrew letter, bet. Exodus 19: 5 (KJV) says:

Now therefore, if ye will obey my voice indeed, and keep my covenant, then ye shall be a peculiar treasure unto me above all people: for all the earth is mine.

The word for covenant is b'rit, a key word that starts with bet and is central to the Bible and to the book of Exodus. Another bet word is, as mentioned above, house. The last 16 chapters of Exodus describe the building and consecration of the Tabernacle – The **House** of the Lord. It is very specific and there are several great websites where you can find depictions, models, and architectural drawings based on these chapters. In our next bet book, Jeremiah, we'll find that Israel has set their abominations in the house of the Lord.

ב Bet + Jeremiah

The Book of Jeremiah is primarily a message of judgment on Judah for rampant idolatry. As a bet b book we should find a connection to bet words like **house** and, indeed, we do. In Jeremiah 7: 30 (KJV) it is written:

For the children of Judah have done evil in my sight, saith the LORD: they have set their abominations in the house which is called by my name, to pollute it.

Other verses pertinent here are Jeremiah 16:10-13; 22:9; 32:29; 44:2-3:

¹⁰ "When you tell these people all this and they ask you, 'Why has the LORD decreed such a great disaster against us? What wrong have we done? What sin have we committed against the LORD our God?' ¹¹ then say to them, 'It is because your ancestors forsook me,' declares the LORD, 'and followed other gods and served and worshiped them. They forsook me and did not keep my law. ¹² But you have behaved more wickedly than your ancestors. See how all of you are following the stubbornness of your evil hearts instead of obeying me. ¹³ So I will throw you out of this land into a land neither you nor your ancestors have known, and there you will serve other gods day and night, for I will show you no favor.'

⁹ And the answer will be: 'Because they have forsaken the covenant of the LORD their God and have worshiped and served other gods.'"

²⁹ The Babylonians who are attacking this city will come in and set it on fire; they will burn it down, along with the houses where the people aroused my anger by burning incense on the roofs to Baal and by pouring out drink offerings to other gods.

² "This is what the LORD Almighty, the God of Israel, says: You saw the great disaster I brought on Jerusalem and on all the towns of Judah. Today they lie deserted and in ruins ³ because of the evil they have done. They aroused my anger by burning incense to and worshiping other gods that neither they nor you nor your ancestors ever knew.

After the death of King Josiah, the last righteous king, the nation of Judah had almost completely abandoned God and His commandments. Jeremiah compares Judah to a prostitute (Jeremiah 2:20; 3:1-3):

²⁰ "Long ago you broke off your yoke
and tore off your bonds;
you said, 'I will not serve you!'
Indeed, on every high hill
and under every spreading tree
you lay down as a prostitute.
¹ "If a man divorces his wife
and she leaves him and marries another man,
should he return to her again?
Would not the land be completely defiled?
But you have lived as a prostitute with many lovers—
would you now return to me?"

    declares the LORD.
² "Look up to the barren heights and see.
  Is there any place where you have not been ravished?
By the roadside you sat waiting for lovers,
  sat like a nomad in the desert.
You have defiled the land
  with your prostitution and wickedness.
³ Therefore the showers have been withheld,
  and no spring rains have fallen.
Yet you have the brazen look of a prostitute;
  you refuse to blush with shame.

    God had promised that He would judge idolatry most severely (Leviticus 26:31-33; Deuteronomy 28:49-68), and Jeremiah was warning Judah that God's judgment was at hand. God had delivered Judah from destruction on countless occasions, but His mercy was at its end. Jeremiah records King Nebuchadnezzar conquering Judah and making it subject to him (Jeremiah 24:1). After further rebellion, God brought Nebuchadnezzar and the Babylonian armies back to destroy and desolate Judah and Jerusalem (Jeremiah 52). Even in this most severe judgment, God promises restoration of Judah back into the land God has given them (Jeremiah 29:10).
    There is a wonderful foreshadowing in Jeremiah 23:5-6:

    ⁵ "The days are coming," declares the LORD,
  "when I will raise up for David a righteous Branch,
a King who will reign wisely
  and do what is just and right in the land.
⁶ In his days Judah will be saved
  and Israel will live in safety.
This is the name by which he will be called:
  The LORD Our Righteous Savior.

    These verses present a prophecy of the coming Messiah, Jesus Christ. The prophet describes Him as a Branch from the house of David (compare verse 5 with Matthew 1), the King who would reign in wisdom and righteousness (compare to Revelation 11:15). It is Christ who will finally be recognized by Israel as her true Messiah as He provides salvation for His chosen ones (compare verse 6 with Romans 11:26). Yes, you have to do a little work here on your own – flip through your Bible and look up these verses for yourself.
    Jeremiah is hugely prophetical. First and foremost there is the prophecy of the Babylonian captivity of 70 years, then the prophecy of the world-wide dispersion of the Jews. There is the prophecy of the final re-gathering, the kingdom age and the Day of Judgment on the Gentile powers and the Remnant of Israel. The words prophet and prophesy occur over a hundred times in this book.

ב Bet + 1st Corinthians

The apostle Paul wrote to the church in Corinth to inform them that he was sending Timothy to them and to give them some much needed reminders and instructions. His major themes are: divisions within the church, his own authority, sexual morality, what to do about food sacrificed to idols, the Lord's supper, spiritual gifts, love, and the resurrection.

Key bet words are "badal" and "bakah" which mean "divide", "beyn" which means "between", "bin" which is Hebrew for "discern" and "binah" which means "understanding". Rattling them off doesn't tell me anything – let's think about them. Divide, between, discern, understanding. We are told in the Scriptures to divide the words – discern their meanings to gain understanding. That's what we're trying to do here. Let's look at the word **division** as it comes up in Young's Literal Translation of 1st Corinthians 1:10 and 3:3:

¹⁰And I call upon you, brethren, through the name of our Lord Jesus Christ, that the same thing ye may all say, and there may not be **divisions** among you, and ye may be perfected in the same mind, and in the same judgment,

³for yet ye are fleshly, for where [there is] among you envying, and strife, and **divisions**, are ye not fleshly, and in the manner of men do walk?

There is a direct correlation to our previous bet book, Exodus. See Exodus 8:23:

²³and I have put a **division** between My people and thy people: to-morrow is this sign.'

Now compare how closely God has related these two books in the following passages from 1st Corinthians 10:1 and Exodus 14:16 where God **divided** the waters:

¹ For I do not want you to be ignorant of the fact, brothers and sisters, that our ancestors were all under the cloud and that **they all passed through** the sea.

¹⁶ Raise your staff and stretch out your hand over the sea to **divide** the water so that the Israelites can go through the sea on dry ground.

We'll look at more alphabetic connections in our three bet books at the end of this chapter.

In 1st Corinthians Paul tells us that the church (the Christian body) is, in essence, the dwelling place of the Holy Spirit. 1st Corinthians 3:16:

¹⁶ Don't you know that you yourselves are God's temple and that God's Spirit dwells in your midst?

Furthermore, we are entrusted with the "secret things" of God (1st Corinthians 4:1) and must prove faithful. He gets to the meat of the matter in chapter 5 and begins by addressing the immorality in the Corinthian church. Apparently a man in the church hooked up with his own step-mother (5:1) and the rest of the church didn't even balk. Read the chapter to see how strongly Paul scolds them. What does Paul command them to do?

Chapter 6 makes some very strong points against suing a fellow Christian and then hits again the topic of sexual immorality. Verses 18 – 20 are the best verses I can think of to show to our sons and daughters:

18 Flee from sexual immorality. All other sins a person commits are outside the body, but whoever sins sexually, sins against their own body. **19** Do you not know that your bodies are temples of the Holy Spirit, who is in you, whom you have received from God? You are not your own; **20** you were bought at a price. Therefore honor God with your bodies.

Read it again aloud. There is much to contemplate there. I found it interesting that Paul asks the question about knowing that your bodies are temples of the Holy Spirit when he had earlier in his letter stated it twice. When something is stated three times . . . you better pay attention! As a Christian, your body is the Holy Spirit's temple, don't smoke Him out. Don't pollute the temple or harm it in any way.

Chapter 3 Gimel

Aleph	1. Genesis	23. Isaiah	45. Romans
Bet	2. Exodus	24. Jeremiah	46. 1st Corinthians
Gimel	*3. Leviticus*	*25. Lamentations*	*47. 2nd Corinthians*
Dalet	4. Numbers	26. Ezekiel	48. Galatians
Hey	5. Deuteronomy	27. Daniel	49. Ephesians
Vav	6. Joshua	28. Hosea	50. Philippians
Zayin	7. Judges	29. Joel	51. Colossians
Het	8. Ruth	30. Amos	52. 1st Thessalonians
Tet	9. 1st Samuel	31. Obadiah	53. 2nd Thessalonians
Yod	10. 2nd Samuel	32. Jonah	54. 1st Timothy
Kaph	11. 1st Kings	33. Micah	55. 2nd Timothy
Lamed	12. 2nd Kings	34. Nahum	56. Titus
Mem	13. 1st Chronicles	35. Habakkuk	57. Philemon
Nun	14. 2nd Chronicles	36. Zephaniah	58. Hebrews
Samek	15. Ezra	37. Haggai	59. James
Ayin	16. Nehemiah	38. Zechariah	60. 1st Peter
Pey	17. Esther	39. Malachi	61. 2nd Peter
Tzaddi	18. Job	40. Matthew	62. 1st John
Quph	19. Psalms	41. Mark	63. 2nd John
Resh	20. Proverbs	42. Luke	64. 3rd John
Shin	21. Ecclesiastes	43. John	65. Jude
Tav	22. Song of Songs	44. Acts	66. Revelation

ג

Gimel + Leviticus

The letter itself, gimel, means "camel". The desert dwelling Bedouins call the camel the "gift of God" because their entire sustenance – food, drink, clothing, fuel, and travel – depends upon it. Camels are frequently used in the Bible as a symbol of wealth and abundance. Picture the wise men with camels, bearing gifts for the Christ child.

Psalm 119:17

¹⁷ Do good to your servant, and I will live;
I will obey your word.

In this alphabetic verse the word for "do good" (or "deal bountifully" in some translations) is the word gamal. The three letters that spell gimel, also spell gamal, gamál, and gomel (vowel points were added centuries later). Gamal means camel, gamál means recompense, reward, deal bountifully or do good and gomel means benefactor or abundant giver. Jewish sages teach that in the alphabet the gimel symbolizes a rich man running after a poor man, the dalet, which is the next letter, to give him charity.

Following the alphabet then we have aleph with its meaning of leader for God, or Av, the father (leader of the house), and bet with its meaning of house with the letter nun (heir) for the word ben (son) (heir of the house) and now we have the third letter which should signify the Holy Spirit, right? Gamal – abundant giver – what do you think? As I see it the first three books of the Old Testament show us the Father, Son, and Holy Spirit.

Leviticus (Va'yikra in Hebrew) means "and He called", which is how verse one starts. We call this book Leviticus because it records the duties of the Levites. The Hebrew title is representative of the content and purpose of the book, namely the calling of God's people, and in particular the calling of the Levites, to minister before Him.

This book was written by Moses and its major themes are like an instruction manual for morals and ethics. There are civil, sanitary, ceremonial, moral and religious regulations for the nation of Israel. There are also instructions for making offerings (burnt, meat, peace, sin, trespass, grain). We have the ordination of Aaron and his son, rules and laws for purification, regulations for atonement, rules for sexual relationships, provisions for festivals, and final instructions and warnings.

All the offerings, as well as the ceremonies and laws, served to constantly remind Israel that God is eminently holy. God could be approached only by the priests, and then only in strict obedience to the detailed instructions for purification. God required the sacrifice of innocent animals for the covering of man's sin. These sacrifices were symbolic of the ultimate sacrifice which would take away the sin of the whole world.

What's really interesting is that in Leviticus you'll find some "divine warnings". There will be terror, the people will be slain and others will be scattered. There are very specific points made in regards to bread and famine, waste and desolation. These exact warnings are echoed in the "divine retribution" fulfilled in the second gimel book, Lamentations.

But such a remarkable link is not confined to just this. Leviticus also hooks up with the third gimel book, 2nd Corinthians, in their matching theme of reconciliation. Specific examples will be given when we reach those books.

Leviticus is clearly a manual for the priests to follow. It explains burnt offerings, grain offerings, fellowship offerings, sin and guilt offerings and how it is forbidden to eat fat and blood. The section on clean and unclean food (chapter 11) makes sense from a scientific point of view as well. As do the chapters (13, 14) about infectious skin diseases and dealing with mildew (mold). Chapter 18 gets uncomfortably specific (for some people) about sexual relations. "Do not have sexual relations" with a relative, someone of the same sex, or an animal, is pretty explicit and unambiguous; these statements cannot be argued away. God says "NO", so don't do it.

Though the Ten Commandments were covered in Exodus 20, they appear again here in Leviticus 19 with some embellishments.

Chapter 23 starts with what I think is a pleasant contrast to all the previous negative prohibitions and sacrifices. The Lord appoints some feasts: The Passover, Feast of Unleavened Bread, Firstfruits, Feast of Weeks, Feast of Trumpets, Day of Atonement (Yom Kippur) and the Feast of Tabernacles. These are wonderful "parties" and have special significance to Israel, but even more significance to Christians. Why? Because they are or will be fulfilled in Christ.

First of all Passover, the Feast of Unleavened Bread and Firstfruits fall on the 14th, 15th and 17th of the Jewish calendar month of Nisan. These are spring feasts. Pentecost is 50 days later on the 6th of Sivan, a summer month. The last three feasts are all autumn festivals falling on the 1st, 10th and 15th of Tishri.

The Passover supper (the Seder meal, explained earlier in the chapter on Exodus) was what Jesus and the disciples were having the night before His crucifixion – The Last Supper! For the Jew Passover celebrates liberation from slavery to Egypt; to the Christian Christ's crucifixion signifies liberation from slavery to sin and death.

The Feast of Unleavened Bread began on the day Christ was crucified – Good Friday! Leaven, or yeast, is symbolic of sin. Jews eat unleavened bread, bread made without yeast called matzah, during the seven days of this feast. Matzah is striped and pierced, an obvious (to a Christian) link to Christ's pre-crucifixion beating and the sword piercing He received on the cross.

The Feast of First Fruits took place on the day Christ rose from the dead! This feast was to present the first fruits of the harvest to God. The priest would wave the first sheaf of grain and it was accepted by God on the people's behalf – just as Jesus now is the "first fruit" accepted on our behalf.

The Feast of Pentecost was the day the Holy Spirit was poured out onto the disciples! The first Pentecost was 7 weeks after the death of the Passover lambs. On that day Moses received the Law on the stone tablets and when he returned to camp 3000 men died because of their sin. Seven weeks after Christ, the Lamb of God, was crucified the disciples received the Holy Spirit and 3000 believed that day (Acts 2:41).

The next three will be fulfilled as prophesied in the Holy Scriptures. The Feast of Trumpets was a day of rest for Israel on which they should "sound the trumpets". This is Rosh Hashanah, the Jewish New Year. At some future date the trumpets will sound Christ's return. Now that will really be a new year!

The Day of Atonement is the day that the priests made atonement for Israel. The people fasted and prayed. On some future Day of Atonement Jesus will be revealed as King and return to this earth.

The Feast of Tabernacles was a feast of joy when the harvest was brought in. Someday it will be the harvest of saved souls and a day that Christ will begin His rule.

These seven feasts, given and explained THOUSANDS of years ago, show us right where we are on God's calendar. Here are two good websites to visit if you want to read more:

http://endtimepilgrim.org/jewishholidays.htm
http://www.luziusschneider.com/Papers/JewishFeasts.htm

ג
Gimel + Lamentations

Remember that gimel g is the letter that means camel and represents the Divine Comforter. Here we have Lamentations, often called the saddest book in existence. In Hebrew this book is called Eichah meaning "how," which is the first word (read vs. 1).

It was written by the prophet Jeremiah who was an eye-witness to the destruction of the temple in Jerusalem. He alternates between accounts of the horrible aftermath of the destruction of the city and the confessions of the people's deep sins, and then to his appeals to God for mercy.

Randomly pick a verse and read it and you'll see why we don't normally read from this book in church. However, the Jews read Lamentations publicly each year at Tisha B'av which is a fast commemorating the destruction of the temple of Jerusalem in both 586 BC and 70 AD.

There are specific parallels between Leviticus (our first gimel book) and Lamentations. The divine warning in Leviticus matches the divine retribution shown in Lamentations. Compare for yourself:

Leviticus 26:17 :
17 I will set my face against you so that you will be defeated by your enemies; those who hate you will rule over you, and you will flee even when no one is pursuing you.

Lamentations 3:52:
52 Those who were my enemies without cause
hunted me like a bird.

Leviticus 26:33:
33 I will scatter you among the nations and will draw out my sword and pursue you. Your land will be laid waste, and your cities will lie in ruins.

Lamentations 2:21:
21 "Young and old lie together
in the dust of the streets;
my young men and maidens
have fallen by the sword.
You have slain them in the day of your anger;
you have slaughtered them without pity.

There are more to check out on your own: Leviticus 26:26 + Lamentations 5:9, Leviticus 26:28 + Lamentations 4:10, and Leviticus 26:31 + Lamentations 3:46.

Notice also the number of verses in Lamentations. Chapters 1, and 4 each have 22 verses. Chapter 3 has 66 verses (3 x 22 = 66). This is a sure give away that Lamentations is full of acrostic verses. In Lamentations 1, 2, and 4 each consecutive Hebrew letter begins a whole verse and in Lamentations 3 each letter begins three verses.

ג

Gimel + 2nd Corinthians

Remember the letter gimel means camel and it is symbolic of a **beneficial giver**. Remember that in our first gimel book, Leviticus, we had the representation of the Holy Spirit, our **Comforter.**

2nd Corinthians was written by the Apostle Paul. Its major theme is always to be faithful to Christ. This epistle shows Paul's state of physical weakness, weariness, and pain as well as his great anguish of heart over the distrust felt toward him by Jews and Jewish Christians. The letters tells us of Paul's principles of action for ministry, the collection for the poor saints at Jerusalem and Paul's defense of his apostolic authority.

2nd Corinthians teaches that God loves a **cheerful giver**. There are two whole chapters on the virtue of giving. The ministry of reconciliation is also a major theme.

Read 2nd Corinthians 1:1-6:

¹Paul, an apostle of Christ Jesus by the will of God, and Timothy our brother,
To the church of God in Corinth, together with all the saints throughout Achaia:
²Grace and peace to you from God our Father and the Lord Jesus Christ.
³Praise be to the God and Father of our Lord Jesus Christ, the Father of compassion and the God of all **comfort**, ⁴who **comforts** us in all our troubles, so that we can **comfort** those in any trouble with the **comfort** we ourselves have received from God. ⁵For just as the sufferings of Christ flow over into our lives, so also through Christ our **comfort** overflows. ⁶If we are distressed, it is for your **comfort** and salvation; if we are **comforted**, it is for your **comfort**, which produces in you patient endurance of the same sufferings we suffer.

Wow, right away in the opening of this letter we get the gimel symbolism of comfort. Would it surprise you to know that we have here the greatest density of the word comfort in the whole Bible? Who is the Comforter? Jesus said in John 14:26 that God would send the Comforter, the Holy Ghost.

Our other gimel books, Leviticus and Lamentations, were linked. Here in 2nd Corinthians we see the great sorrow of Lamentations reflected in this letter which has been called the "epistle of tears." In fact, the words sorry and sorrow come up over a dozen times in this short letter.

There are several verses in Lamentations like these from the King James version: "mine eye runneth down with water, because the **comforter** that should relieve my soul is far from me", "Zion spreadeth forth her hands, and there is none to **comfort** her", "they have heard that I sigh: there is none to **comfort** me". Whereas Lamentations specifically declares that the Comforter is missing, we just saw that the promise of a Comforter dominated the opening of 2nd Corinthians. How marvelously are the books of His Holy Word linked!

Next there is the ministry of reconciliation. Read 2nd Corinthians 5: 17 – 21:

17 Therefore, if anyone is in Christ, the new creation has come: The old has gone, the new is here! **18** All this is from God, who reconciled us to himself through Christ and gave us the **ministry of reconciliation**: **19** that **God was reconciling the world to himself in Christ, not counting people's sins against them.** And he has committed to us the message of reconciliation. **20** We are therefore Christ's ambassadors, as though God were making his appeal through us. We implore you on Christ's behalf: Be reconciled to God. **21** God made him who had no sin to be sin for us, so that in him we might become the righteousness of God.

Why is this important? Because it matches up to the first gimel book, Leviticus. See Leviticus 16:32 – 34:

32 The priest who is anointed and ordained to succeed his father as high priest is to make atonement. He is to put on the sacred linen garments **33** and make atonement for the Most Holy Place, for the tent of meeting and the altar, and for the priests and all the members of the community.
34 "This is to be a lasting ordinance for you: Atonement is to be made once a year for all the sins of the Israelites."
And it was done, as the LORD commanded Moses.

In Leviticus it was the priest's duty to make atonement and **reconcile** the people to God. The entire premise of the book of Leviticus is instructions for the priests (the Levites). But now in the New Testament we have Christ doing the work of the priest – once and for all. Hooray! Or rather, halleluia!

And there's more. Keep reading and you'll find this ministry of reconciliation blossoming into a ministry of the Spirit. 2nd Corinthians 3: 3 – 9:

3 You show that you are a letter from Christ, the result of our ministry, written not with ink but with the Spirit of the living God, not on tablets of stone but on tablets of human hearts.
4 Such confidence we have through Christ before God. **5** Not that we are competent in ourselves to claim anything for ourselves, but our competence comes from God. **6** He has made us competent as ministers of a new covenant—not of the letter but of the Spirit; for the letter kills, but the Spirit gives life.
7 Now if the ministry that brought death, which was engraved in letters on stone, came with glory, so that the Israelites could not look steadily at the face of Moses because of its glory, transitory though it was, **8** will not the ministry of the Spirit be even more glorious? **9** If the ministry that brought condemnation was glorious, how much more glorious is the ministry that brings righteousness!

They didn't have this ministry of the spirit in Leviticus, but rather it was all about ministry of the priests – the burnt offerings, the sin offerings, the meat offerings, the trespass offerings, and so on. (See Leviticus 7: 35 – 38.)

Something to remember if you witness to someone: 2nd Corinthians 2: 14:

14 But thanks be to God, who always leads us as captives in Christ's triumphal procession and uses us to spread the aroma of the knowledge of him everywhere.

Pretty, isn't it? What gloriously creative imagery there is here. Can you see yourself as a "captive" of Christ? Can you see yourself led away in a "triumphal procession"? The two ideas seem dissimilar. Yet there is an "aroma" of the knowledge of Christ that should follow you. Will you let it?

There are verses in 2nd Corinthians that encourage those who may be discouraged. When you are feeling down meditate on these verses:

2nd Corinthians 4:8; 4:16-18:

8 We are hard pressed on every side, but not crushed; perplexed, but not in despair;
16 Therefore we do not lose heart. Though outwardly we are wasting away, yet inwardly we are being renewed day by day. **17** For our light and momentary troubles are achieving for us an eternal glory that far outweighs them all. **18** So we fix our eyes not on what is seen, but on what is unseen, since what is seen is temporary, but what is unseen is eternal.

Last thing, it is in 2nd Corinthians that we find a warning not to marry a non-Christian. Read 2nd Corinthians 6: 14 for yourself to learn why.

Chapter 4 Dalet

Aleph	1. Genesis		23. Isaiah		45. Romans
Bet	2. Exodus		24. Jeremiah		46. 1st Corinthians
Gimel	3. Leviticus		25. Lamentations		47. 2nd Corinthians
Dalet	*4. Numbers*		*26. Ezekiel*		*48. Galatians*
Hey	5. Deuteronomy		27. Daniel		49. Ephesians
Vav	6. Joshua		28. Hosea		50. Philippians
Zayin	7. Judges		29. Joel		51. Colossians
Het	8. Ruth		30. Amos		52. 1st Thessalonians
Tet	9. 1st Samuel		31. Obadiah		53. 2nd Thessalonians
Yod	10. 2nd Samuel		32. Jonah		54. 1st Timothy
Kaph	11. 1st Kings		33. Micah		55. 2nd Timothy
Lamed	12. 2nd Kings		34. Nahum		56. Titus
Mem	13. 1st Chronicles		35. Habakkuk		57. Philemon
Nun	14. 2nd Chronicles		36. Zephaniah		58. Hebrews
Samek	15. Ezra		37. Haggai		59. James
Ayin	16. Nehemiah		38. Zechariah		60. 1st Peter
Pey	17. Esther		39. Malachi		61. 2nd Peter
Tzaddi	18. Job		40. Matthew		62. 1st John
Quph	19. Psalms		41. Mark		63. 2nd John
Resh	20. Proverbs		42. Luke		64. 3rd John
Shin	21. Ecclesiastes		43. John		65. Jude
Tav	22. Song of Songs		44. Acts		66. Revelation

ד
Dalet + Numbers

Dalet means **door**. It kind of looks like a doorway, perhaps into a tent. In the alphabetic (acrostic) verses some dalet words (among others) are derek (way), dam (blood) and damam (rest).

So far we've had Genesis, the book of the creation and fall, Exodus, the book of redemption, and Leviticus, the book of worship and fellowship. Now we get to Numbers, the book of service and walk.

Numbers records the population numbers of the Hebrews thus the title seems obvious. In Hebrew it is called B'midbar because the first words are "In the wilderness" (b'midbar), appropriate because it contains the 40 years of wandering. This book was written by Moses. Its major themes are that every servant (person) was numbered, knew his place in the family, and had his own definitely assigned service. Read Numbers 1:1-3 (bold added):

¹The LORD spoke to Moses in the Tent of Meeting in the Desert of Sinai on the first day of the second month of the second year after the Israelites came out of Egypt. He said: ² "Take a census of the whole Israelite community by their clans and families, **listing every man by name, one by one**. ³ You and Aaron are to number by their divisions all the men in Israel twenty years old or more who are able to serve in the army.

The book of Numbers can be divided into sections. The first 10 chapters show the preparation for the journey into the Promised Land. Read chapter 2 below (or at least scan the bold print I added):

¹ The LORD said to Moses and Aaron: ² "The Israelites are to **camp around the Tent of Meeting** some distance from it, each man under his standard with the banners of his family."
³ **On the east**, toward the sunrise, the divisions of **the camp of Judah** are to encamp under their standard. The leader of the people of Judah is Nahshon son of Amminadab. ⁴ His division numbers 74,600.
⁵ The tribe of Issachar will camp next to them. The leader of the people of Issachar is Nethanel son of Zuar. ⁶ His division numbers 54,400.
⁷ The tribe of Zebulun will be next. The leader of the people of Zebulun is Eliab son of Helon. ⁸ His division numbers 57,400.
⁹ **All the men assigned to the camp of Judah, according to their divisions, number 186,400**. They will set out first.
¹⁰ **On the south** will be the divisions of **the camp of Reuben** under their standard. The leader of the people of Reuben is Elizur son of Shedeur. ¹¹ His division numbers 46,500.
¹² The tribe of Simeon will camp next to them. The leader of the people of Simeon is Shelumiel son of Zurishaddai. ¹³ His division numbers 59,300.
¹⁴ The tribe of Gad will be next. The leader of the people of Gad is Eliasaph son of Deuel. ¹⁵ His division numbers 45,650.
¹⁶ **All the men assigned to the camp of Reuben, according to their divisions, number 151,450**. They will set out second.

¹⁷ Then the Tent of Meeting and the camp of the Levites will set out in the middle of the camps. They will set out in the same order as they encamp, each in his own place under his standard.

¹⁸ On the west will be the divisions of **the camp of Ephraim** under their standard. The leader of the people of Ephraim is Elishama son of Ammihud. **¹⁹** His division numbers 40,500.

²⁰ The tribe of Manasseh will be next to them. The leader of the people of Manasseh is Gamaliel son of Pedahzur. **²¹** His division numbers 32,200.

²² The tribe of Benjamin will be next. The leader of the people of Benjamin is Abidan son of Gideoni. **²³** His division numbers 35,400.

²⁴ All the men assigned to the camp of Ephraim, according to their divisions, number 108,100. They will set out third.

²⁵ On the north will be the divisions of **the camp of Dan**, under their standard. The leader of the people of Dan is Ahiezer son of Ammishaddai. **²⁶** His division numbers 62,700.

²⁷ The tribe of Asher will camp next to them. The leader of the people of Asher is Pagiel son of Ocran. **²⁸** His division numbers 41,500.

²⁹ The tribe of Naphtali will be next. The leader of the people of Naphtali is Ahira son of Enan. **³⁰** His division numbers 53,400.

³¹ All the men assigned to the camp of Dan number 157,600. They will set out last, under their standards.

³² These are the Israelites, counted according to their families. All those in the camps, by their divisions, number 603,550. **³³** The Levites, however, were not counted along with the other Israelites, as the LORD commanded Moses.

³⁴ So the Israelites did everything the LORD commanded Moses; that is the way they encamped under their standards, and that is the way they set out, each with his clan and family.

On the next page is one way that the camp might have looked:

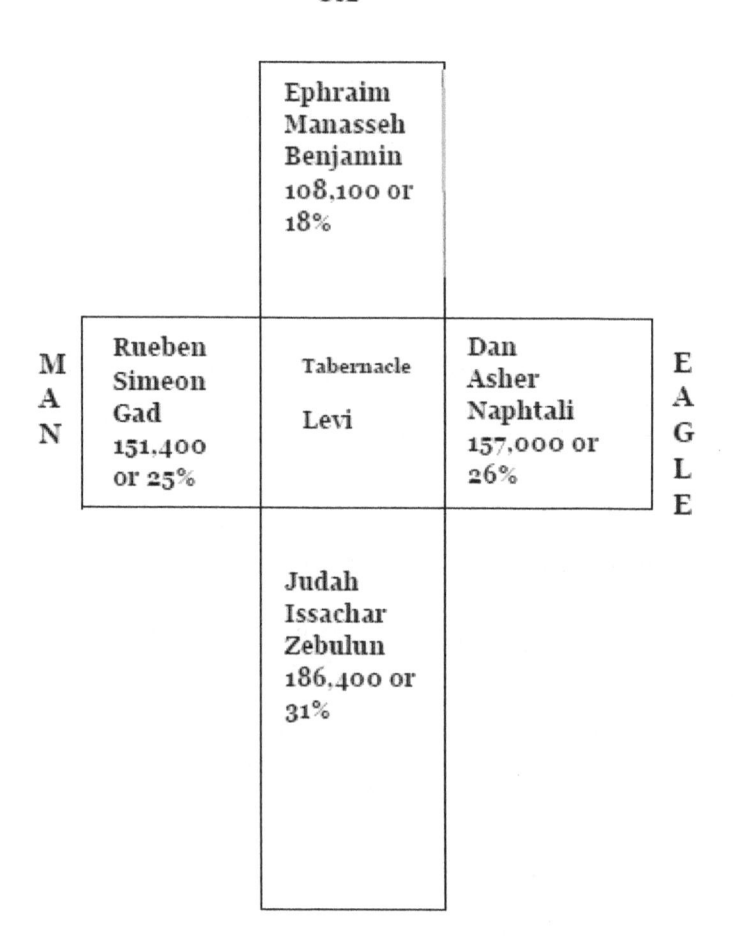

```
                          OX

              ┌───────────────┐
              │ Ephraim       │
              │ Manasseh      │
              │ Benjamin      │
              │ 108,100 or    │
              │ 18%           │
              │               │
      ┌───────┼───────────────┼───────┐
  M   │ Rueben│               │ Dan   │   E
  A   │ Simeon│  Tabernacle   │ Asher │   A
  N   │ Gad   │               │Naphtali│  G
      │151,400│    Levi       │157,000 │  L
      │ or 25%│               │ or 26% │  E
      └───────┼───────────────┼───────┘
              │ Judah         │
              │ Issachar      │
              │ Zebulun       │
              │ 186,400 or    │
              │ 31%           │
              │               │
              └───────────────┘

                         LION
```

Personally, I like the idea of the cross configuration. A second thing to notice is the standards or banners that they camped under: man, ox, eagle, lion. These four symbols come up again in Revelation 4:7:

> The first living creature was like a **lion**, the second was like an **ox**, the third had a face like a **man**, the fourth was like a flying **eagle**.

But that's not all. As will be pointed out in the sections on the Gospel books, these four creatures are apparent in each of those books as representative of a certain facet of Jesus. That is, that in the book of Matthew Jesus is portrayed as the **lion** of the tribe of Judah, in Mark he is the servant and workman (like an **ox**), in Luke he is the great physician and friend of sinners (a **man**), and in John he is the Word, the Living Bread "that came down from heaven" (like an **eagle**).

The next section of the book of Numbers is chapters 11-15: Rebellion in the wilderness. This section shows their refusal to obey the Lord when commanded to enter the Promised Land, hence the wandering.

Chapters 16-36 are the third section: Death in the wilderness – 40 years of wandering until all of that generation died out.

As stated before, Numbers describes the Israelite people's journey in the desert wilderness. There they learn how God wishes them to be organized, and how the Levites are to help Israel's priests. They also find out who will be chosen to lead them when they enter Canaan.

But the Israelites' desert journey also shows the rebellious side of the people. They complain that God has brought them out to the wilderness to starve or to die of thirst. They plot to get rid of their leaders, Moses and Aaron. Because of these sins, God does not allow them an easy, straight path to the land of promise. Instead, all those in the older generation who left Egypt (including Moses) must wander for forty years and eventually die in the desert wilderness. Only those in the younger generation (see chapter 14: 22, 23, 29, 30) would follow the faithful leaders, Joshua and Caleb, into Canaan. The lesson is about trust in God. Those who obey and trust God will receive God's blessings. Those who don't obey will not receive the blessings connected with God's promises. Read the following selection and underline the words you think should be in bold print. Numbers 14: 18 – 35:

18The LORD is slow to anger, abounding in love and forgiving sin and rebellion. Yet he does not leave the guilty unpunished; he punishes the children for the sin of the fathers to the third and fourth generation.' **19** In accordance with your great love, forgive the sin of these people, just as you have pardoned them from the time they left Egypt until now."

20 The LORD replied, "I have forgiven them, as you asked. **21** Nevertheless, as surely as I live and as surely as the glory of the LORD fills the whole earth, **22** not one of the men who saw my glory and the miraculous signs I performed in Egypt and in the desert but who disobeyed me and tested me ten times- **23** not one of them will ever see the land I promised on oath to their forefathers. No one who has treated me with contempt will ever see it. **24** But because my servant Caleb has a different spirit and follows me wholeheartedly, I will bring him into the land he went to, and his descendants will inherit it. **25** Since the Amalekites and Canaanites are living in the valleys, turn back tomorrow and set out toward the desert along the route to the Red Sea."

26 The LORD said to Moses and Aaron: **27** "How long will this wicked community grumble against me? I have heard the complaints of these grumbling Israelites. **28** So tell them, 'As surely as I live, declares the LORD, I will do to you the very things I heard you say: **29** In this desert your bodies will fall—every one of you twenty years old or more who was counted in the census and who has grumbled against me. **30** Not one of you will enter the land I swore with uplifted hand to make your home, except Caleb son of Jephunneh and Joshua son of Nun. **31** As for your children that you said would be taken as plunder, I will bring them in to enjoy the land you have rejected. **32** But you—your bodies will fall in this desert. **33** Your children will be shepherds here for forty years, suffering for your unfaithfulness, until the last of your bodies lies in the desert. **34** For forty years—one year for each of the forty days you explored the land—you will suffer for your sins and know what it is like to have me against you.' **35** I, the LORD, have spoken, and I will surely do these things to this whole wicked community, which has banded together against me. They will meet their end in this desert; here they will die."

Is Jesus in Numbers? Read Numbers 24:17 :

"I see him, but not now;
I behold him, but not near.
A star will come out of Jacob;
a scepter will rise out of Israel.
He will crush the foreheads of Moab,
the skulls of all the sons of Sheth.

– This is a Messianic Kingdom prophecy.

ד
Dalet + Ezekiel

The Name of the Fourth Letter, dalet, signifies a **door**. It represents the two universal doors by which we all enter and exit this world, **birth** and **death**. Key dalet words (among others) are derek (way), dam (blood) and damam (rest). Ezekiel 41: 23-25 describes some very important doors:

> 23 Both the outer sanctuary and the Most Holy Place had double doors. 24 Each door had two leaves—two hinged leaves for each door. 25 And on the doors of the outer sanctuary were carved cherubim and palm trees like those carved on the walls, and there was a wooden overhang on the front of the portico.

I did a search for the word door in the Bible and found 239 verses containing this word. Here's how it looks in a graph matching the books up 3 at a time:

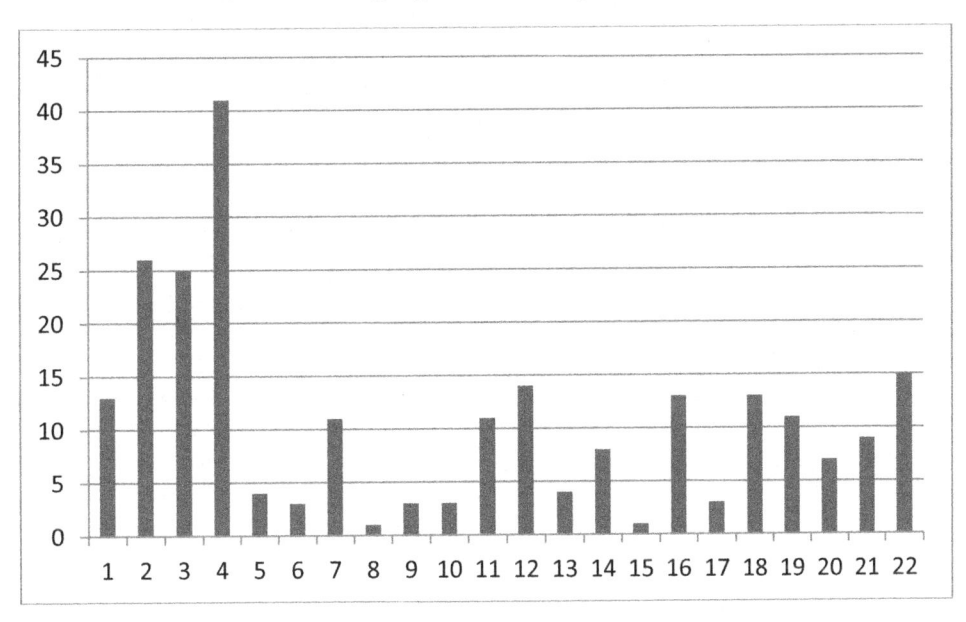

It is rather amazing that the meaning of the 4th letter peaks right where it should.
(Other interesting "connect 4" tidbits: Numbers records the fourfold camp and the first violation of the 4th commandment. Ezekiel has the greatest density of the number 4 and records the fourfold temple and the four living creatures that had four faces. Galatians speaks of the four "weak and beggarly elements" (days, months, times and years) in chapter 4.)

Ezekiel in Hebrew is "Y'chkezkiel" meaning "God will strengthen". The book was written by Ezekiel who was carried away to Babylon during the exile (remember Jeremiah prophesied about the Temple destruction and the 70 year exile). Ezekiel's main purpose was to keep before the generation born in exile the national sins which had brought Israel so low. He also sustained the faith of the exiles by predictions of national restoration, justice upon their oppressors and national glory.

Ezekiel's book can be divided into four sections: Chapters 1-24 contain the prophecies about the ruin of Jerusalem; Chapters 25-32 have the prophecies of God's judgment on nearby nations; Chapter 33 has a last call for repentance to Israel; and Chapters 34-48 hold prophecies concerning the future restoration of Israel.

Let's start with Ezekiel's 1st vision in chapter 1, verses 4 through 10:

"And I looked, and, behold, a whirlwind came out of the north, a great cloud, and a fire infolding itself, and a brightness was about it, and out of the midst thereof as the colour of amber, out of the midst of the fire. Also out of the midst thereof came the likeness of four living creatures. And this was their appearance; they had the likeness of a man. And every one had four faces, and every one had four wings. And their feet were straight feet; and the sole of their feet was like the sole of a calf's foot: and they sparkled like the colour of burnished brass. And they had the hands of a man under their wings on their four sides; and they four had their faces and their wings. Their wings were joined one to another; they turned not when they went; they went every one straight forward. As for the likeness of their faces, they four had the face of a man, and the face of a lion, on the right side: and they four had the face of an ox on the left side; they four also had the face of an eagle."

You can find many artists' renditions of this description and some look eerily like something from our present day. Another vision of Ezekiel is several chapters long about the temple:

1 In the twenty-fifth year of our exile, at the beginning of the year, on the tenth of the month, in the fourteenth year after the fall of the city—on that very day the hand of the LORD was on me and he took me there. **2** In visions of God he took me to the land of Israel and set me on a very high mountain, on whose south side were some buildings that looked like a city. **3** He took me there, and I saw a man whose appearance was like bronze; he was standing in the gateway with a linen cord and a measuring rod in his hand. **4** The man said to me, "Son of man, look carefully and listen closely and pay attention to everything I am going to show you, for that is why you have been brought here. Tell the people of Israel everything you see."

It goes on to describe all the gates and the rooms. A picture is worth these thousand words, so read the description for yourself and sketch out the courts and gates and rooms. Don't forget the palm tree decorations.

Ezekiel links back to Numbers, the first dalet book, in the following way. Compare these verses, Numbers 14:33-34 and Ezekiel 4:5-6 :

33 Your children will be shepherds here for forty years, suffering for your unfaithfulness, until the last of your bodies lies in the wilderness. **34** For forty years—**one year for each of the forty days** you explored the land—you will suffer for your sins and know what it is like to have me against you.'

5 I have assigned you the **same number of days as the years** of their sin. So for 390 days you will bear the sin of the people of Israel.

⁶ "After you have finished this, lie down again, this time on your right side, and bear the sin of the people of Judah. I have assigned you **40 days, a day for each year**.

When God calculated His judgment using "a day for a year", He commanded His Prophet to lie 390 days on his left side for the sins of Israel, and 40 days on his right for the sins of Judah. The total, therefore, is 390 +40 = 430, the same number Paul uses below in reference to the Law in the third dalet book Galatians (3:17):

¹⁷ What I mean is this: The law, introduced 430 years later, does not set aside the covenant previously established by God and thus do away with the promise. ¹⁸ For if the inheritance depends on the law, then it no longer depends on the promise; but God in his grace gave it to Abraham through a promise.

Furthermore, Paul speaks of a covenant. Read Numbers 25:12:

¹² Therefore tell him I am making my **covenant of peace** with him.

And Ezekiel 37:26:

²⁶ I will make a **covenant of peace** with them; it will be an everlasting covenant. I will establish them and increase their numbers, and I will put my sanctuary among them forever.

How perfectly aligned are the words of the Holy Scriptures!

ד
Dalet + Galatians
Galatians is the third dalet book. Remember the letter and what it means? Door.
Galatians was written by the apostle Paul. The Galatians had become the prey of the legalizers, the Judaizing missionaries from Palestine. They believed 2 false doctrines: one was that obedience to the law was mingled with faith as the grounds of the sinner's justification and the other was that the justified believer was made perfect by keeping the law. Think about that. You might find that false doctrine resurfacing today. A sinner is justified by faith alone; there is no salvation by keeping the law. Don't let someone tell you that you're not getting into Heaven if you don't obey the 10 commandments.

Read Galatians 2:16, 3:11,13 and 3:23-24:

¹⁶know that a man is not justified by observing the law, but by faith in Jesus Christ. So we, too, have put our faith in Christ Jesus that we may be **justified by faith in Christ and not by observing the law**, because by observing the law no one will be justified.

¹¹Clearly **no one is justified before God by the law**, because, "The righteous will live by faith."

¹³**Christ redeemed us from the curse of the law** by becoming a curse for us, for it is written: "Cursed is everyone who is hung on a tree."

²³Before this faith came, we were held prisoners by the law, locked up until faith should be revealed. ²⁴So the law was put in charge to lead us to Christ that we might be **justified by faith**.

In chapter 4 Paul shows great concern for the Galatians:

⁸Formerly, when you did not know God, you were slaves to those who by nature are not gods. ⁹But now that you know God—or rather are known by God—how is it that you are turning back to those weak and miserable principles? Do you wish to be enslaved by them all over again? ¹⁰You are observing special days and months and seasons and years!

Paul marvels, "You are observing special days and months and seasons and years!" Yet these are not pagan festivals that he is referring to, but important dates on the Jewish calendar. We understand that there is a sense in which the observance of special days could be tolerated (Romans 14:5-6), but the Galatians are taught to observe them for justification before God and other spiritual attainments. Paul's position is that this is like returning to paganism, back to ignorance and enslavement. And this is also his assessment of the Judaizers' religion.

As a dalet book Galatians should link in some way with Numbers and Ezekiel. Here's how. In Numbers 14: 33 – 35 God says:

³³ Your children will be shepherds here for forty years, suffering for your unfaithfulness, until the last of your bodies lies in the desert. ³⁴ For forty years—**one year for each of the forty days** you explored the land—you will suffer for your sins and know what it is like to

have me against you.' **35** I, the LORD, have spoken, and I will surely do these things to this whole wicked community, which has banded together against me. They will meet their end in this desert; here they will die."
Then in Ezekiel 4: 4 – 6

4 "Then lie on your left side and put the sin of the house of Israel upon yourself. You are to bear their sin for the number of days you lie on your side. **5** I have assigned you the same number of days as the years of their sin. So for 390 days you will bear the sin of the house of Israel.
6 "After you have finished this, lie down again, this time on your right side, and bear the sin of the house of Judah. I have assigned you 40 days, **a day for each year**.

When God calculated His judgment using "a day for a year", He commanded His Prophet to lie 390 days on his left side for the sins of Israel, and 40 days on his right for the sins of Judah. 390 +40 = **430**. Now for the really cool, amazing stuff: In Galatians Paul uses the same number in reference to the Law in chapter 3: 17-18:

17What I mean is this: The law, introduced **430** years later, does not set aside the covenant previously established by God and thus do away with the promise. **18**For if the inheritance depends on the law, then it no longer depends on a promise; but God in his grace gave it to Abraham through a promise.

Sound familiar? It should, I'm repeating part of the connections here that I explained under the book of Ezekiel.

Chapter 5 Hey

Aleph	1. Genesis		23. Isaiah		45. Romans
Bet	2. Exodus		24. Jeremiah		46. 1st Corinthians
Gimel	3. Leviticus		25. Lamentations		47. 2nd Corinthians
Dalet	4. Numbers		26. Ezekiel		48. Galatians
Hey	*5. Deuteronomy*		*27. Daniel*		*49. Ephesians*
Vav	6. Joshua		28. Hosea		50. Philippians
Zayin	7. Judges		29. Joel		51. Colossians
Het	8. Ruth		30. Amos		52. 1st Thessalonians
Tet	9. 1st Samuel		31. Obadiah		53. 2nd Thessalonians
Yod	10. 2nd Samuel		32. Jonah		54. 1st Timothy
Kaph	11. 1st Kings		33. Micah		55. 2nd Timothy
Lamed	12. 2nd Kings		34. Nahum		56. Titus
Mem	13. 1st Chronicles		35. Habakkuk		57. Philemon
Nun	14. 2nd Chronicles		36. Zephaniah		58. Hebrews
Samek	15. Ezra		37. Haggai		59. James
Ayin	16. Nehemiah		38. Zechariah		60. 1st Peter
Pey	17. Esther		39. Malachi		61. 2nd Peter
Tzaddi	18. Job		40. Matthew		62. 1st John
Quph	19. Psalms		41. Mark		63. 2nd John
Resh	20. Proverbs		42. Luke		64. 3rd John
Shin	21. Ecclesiastes		43. John		65. Jude
Tav	22. Song of Songs		44. Acts		66. Revelation

ה

Hey + Deuteronomy

Hey means **Behold**, See or Look! We also translate it "Lo." Its lengthened form is "Hinney" appearing over a thousand times in the OT, still meaning Behold or Look!

Deuteronomy means "a recapitulation of the law" or in Latin second (deutero) law (nomos). In Hebrew this book is called d'varim which means "words" or "things". It was written by Moses.

Deuteronomy holds the parting counsels of Moses just before they enter the Promised Land. There is a summary of the wilderness wanderings and a repeating of the Law (10 commandments, etc.). Warnings, instructions and prophecies follow and then we have Moses's parting blessings and then his death.

Look at Deuteronomy 5: 7 – 21:

7 "You shall have no other gods before me.

8 "You shall not make for yourself an image in the form of anything in heaven above or on the earth beneath or in the waters below. 9 You shall not bow down to them or worship them; for I, the LORD your God, am a jealous God, punishing the children for the sin of the parents to the third and fourth generation of those who hate me, 10 but showing love to a thousand generations of those who love me and keep my commandments.

11 "You shall not misuse the name of the LORD your God, for the LORD will not hold anyone guiltless who misuses his name.

12 "Observe the Sabbath day by keeping it holy, as the LORD your God has commanded you. 13 Six days you shall labor and do all your work, 14 but the seventh day is a sabbath to the LORD your God. On it you shall not do any work, neither you, nor your son or daughter, nor your male or female servant, nor your ox, your donkey or any of your animals, nor any foreigner residing in your towns, so that your male and female servants may rest, as you do. 15 Remember that you were slaves in Egypt and that the LORD your God brought you out of there with a mighty hand and an outstretched arm. Therefore the LORD your God has commanded you to observe the Sabbath day.

16 "Honor your father and your mother, as the LORD your God has commanded you, so that you may live long and that it may go well with you in the land the LORD your God is giving you.

17 "You shall not murder.

18 "You shall not commit adultery.

19 "You shall not steal.

20 "You shall not give false testimony against your neighbor.

21 "You shall not covet your neighbor's wife. You shall not set your desire on your neighbor's house or land, his male or female servant, his ox or donkey, or anything that belongs to your neighbor."

Which commandment has a blessing? The **5th** one: "Honor your father and your mother". See what the upside is – that you may live long and it may go well with you. Now look at Matthew 22: 36 – 37:

³⁶ "Teacher, which is the greatest commandment in the Law?"
³⁷ Jesus replied: **"'Love the Lord your God with all your heart and with all your soul and with all your mind.'**

And compare that to Deuteronomy 6:5:

⁵ **Love the LORD your God with all your heart and with all your soul and with all your strength.**

Jesus wasn't telling us anything new, He was quoting Scripture. Next he says in verse 39:

³⁹ And the second is like it: **'Love your neighbor as yourself.'**

Could He have gotten that from Leviticus 19:18?

¹⁸ "'Do not seek revenge or bear a grudge against anyone among your people, but **love your neighbor as yourself.** I am the LORD.

Remember Jesus' temptation in the wilderness? He told Satan in Matthew 4:4:

⁴ Jesus answered, "It is written: 'Man shall not live on bread alone, but on every word that comes from the mouth of God.'"

Now look at Deuteronomy 8:3:

³ He humbled you, causing you to hunger and then feeding you with manna, which neither you nor your ancestors had known, to teach you that **man does not live on bread alone but on every word that comes from the mouth of the LORD.**

Key verses of Deuteronomy (11:26-28) start with the Hebrew word Hey – Behold:

²⁶ See (Behold!), I am setting before you today a blessing and a curse— ²⁷ the blessing if you obey the commands of the LORD your God that I am giving you today; ²⁸ the curse if you disobey the commands of the LORD your God and turn from the way that I command you today by following other gods, which you have not known.

Hey! It looks like Deuteronomy is the book to head to for commandments. Check out this prophecy from chapter 28:1 – 2:

¹ If you fully obey the LORD your God and carefully follow all his commands I give you today, the LORD your God will set you high above all the nations on earth. ² All these blessings will come on you and accompany you if you obey the LORD your God:

But there are conditions and the rest of the chapter names dozens of specific curses, like going crazy, if they do not observe all of the Lord's commandments:

³⁴ The sights you see will drive you mad.

Next we have the Palestinian Covenant which gives the conditions under which Israel entered the land of promise. I just want to focus on one verse: chapter 29:29:

29 The secret things belong to the LORD our God, but the things revealed belong to us and to our children forever, that we may follow all the words of this law.

According to Rabbinical tradition, the letter hey is the letter of **revelation**, that is, the letter of secrets revealed. The next hey book is Daniel, wherein secrets are revealed.

ה

Hey + Daniel

Our second hey book is Daniel. In Hebrew this book is called Dan'yiel meaning "judge of God" or "the strong man of God". It was written by Daniel who, like Ezekiel, was a Jewish captive in Babylon. Daniel was of royal or princely ancestry. He was one of Israel's major prophets yet he was distinctively the prophet of the "times of the Gentiles". His vision envelops the whole course of Gentile world-rule to its catastrophic end and to the setting up of the Messianic kingdom. Heavy stuff.

The book is in four divisions. First there is the personal history of Daniel, then the visions of Nebuchadnezzar and their results. More personal history follows and then Daniel's visions.

Daniel interpreted Nebuchadnezzar's dream after the magi (Persian astrologer/priests) failed. That dream's interpretation revealed the course of Gentile rule and the end times. Daniel's buddies (who hasn't heard of Shadrach, Meshach and Abednego?) got thrown into the fiery furnace and survived. Next we learn how Daniel interprets the "writing on the wall". Clearly, God gave Daniel the power to reveal secrets. Next comes the story of Daniel in the lion's den. But from chapter 7 on we have end times visions of the beast and the second coming of Christ, many of which are identical to scenes in the book of Revelation.

What I want to look at is Chapter 9 verses 21 – 27:

21 while I was still in prayer, Gabriel, the man I had seen in the earlier vision, came to me in swift flight about the time of the evening sacrifice. **22** He instructed me and said to me, "Daniel, I have now come to give you insight and understanding. **23** As soon as you began to pray, a word went out, which I have come to tell you, for you are highly esteemed. Therefore, consider the word and understand the vision:
24 "Seventy 'sevens' are decreed for your people and your holy city to finish transgression, to put an end to sin, to atone for wickedness, to bring in everlasting righteousness, to seal up vision and prophecy and to anoint the Most Holy Place.
25 "Know and understand this: From the time the word goes out to restore and rebuild Jerusalem until the Anointed One, the ruler, comes, there will be seven 'sevens,' and sixty-two 'sevens.' It will be rebuilt with streets and a trench, but in times of trouble. **26** After the sixty-two 'sevens,' the Anointed One will be put to death and will have nothing. The people of the ruler who will come will destroy the city and the sanctuary. The end will come like a flood: War will continue until the end, and desolations have been decreed. **27** He will confirm a covenant with many for one 'seven.' In the middle of the 'seven' he will put an end to sacrifice and offering. And at the temple he will set up an abomination that causes desolation, until the end that is decreed is poured out on him."

These events were fulfilled in the same order they were prophesied as follows:
First: there would be a decree to rebuild Jerusalem. After the Medo-Persians had conquered the Babylonian empire about 2540 years ago, they ruled an empire that included the land of Israel. About 2446 years ago, around 445 B.C., the Persian king

Artaxerxes gave permission to the Jews to rebuild Jerusalem. Jerusalem was still in ruins from when it had been destroyed by the Babylonians.

Second: Jerusalem and the Temple would be rebuilt. It was.

Third: Then an anointed one (messiah) would make his appearance and then be "cut off". In approximately 33 A.D. Jesus entered Jerusalem as the Messiah promised by the Old Testament prophets, but many people rejected him and he was crucified by the Romans (cut off).

Fourth: Then Jerusalem and the Temple would be destroyed again. In 70 A.D., about 40 years after the crucifixion and resurrection of Jesus, Jerusalem and the Temple were destroyed by the Romans and the Temple has not yet been rebuilt.

The amazing fulfillment of these prophecies in Daniel is indisputable. Now, look at verse 25 again. The seventy "sevens" are divided into seven "sevens" and sixty-two "sevens". Later in verse 27 the last "seven" is addressed. What are these "sevens?" They are years.

Working from March 14, 445 B. C. (the date of Artaxerxes' second decree according to our calendar), it has been calculated by the use of astronomical calendars and charts that the day of the coming of the Messiah was April 6, A. D. 32. The timing of the Jewish new moons by which the Passovers are determined had to be considered in order to figure out that this was the accurate date that Christian scholars agree on.

Between the decree of Artaxerxes and the triumphal entry of Jesus into Jerusalem is a period of 477 years and 24 days. To fit the prophecy it needs to be 483 years (7 x 7 + 62 x 7 = 483 Jewish years, Jewish years are 360 days, then 483 x 360 days = 173,880 days). After deducting one year to account for the fact that 1 B. C. and A. D. 1 are not two years but one, that leaves a total of 476 years 24 days or a total of 173,764 days. Oops, that's still not the necessary 173,880 days.

But wait! When you add 119 days to this figure to include the 119 leap years represented by 476 years, then that results in a figure of 173,883 days. Closer, but three days too many. Hmm, someone realized that the Julian calendar (which we base our 365 day year on) is slightly inaccurate compared to an actual solar year. Well, well, well, someone by the name of Sir Robert Anderson checked with the Royal Observatory in London and found that a 365 day year exceeds a solar year by 1/128th of a day. That fraction of 476 years is three days, which when subtracted from 173,883 yields a difference of 173,880 days. Hooray! I mean, Hallelujah! That is exactly the number of days predicted in Daniel 9:25!

Since Jesus was crucified after the end of the sixty-ninth week we still have one more "week of sevens" or seven years left. (Dan. 9:24). Verse 27 says that "he" (the Antichrist) "shall confirm the covenant with many". That hasn't happened yet and so we find a long, long gap of time between the 69th and the 70th weeks. Guess what? We are living in that gap right now. The last "seven" will be the seven years of Tribulation. When will it begin? Watch and listen because it will begin when the Antichrist comes to confirm a covenant with Israel (v. 27).

When we looked at the first hey book, Deuteronomy, I promised that secrets would be revealed. Compare Deuteronomy 29:29 to Daniel 2:22:

29 The **secret things** belong to the LORD our God, but the things **revealed** belong to us and to our children forever, that we may follow all the words of this law.
22 He **reveals** deep and **hidden things**;
he knows what lies in darkness,
and light dwells with him.

That's pretty cool, but wouldn't it be really awesome if the third hey book, Ephesians, had something similar? Check it out – Ephesians 3: 2-3:

2 Surely you have heard about the administration of God's grace that was given to me for you, **3** that is, the **mystery** made known to me by **revelation**, as I have already written briefly.

ה
Hey + Ephesians

Our last hey h book is Ephesians, another beautiful letter by St. Paul, written to the saints in Ephesus. He covers the believer's status in Christ through pure grace. He also writes about the walk, service and warfare of the Spirit-filled believer.

Our Hebrew letter hey means "Behold!" so let's pay attention. Turn in your Bible to Ephesians and read the first 14 verses of the first chapter.

Ask yourself some questions. I've put the verse in parentheses to help you.
    1) How many spiritual blessings do we get? (vs. 3)
    2) Does God see our sin? (vs. 4)
    3) How do we have redemption? (vs. 7)
    4) How are we marked or sealed? (vs. 13)

We get *every* spiritual blessing, God *doesn't* see our sin, he *predestined* us to be adopted through Christ, *redeemed* by his blood and *sealed* by the Holy Spirit. The issue of predestination isn't as hard as it sounds. It just means that God chose everyone, but not everyone chooses God.

Look at these verses again and check the punctuation in your translation. Would it surprise you to know that in the original Greek verses 3 through 14 are all one sentence? This one sentence is a doxology or a liturgical praise to God.

There are lots of wonderful verses in Ephesians, a few of which I'm going to pull out and paraphrase, but you should read them for yourself:

Ephesians 2: 8, 9: I don't have to do anything to be saved.

Ephesians 3: 6: Jews and Gentiles get to share in the blessing through Christ.

Ephesians 4: 4-6: Perfect unity in Christ – 7 phrases of oneness: 1 body, 1 Spirit, 1 hope, 1 Lord, 1 faith, 1 baptism, 1 God

Ephesians 5: 21 – 6: 4: There is a divine order to marriage and family. Love, respect and sacrifice for one another. There should be mutual submission.

Ephesians 6: 10 – 18: The "armor" of God is truth, righteousness, peace, faith, salvation and the word of God. Pray a lot.

How does this hey book relate back to the first and second hey books? Like this, compare Ephesians 6:1 – 3 with Deuteronomy 5: 16:

> [1] Children, obey your parents in the Lord, for this is right. [2] "Honor your father and mother"—which is the first commandment with a promise— [3] "so that it may go well with you and that you may enjoy long life on the earth."
>
> [16] "Honor your father and your mother, as the LORD your God has commanded you, so that you may live long and that it may go well with you in the land the LORD your God is giving you.

This commandment is found in Exodus, too, but does not include the blessing of long life there. Only in these hey books do things match up so nicely. Hey! There are other cool links among the hey books, but I encourage you to read Richard Amiel McGough's book *The Bible Wheel* to find them all.

Chapter 6 Vav

Aleph	1. Genesis	23. Isaiah	45. Romans
Bet	2. Exodus	24. Jeremiah	46. 1st Corinthians
Gimel	3. Leviticus	25. Lamentations	47. 2nd Corinthians
Dalet	4. Numbers	26. Ezekiel	48. Galatians
Hey	5. Deuteronomy	27. Daniel	49. Ephesians
Vav	*6. Joshua*	*28. Hosea*	*50. Philippians*
Zayin	7. Judges	29. Joel	51. Colossians
Het	8. Ruth	30. Amos	52. 1st Thessalonians
Tet	9. 1st Samuel	31. Obadiah	53. 2nd Thessalonians
Yod	10. 2nd Samuel	32. Jonah	54. 1st Timothy
Kaph	11. 1st Kings	33. Micah	55. 2nd Timothy
Lamed	12. 2nd Kings	34. Nahum	56. Titus
Mem	13. 1st Chronicles	35. Habakkuk	57. Philemon
Nun	14. 2nd Chronicles	36. Zephaniah	58. Hebrews
Samek	15. Ezra	37. Haggai	59. James
Ayin	16. Nehemiah	38. Zechariah	60. 1st Peter
Pey	17. Esther	39. Malachi	61. 2nd Peter
Tzaddi	18. Job	40. Matthew	62. 1st John
Quph	19. Psalms	41. Mark	63. 2nd John
Resh	20. Proverbs	42. Luke	64. 3rd John
Shin	21. Ecclesiastes	43. John	65. Jude
Tav	22. Song of Songs	44. Acts	66. Revelation

ו

Vav + Joshua

Vav u means **nail** or **hook** and by itself it appears 13 times in Exodus to describe the hooks holding each curtain to its pillar in the Tabernacle. Grammatically it serves to hook words together and link them in a sentence as a conjunction meaning "and", "so" or "but".

In the alphabetic verses in Psalms 119: 41 -48, every verse, of course, starts with the letter vav working as a connector, but some translations have lost some or all of the meaning. Let's read Young's Literal Translation of these verses to detect all of the **ands**:

[41][Waw.] And meet me doth Thy kindness, O Jehovah, Thy salvation according to Thy saying.
[42]And I answer him who is reproaching me a word, For I have trusted in Thy word.
[43]And Thou takest not utterly away From my mouth the word of truth, Because for Thy judgment I have hoped.
[44]And I keep Thy law continually, To the age and for ever.
[45]And I walk habitually in a broad place, For Thy precepts I have sought.
[46]And I speak of Thy testimonies before kings, And I am not ashamed.
[47]And I delight myself in Thy commands, That I have loved,
[48]And I lift up my hands unto Thy commands, That I have loved, And I do meditate on Thy statutes!

Another interesting thing is that there are only 10 words that start with vav. Its primary use therefore is as a hook, a connector. In fact it connects the historical books together from Genesis to Malachi, where it appears as the first letter in all but 4. Example: Exodus starts with "**and** these are the names", Leviticus opens with "**and** the Lord called", and Numbers begins with "**and** the Lord spoke". (In Joshua, "**and** it came to pass after the death of Moses".)

Joshua, the 6th book, acts as the letter vav does in that it links the first 5 books of Moses, which lead Israel up to Canaan, with the 12 succeeding books, which cover Israel's history inside Canaan.

Joshua's name means salvation. In Hebrew it is Y'hoshua, the 1st of the 12 books of Old Testament history.

Joshua records the consummation of the redemption of Israel out of Egypt. The book is divided into 4 parts: the conquest, the partition of the inheritance, developing discord, and Joshua's last counsels and his death.

Joshua records the passage of Israel from the wilderness where they wandered forty years to the Promised Land. There is powerful symbolism here. Moses the Lawgiver died, and Joshua, whose name is the equivalent of Jesus, led them through the "baptism" in the Jordan into the Promised Land. Does it sound like the gospel? Joshua was a helper to Moses. He led the army against the Amalekites. He went with Moses up Sinai mountain when God gave instructions about the ark. He was one of 12 who Moses sent in secret to look at the Promised Land. Only Joshua and Caleb brought good news back. Joshua had faith that God would provide.

Read Joshua 20: 1-6 and think about how these cities of refuge compare to Jesus.

¹ Then the LORD said to Joshua: ² "Tell the Israelites to designate the cities of refuge, as I instructed you through Moses, ³ so that anyone who kills a person accidentally and unintentionally may flee there and find protection from the avenger of blood. ⁴ When they flee to one of these cities, they are to stand in the entrance of the city gate and state their case before the elders of that city. Then the elders are to admit the fugitive into their city and provide a place to live among them. ⁵ If the avenger of blood comes in pursuit, the elders must not surrender the fugitive, because the fugitive killed their neighbor unintentionally and without malice aforethought. ⁶ They are to stay in that city until they have stood trial before the assembly and until the death of the high priest who is serving at that time. Then they may go back to their own home in the town from which they fled."

The cities of refuge are like a picture of Jesus: We are all guilty. We have all sinned. We can go to Jesus as a place of refuge. He will forgive us. He will keep us safe. We must confess that we have sinned. We do not need to wait for the death of the high priest. Our high priest (Jesus) has died for us already. Our high priest became alive again. He argues our case for us before God.

Read vs. 7 & 8:

⁷ So they set apart Kedesh in Galilee in the hill country of Naphtali, Shechem in the hill country of Ephraim, and Kiriath Arba (that is, Hebron) in the hill country of Judah. ⁸ East of the Jordan (on the other side from Jericho) they designated Bezer in the wilderness on the plateau in the tribe of Reuben, Ramoth in Gilead in the tribe of Gad, and Golan in Bashan in the tribe of Manasseh.

The names of the cities of refuge are interesting. Kedesh means "right with God." Jesus makes us to be right with God. Shechem, "shoulder," Jesus cares about us, especially when we are weak. He is like a farmer who carries a young sheep on his shoulder. Hebron, "fellowship," we have fellowship with God and with other Christians. Bezer, "a place of safety," Jesus is our place of safety. Ramoth, "high places," certainly you can see the symbolism here. And finally, Golan, which means "captive" or "exiles;" we are like exiles in this world.

Note the relationship to the 6th commandment. The refuge cities relate to the 6th commandment, the unjust destruction of man. And remember that man was created on the 6th day.

Last thing I want to mention about Joshua is his name. Originally it was Hosea (Hoshea), but Moses prefixed one letter to it and it became Joshua which I said meant salvation, but what did Hosea mean? . . . Miraculously, Hosea is connected to the same Hebrew letter, vav, so read on.

ו

Vav + Hosea

As we saw in our chapter on the first vav book, Joshua, this Hebrew letter means **nail** or hook and grammatically serves as a conjunction meaning "and," "so" or "but." We saw this quite obviously in the literal translation of Psalm 119: 41 – 48.

The book of Hosea was written by the prophet Hosea. Hosea was a contemporary of the prophets Amos, Isaiah and Micah and prophesied around the years of 758 B.C. to 725 B.C. during the reign of king Uzziah. Now is the time to look at all the prophets and notice that the Bible is not ordered chronologically.

The Prophets in Chronological Order:

Prophet	Time Period
Joel	during 9th century BC
Obadiah	during 9th century BC - or after 586 BC?
Jonah	800 - 790 BC
Hosea	772/752 - 722 BC
Isaiah	767 - 697 BC
Amos	767 - 753 BC
Micah	750 - 700 BC
Nahum	663 - 612 BC
Jeremiah	627 - 586 BC
Zephaniah	622 - 606 BC
Habakkuk	612 - 605 BC
Daniel	605 - 536/535 BC
Ezekiel	593 - 571 BC
Haggai	around 520 BC
Zechariah	520 - 480 BC
Malachi	450 - 425 BC

Why aren't the prophetical books in their chronological order? Because God had infinitely better plans for the order and construct of His Most Holy Word.

The major theme of the book of Hosea is that Israel is Jehovah's adulterous wife, apostate, sinful and rejected, but ultimately to be purified and restored. The book is in 3 parts: the dishonored wife, the sinful people and the ultimate blessing and glory of Israel.

Here is a summary of the story of Hosea:

God tells him to take "an adulterous wife" so he marries a woman named Gomer. Think about how humiliating that must have been for Hosea. (After all, Jesus was judged as "no prophet" when He merely let a prostitute touch His feet.) Gomer has two sons and a daughter. God tells him to name the first son Jezreel, the daughter Lo-Ruhamah and the second son Lo-Ammi. The names are important to the story. They mean "God scatters," "not loved" and "not my people." Take a moment and think about how significant those names are.

Gomer is, as expected, an adulterous wife and Hosea rebukes her for the adultery. She leaves to be with her lovers, but we read a poetic declaration of Hosea's (God's) love and promise of mercy. Look at Hosea 2: 14-23:

> ¹⁴ "Therefore I am now going to allure her;
> I will lead her into the wilderness
> and speak tenderly to her.
> ¹⁵ There I will give her back her vineyards,
> and will make the Valley of Achor a door of hope.
> There she will respond as in the days of her youth,
> as in the day she came up out of Egypt.
> ¹⁶ "In that day," declares the LORD,
> "you will call me 'my husband';
> you will no longer call me 'my master.'
> ¹⁷ I will remove the names of the Baals from her lips;
> no longer will their names be invoked.
> ¹⁸ In that day I will make a covenant for them
> with the beasts of the field, the birds in the sky
> and the creatures that move along the ground.
> Bow and sword and battle
> I will abolish from the land,
> so that all may lie down in safety.
> ¹⁹ I will betroth you to me forever;
> I will betroth you in righteousness and justice,
> in love and compassion.
> ²⁰ I will betroth you in faithfulness,
> and you will acknowledge the LORD.
> ²¹ "In that day I will respond,"
> declares the LORD—
> "I will respond to the skies,
> and they will respond to the earth;
> ²² and the earth will respond to the grain,
> the new wine and the olive oil,
> and they will respond to Jezreel.
> ²³ I will plant her for myself in the land;
> I will show my love to the one I called 'Not my loved one.'
> I will say to those called 'Not my people,' 'You are my people';
> and they will say, 'You are my God.'"

Did you notice at the end the wonderful references to the names of Hosea's children? Remember what they meant? Do you see the prophetic story of God's persistent love for His children? Since the beginning of time God's ungrateful and undeserving creation has been accepting God's love, grace, and mercy while still unable to abstain from sin and wickedness.

Hosea reconciles with his wife. In fact, he has to buy her back from the sex trade. The last part of Hosea shows how God's love once again restores His children as He forgets their transgressions when they turn back to Him with a repentant heart.

The prophetic message of Hosea foretells the coming of Israel's Messiah 700 years in the future. Hosea is quoted often in the New Testament and is one of the most significant books of the Old Testament. No other messenger gives as full a summary of the ways of God with man as this book does. For example, Hosea reveals that God suffers when His people are unfaithful to Him. Hosea shows that God cannot condone sin.

Yet through the marvelous analogy of Hosea's love for Gomer we see that God will never cease to love His people. And most marvelously of all we learn that God seeks us and will not fail to win us back no matter how far we have sunk and abandoned Him.

To backtrack just a moment – in the book of Joshua we learn that Joshua sent out two men to spy out Jericho. They went and stayed with the harlot, Rahab, who helped them. She is remembered and mentioned in the new testament as the harlot who was saved by faith. Rahab was also the great-great- many greats- grandmother of Jesus. Think of that symbolism.

ו

Vav + Philippians
Our third vav book is Philippians. Remember that the symbolic meaning of this little letter is **nail** or hook. It plays a very important part in Jehovah's name:. Remember the symbolic meanings of these letters are Hand, Behold, Nail, Behold.

Philippians was written by the Apostle Paul to the Christians at Philippi. The major themes are that Christian experience is not what is going on around the Christian, but what is going on inside him and also that joy triumphs over suffering. The key verse to this letter is found in the first chapter, verse 21:

²¹ For to me, to live is Christ and to die is gain.

Three of Philippians' four chapters contain Paul's discourse on rejoicing in spite of suffering, rejoicing in lowly service and rejoicing over anxiety, with Christ being the believer's strength. One chapter contains warnings against Judaizers and legal righteousness.

Read this beautiful passage on humility from Philippians 2: 5-11 and notice what I have put in bold print:

⁵ In your relationships with one another, have the same mindset as Christ Jesus:
⁶ Who, being in very nature God,
did not consider equality with God something to be used to his own advantage;
⁷ rather, **he made himself nothing**
by taking the very **nature of a servant**,
being made in human likeness.
⁸ And being found in appearance as a man,
he humbled himself
by **becoming obedient to death**—
even death on a cross!
⁹ Therefore God exalted him to the highest place
and gave him the name that is above every name,
¹⁰ that at the name of Jesus every knee should bow,
in heaven and on earth and under the earth,
¹¹ and every tongue acknowledge that Jesus Christ is Lord,
to the glory of God the Father.

Remember our second vav u book Hosea? Remember how he was obedient to God as he had to humble himself by marrying the prostitute Gomer? Jesus' humility was far more demeaning, of course, but isn't this a perfect vav match?

Now look at Philippians 4: 4 – 9:

⁴ Rejoice in the Lord always. I will say it again: Rejoice! ⁵ Let your gentleness be evident to all. The Lord is near. ⁶ Do not be anxious about anything, but in every situation, by prayer

and petition, with thanksgiving, present your requests to God. **⁷** And the peace of God, which transcends all understanding, will guard your hearts and your minds in Christ Jesus.

⁸ Finally, brothers and sisters, whatever is true, whatever is noble, whatever is right, whatever is pure, whatever is lovely, whatever is admirable—if anything is excellent or praiseworthy—think about such things. **⁹** Whatever you have learned or received or heard from me, or seen in me—put it into practice. And the God of peace will be with you.

Okay, let's do the old list exercise for this passage.
1. Rejoice
2. Be gentle
3. Don't be anxious
4. Pray
5. Think about true stuff
6. Think about pure stuff
7. Think about lovely stuff
8. Think about admirable, excellent and praiseworthy stuff
9. Practice what you learn in the Bible

Chapter 7 Zayin

Aleph	1. Genesis	23. Isaiah	45. Romans
Bet	2. Exodus	24. Jeremiah	46. 1st Corinthians
Gimel	3. Leviticus	25. Lamentations	47. 2nd Corinthians
Dalet	4. Numbers	26. Ezekiel	48. Galatians
Hey	5. Deuteronomy	27. Daniel	49. Ephesians
Vav	6. Joshua	28. Hosea	50. Philippians
Zayin	*7. Judges*	*29. Joel*	*51. Colossians*
Het	8. Ruth	30. Amos	52. 1st Thessalonians
Tet	9. 1st Samuel	31. Obadiah	53. 2nd Thessalonians
Yod	10. 2nd Samuel	32. Jonah	54. 1st Timothy
Kaph	11. 1st Kings	33. Micah	55. 2nd Timothy
Lamed	12. 2nd Kings	34. Nahum	56. Titus
Mem	13. 1st Chronicles	35. Habakkuk	57. Philemon
Nun	14. 2nd Chronicles	36. Zephaniah	58. Hebrews
Samek	15. Ezra	37. Haggai	59. James
Ayin	16. Nehemiah	38. Zechariah	60. 1st Peter
Pey	17. Esther	39. Malachi	61. 2nd Peter
Tzaddi	18. Job	40. Matthew	62. 1st John
Quph	19. Psalms	41. Mark	63. 2nd John
Resh	20. Proverbs	42. Luke	64. 3rd John
Shin	21. Ecclesiastes	43. John	65. Jude
Tav	22. Song of Songs	44. Acts	66. Revelation

Zayin + Judges

Zayin is the 7th Hebrew letter and means **weapon** or **sword**. In Modern Hebrew it means to be armed and that is the primary theme of the 7th book, Judges. Zayin sounds like an English "Z" and was drawn like a "Z" in ancient Hebrew. Key Bible words that start with this letter are zayin (weapon, sword), zakar (remember), zamam (think, consider), zuah (tremble), and zanah (to fornicate, to be a whore). Think about these words in relation to the Bible. Two more zayin key words are zavav which means buzz and zevuv (zebub) which means a fly. I'll bet you already knew this from the Hebrew for "Lord of the flies". Remember they'd get off track and worship Baal? Baal means "lord" so Baalzebub means lord of flies.

Judges, (Shof'tim in the Hebrew) takes its name from the 13 men raised up to deliver Israel in the falling away and division following the death of Joshua. It was probably written by Samuel. Judges, the 7th book, records 7 apostasies, 7 servitudes to 7 heathen nations and 7 deliverances. Key verses are 2:16-19, 17:6 and 21:25 and I've bolded some important parts:

16 Then **the LORD raised up judges**, who saved them out of the hands of these raiders. **17 Yet they would not listen to their judges** but prostituted themselves to other gods and worshiped them. They quickly turned from the ways of their ancestors, who had been obedient to the LORD's commands. **18** Whenever the LORD raised up a judge for them, he was with the judge and saved them out of the hands of their enemies as long as the judge lived; for the LORD relented because of their groaning under those who oppressed and afflicted them. **19** But when the judge died, the people returned to ways even more corrupt than those of their ancestors, following other gods and serving and worshiping them. **They refused to give up their evil practices and stubborn ways**.
6 In those days Israel had no king; everyone did as they saw fit.
25 In those days Israel had no king; everyone did as they saw fit.

That's right, chapters 17 and 21 reiterate the same thing. I think this helps us a lot to understand why the Bible has so much of what those who criticize the Bible call senseless violence and bloodshed. After the death of Joshua and his contemporaries, the Israelites returned to serving Baal and Ashtaroth. God allowed the Israelites to suffer the consequences of worshiping false gods. It was then that the people of God would cry out to Yahweh for help. God sent judges to His children to lead them in righteous living. But time after time they would turn their backs on God and return to their lives of wickedness. However, keeping His part of the covenant with Abraham, God would save His people from their oppressors throughout this time.

Probably the most notable judge was the 12th judge, Samson, who came to lead the Israelites after a 40-year captivity under the rule of the ruthless Philistines. Samson led God's people to victory over the Philistines where he lost his own life after 20 years as judge of Israel. The announcement to Samson's mother that she would bear a son to lead

Israel is a foreshadowing of the announcement to Mary of the birth of the Messiah. God sent His Angel to both women and told them they would "conceive and bear a son" (Judges 13:7) who would lead God's people.

Let's compare Samson to Jesus. Most of us have heard the incredible story of Samson, the judge, who killed a thousand Philistines with a jawbone. We know that he died by pushing apart two pillars of a temple. And who doesn't know how he was tempted by Delilah? If we read the story carefully we find out that he was married once, visited a prostitute, and loved another woman, Delilah, who betrayed him.

Forget about the Hollywood production movies and let's look at Samson strictly as God describes him to us: all we know are the facts about his birth, relationships with three women, and his death. And one more thing: He is listed in the New Testament book of Hebrews, chapter 11, as being a man who lived by faith!

Samson's story is also a set of parallels depicting Jesus' birth, Jesus' relationships with the three groups of mankind, and His death.

The meanings of Hebrew names can almost tell the whole story by themselves. They show how the allegory is assembled. Here are three examples: Samson means "the light." The reference is of course to Jesus who is "the Light of men." Samson's father's name is Manoah which means "peace or rest." In this case the reference is to our heavenly Father who provided peace between Himself and man. He reconciled us through the death of His Son. Delilah means "one who is heavily burdened." She depicts the bride of Christ – those He told "Come to me all you who are weary and burdened."

There are three women in the story of Samson. All were Philistines (Philistine means "to roll in the dust") – the Philistines were Israel's enemy who had been ruling over them for some time. Each of the women portrays one of the three divisions of mankind – all initially enemies of God – and how they relate to God. Based on the symbolism, the time frame begins with Jesus' introduction to the respective people and ends with Judgment Day.

The first is a woman that Samson has chosen to marry (Judges 14); she is from Timnah which means the allotted (or chosen) place. The name of the place foreshadows the fact that Jesus was predestined to come to live in His humanity to bring reconciliation between God and man. She represents the relationship between mankind and God. Her story begins with Jesus desiring and pursuing her – that's equivalent to His pursuing mankind since the fall in the Garden of Eden. It ends with a description of what she became –the great city of Babylon– and her final destruction.

The second woman's story is contained in just three verses (Judges 15: 1-3). She is a prostitute from the town of Gaza (which means "fierce enemy"). She is indicative of the hostility that Jesus encountered when He came to His own people and they rejected Him. Her story ends with the city gates –the only thing that separated it from the rest of the world– taken up onto a nearby hill. It is a picture of the law being taken away from the Jews (the law made the Jews separate from the world.) Jesus carried the law (in the form of the cross) up on the hill and was crucified on it.

The third woman is Delilah (Judges 16: 4 - 22). She is from the Valley of Sorek which means the valley of the true (or choice) vine. Even with all of her betrayals, she is Samson's true love –representing the Bride of Christ. She is the ultimate cause of His death. He was displayed and mocked in a religious forum and died a crushing death for the sins of the people.

Isn't this amazing? I love how Christ appears throughout the Old Testament.

ז

Zayin + Joel

The name Joel means "Jehovah is God." What a wonderful name for a prophet. Joel did indeed write this book. He was a contemporary of Elijah and Elisha.

There was an actual plague of locusts in the land - read chapter 1 verse 4– the palmerworm, locust, cankerworm and caterpillar are all developmental stages of the desert locust which as recently as 1915 devastated Palestine. All of chapter 1 deals with an actual event. Here it is:

¹ The word of the LORD that came to Joel son of Pethuel.
² Hear this, you elders;
  listen, all who live in the land.
Has anything like this ever happened in your days
  or in the days of your ancestors?
³ Tell it to your children,
  and let your children tell it to their children,
  and their children to the next generation.
⁴ What the locust swarm has left
  the great locusts have eaten;
what the great locusts have left
  the young locusts have eaten;
what the young locusts have left
  other locusts have eaten.
    ⁵ Wake up, you drunkards, and weep!
  Wail, all you drinkers of wine;
wail because of the new wine,
  for it has been snatched from your lips.
⁶ A nation has invaded my land,
  a mighty army without number;
it has the teeth of a lion,
  the fangs of a lioness.
⁷ It has laid waste my vines
  and ruined my fig trees.
It has stripped off their bark
  and thrown it away,
  leaving their branches white.
    ⁸ Mourn like a virgin in sackcloth
  grieving for the betrothed of her youth.
⁹ Grain offerings and drink offerings
  are cut off from the house of the LORD.
The priests are in mourning,
  those who minister before the LORD.
¹⁰ The fields are ruined,
  the ground is dried up;
the grain is destroyed,

   the new wine is dried up,
   the olive oil fails.
    11 Despair, you farmers,
  wail, you vine growers;
grieve for the wheat and the barley,
   because the harvest of the field is destroyed.
    12 The vine is dried up
  and the fig tree is withered;
the pomegranate, the palm and the apple tree—
   all the trees of the field—are dried up.
Surely the people's joy
   is withered away.
    13 Put on sackcloth, you priests, and mourn;
  wail, you who minister before the altar.
Come, spend the night in sackcloth,
   you who minister before my God;
for the grain offerings and drink offerings
   are withheld from the house of your God.
14 Declare a holy fast;
  call a sacred assembly.
Summon the elders
   and all who live in the land
to the house of the LORD your God,
   and cry out to the LORD.
    15 Alas for that day!
For the day of the LORD is near;
   it will come like destruction from the Almighty.
    16 Has not the food been cut off
  before our very eyes—
joy and gladness
   from the house of our God?
17 The seeds are shriveled
   beneath the clods.
The storehouses are in ruins,
   the granaries have been broken down,
   for the grain has dried up.
18 How the cattle moan!
  The herds mill about
because they have no pasture;
   even the flocks of sheep are suffering.
    19 To you, LORD, I call,
   for fire has devoured the pastures in the wilderness
   and flames have burned up all the trees of the field.
20 Even the wild animals pant for you;
   the streams of water have dried up
   and fire has devoured the pastures in the wilderness.

That was a cry for repentance, wasn't it? He appeals to drunkards, the people, priests and elders. All of the prophets seem to follow this theme: repent before the judgment. There will be judgment and then there will be an eventual blessing for Israel.

Chapter 2 changes to a prophecy of an invasion of locusts as "the day of the Lord". That is, the locusts now represent an invading army from the north before the day of Armageddon (this army is described in Revelation 19). Read Joel 2:12 and 13:

> [12] "Even now," declares the LORD,
> "return to me with all your heart,
> with fasting and weeping and mourning."
> [13] Rend your heart
> and not your garments.
> Return to the LORD your God,
> for he is gracious and compassionate,
> slow to anger and abounding in love,
> and he relents from sending calamity.

The Lord wants repentance and later offers a promise of deliverance and a promise of the Holy Spirit. In my Bible I underlined the phrase above about the Lord being slow to anger and abounding in love. That's something we should remember. If you want a model of how a parent should behave, this is it.

Chapter 2 also gives the signs that will precede the 2nd advent and the day of the Lord: verses 28 – 31 say that sons and daughters will prophesy, old men will dream dreams, young men will see visions, there will be wonders in the heavens and on the earth, the sun will be turned to darkness and the moon to blood. There will be an invader and the accompanying description is chilling if you imagine with your 21st century knowledge a picture of what is described in verses 2 – 6:

> [2] a day of darkness and gloom,
> a day of clouds and blackness.
> Like dawn spreading across the mountains
> a large and mighty army comes,
> such as never was in ancient times
> nor ever will be in ages to come.
> [3] Before them fire devours,
> behind them a flame blazes.
> Before them the land is like the garden of Eden,
> behind them, a desert waste—
> nothing escapes them.
> [4] They have the appearance of horses;
> they gallop along like cavalry.
> [5] With a noise like that of chariots
> they leap over the mountaintops,
> like a crackling fire consuming stubble,
> like a mighty army drawn up for battle.

⁶ At the sight of them, nations are in anguish;
every face turns pale.

Really try to imagine the noise, the way they "leap" over mountaintops, the way the land is left like a desert waste, nothing escaping . . . But there's good news. Keep reading the chapter and see how the Lord takes pity, drives the army away and restores the land. And remember, this is a zayin book and zayin means **weapon**.

Chapter 3 outlines the restoration of Israel and the judgment of the Gentile nations and the day of the Lord. You'll find the reasons for the judgment and then its implementation. The final verses of this chapter tell of the blessings for God's people:

¹⁷ "Then you will know that I, the LORD your God,
   dwell in Zion, my holy hill.
Jerusalem will be holy;
   never again will foreigners invade her.
    ¹⁸ "In that day the mountains will drip new wine,
   and the hills will flow with milk;
all the ravines of Judah will run with water.
A fountain will flow out of the LORD's house
   and will water the valley of acacias.
¹⁹ But Egypt will be desolate,
   Edom a desert waste,
because of violence done to the people of Judah,
   in whose land they shed innocent blood.
²⁰ Judah will be inhabited forever
   and Jerusalem through all generations.
²¹ Shall I leave their innocent blood unavenged?
   No, I will not."
      The LORD dwells in Zion!

Is the Messiah found in the book of Joel? Most definitely. Young's Literal Translation of Joel 2:23 is:

²³And ye sons of Zion, joy and rejoice, In Jehovah your God, For He hath given to you the Teacher for righteousness, And causeth to come down to you a shower, Sprinkling and gathered -- in the beginning.

The Messiah is the Teacher for righteousness. Jesus is that Teacher.

Now here's some other cool stuff about this zayin book: Joel prophesies that the Lord will do the judging in the valley of *Jehoshaphat*. (I always liked that name because my father used to say "jumpin' Jehoshaphat" as an exclamation.) In studying Hebrew I learned that this word is made up of two words: shaphat which means judge and yeho which is the beginning of God's name, Jehovah. So you get Jeho . . . shaphat – God judges. This links divinely back to the first zayin book, Judges, because in Judges (and only in Judges) is God given the title "the Lord the Judge" (Judges 11:27). The name

Jehoshaphat appears dozens of times in Samuel, Kings and Chronicles, but "the valley of Jehoshaphat" appears ONLY in Joel, the second zayin book.

ז

Zayin + Colossians

Our third zayin book was written by St. Paul to the Christians at Colosse. Paul had not visited Colosse, but he often prayed for the Christians there. In fact, he says early on in his letter (1:9) that he had not stopped praying for them. This is a short book and you can easily read it straight through right now before going on.

Paul reminded the Christians about the importance of Jesus: Jesus is God, and He created everything. He became a man so that He could die for us and because Jesus paid our "death debt", God will accept us and forgive us our sins. If we invite Jesus into our lives, we will become friends of God (Colossians 1:15-23).

Then, Paul warned the Christians about some people (Colossians 2). These people wanted the Christians to obey the ancient rules of the Hebrew nation saying that real Christians must obey all such rules. Paul did not agree. He wrote that these rules were human traditions (Colossians 2:8). Christians ought to obey Christ, instead of tradition. The ancient Hebrew traditions might seem wise, but they cannot help us to live good lives (Colossians 2:23).

Paul reminded the Christians how they should live. They should think about the things in heaven (Colossians 3:2), because they belong with Christ (Colossians 3:3-4). They should not do evil deeds (Colossians 3:5-11). Instead, they should love other people (Colossians 3:12-14). And they should serve God (Colossians 3:15-17).

Let's look specifically at the rules for holy living found in chapter 3. Read the chapter and then see if you can answer these:

Where should you set your heart?
Where should you set your mind?
Should you "put to death" sexual immorality?
Should you "put to death" impurity? What is impurity?
Besides lust, evil desires and greed, what else should you "put to death"?
What are the 5 things you should rid your lips of?
What are the 5 things you should clothe yourself with?
What should wives do?
What should husbands do?
What should children do?
What should fathers **not** do?
How can you make verse 23 central to your life?

Chapter 8 Het

Aleph	1. Genesis	23. Isaiah	45. Romans
Bet	2. Exodus	24. Jeremiah	46. 1st Corinthians
Gimel	3. Leviticus	25. Lamentations	47. 2nd Corinthians
Dalet	4. Numbers	26. Ezekiel	48. Galatians
Hey	5. Deuteronomy	27. Daniel	49. Ephesians
Vav	6. Joshua	28. Hosea	50. Philippians
Zayin	7. Judges	29. Joel	51. Colossians
Het	*8. Ruth*	*30. Amos*	*52. 1st Thessalonians*
Tet	9. 1st Samuel	31. Obadiah	53. 2nd Thessalonians
Yod	10. 2nd Samuel	32. Jonah	54. 1st Timothy
Kaph	11. 1st Kings	33. Micah	55. 2nd Timothy
Lamed	12. 2nd Kings	34. Nahum	56. Titus
Mem	13. 1st Chronicles	35. Habakkuk	57. Philemon
Nun	14. 2nd Chronicles	36. Zephaniah	58. Hebrews
Samek	15. Ezra	37. Haggai	59. James
Ayin	16. Nehemiah	38. Zechariah	60. 1st Peter
Pey	17. Esther	39. Malachi	61. 2nd Peter
Tzaddi	18. Job	40. Matthew	62. 1st John
Quph	19. Psalms	41. Mark	63. 2nd John
Resh	20. Proverbs	42. Luke	64. 3rd John
Shin	21. Ecclesiastes	43. John	65. Jude
Tav	22. Song of Songs	44. Acts	66. Revelation

ח

Het + Ruth

Het or sometimes you see it as Chet (the h sound is a bit guttural) means **fence**, hedge, **wall**, or enclosure. The ancient form looked like a capital H but with 2 or three lines across the center.

In the Alphabetic verses the het words are "to bind," "companion" or "friend," "to love fervently," "to cherish," "to embrace," "to enclose," "to trust," "refuge" and "encamp". These establish the fundamental meaning of het as signifying something like a fence which surrounds one in friendship and love. The word we see often in the Bible translated as "mercy" is the Hebrew word "hesed" which actually means "lovingkindness."

Our first het book is Ruth. Her name means friendship (possibly) or mercy. We don't know by whom it was written, but it is generally credited to Samuel as is the book of Judges. Ruth was originally part of the book of Judges.

Let's start with Chapter 1 verses 1 through 17:

¹ In the days when the judges ruled, there was a famine in the land. So a man from Bethlehem in Judah, together with his wife and two sons, went to live for a while in the country of Moab. ² The man's name was Elimelek, his wife's name was Naomi, and the names of his two sons were Mahlon and Kilion. They were Ephrathites from Bethlehem, Judah. And they went to Moab and lived there.

³ Now Elimelek, Naomi's husband, died, and she was left with her two sons. ⁴ They married Moabite women, one named Orpah and the other Ruth. After they had lived there about ten years, ⁵ both Mahlon and Kilion also died, and Naomi was left without her two sons and her husband.

⁶ When Naomi heard in Moab that the LORD had come to the aid of his people by providing food for them, she and her daughters-in-law prepared to return home from there. ⁷ With her two daughters-in-law she left the place where she had been living and set out on the road that would take them back to the land of Judah.

⁸ Then Naomi said to her two daughters-in-law, "Go back, each of you, to your mother's home. May the LORD show you kindness, as you have shown kindness to your dead husbands and to me. ⁹ May the LORD grant that each of you will find rest in the home of another husband."

Then she kissed them goodbye and they wept aloud ¹⁰ and said to her, "We will go back with you to your people."

¹¹ But Naomi said, "Return home, my daughters. Why would you come with me? Am I going to have any more sons, who could become your husbands? ¹² Return home, my daughters; I am too old to have another husband. Even if I thought there was still hope for me—even if I had a husband tonight and then gave birth to sons— ¹³ would you wait until they grew up? Would you remain unmarried for them? No, my daughters. It is more bitter for me than for you, because the LORD's hand has turned against me!"

¹⁴ At this they wept aloud again. Then Orpah kissed her mother-in-law goodbye, but Ruth clung to her.

¹⁵ "Look," said Naomi, "your sister-in-law is going back to her people and her gods. Go back with her."

16 But Ruth replied, "Don't urge me to leave you or to turn back from you. Where you go I will go, and where you stay I will stay. Your people will be my people and your God my God. **17** Where you die I will die, and there I will be buried. May the LORD deal with me, be it ever so severely, if even death separates you and me."

We need to look at some background. In Deuteronomy 25: 5 it says:

5 If brothers are living together and one of them dies without a son, his widow must not marry outside the family. Her husband's brother shall take her and marry her and fulfill the duty of a brother-in-law to her.

Now we can see why Naomi says what she does in verses 11 – 13. One daughter-in-law takes her advice and heads home, but Ruth decides to stay. This is an incredible testament to Naomi. She must have been a wonderful example for Ruth to want to go back with her to a strange land with strange customs and a different religion. Ruth must have seen something she wanted for herself. In verse 16 we see the importance of her bond to her mother-in-law (hamoth, a het word). In fact Naomi is to Ruth like a protecting wall. Ruth is rightly remembered for her pledge of total devotion and loyalty to Naomi. She clung to Naomi even at the cost of renouncing her people and her gods in favor of Naomi's people, the Israelites, and Naomi's God, Yahweh: "Your people will be my people and your God my God" (merely four words long in the Hebrew: *'amekh 'ami we'lohaikh 'elohai*, which literally means "your people my people; your God my God").

Yet Ruth extended her commitment still further, beyond death itself: "Where you die I will die, and there I will be buried". These words may sound anticlimactic compared to accepting Naomi's people and her God. But to understand their significance, we must appreciate the cultural mind-set of the ancient Near Eastern peoples. All the death accounts of the patriarchs mention their burials, often at length. When a patriarch died, he was "gathered to his people." Jacob and Joseph died in Egypt, but their bones were laid to rest in the Promised Land. The location of burial was important. Ruth concluded her pledge by calling down God's punishment on herself if "even death" parted her from Naomi. Even after the death of Naomi, Ruth would live, die and be buried in Bethlehem. In so doing, Ruth identified herself with Naomi's community in the most absolute manner possible. This really tells us something special about Naomi, doesn't it?

The rest of the story: Boaz. First look at Leviticus 25:25, 48, 49:

25 "'If one of your fellow Israelites becomes poor and sells some of their property, their nearest relative is to come and redeem what they have sold.
48 they retain the right of redemption after they have sold themselves. One of their relatives may redeem them:
49 An uncle or a cousin or any blood relative in their clan may redeem them. Or if they prosper, they may redeem themselves.

The kinsman redeemer requirements were relationship, financial ability and willingness. There was a closer kinsman, but he was unwilling, so it fell to Boaz who was next, able and willing which is a picture of our redeemer, Christ, who came as a man (close relative), was able (because he was God) and was willing (went to the cross for us). It is interesting to note that Boaz was a descendant of Rahab (the harlot in Jericho); Boaz and Ruth were great-grandparents to King David and thus in Jesus' human lineage. Ruth was a Moabite, a Gentile, so we see the Gentile line grafted in early on.

This is a beautiful story, only 4 chapters long, so go read it in your own Bible right now.

ח
Het + Amos

Our second het book is Amos. His name means "burden". Amos prophesied during the reign of Jeroboam II who brought the kingdom to the height of its power. Amos's warnings seemed improbable yet within 50 years the kingdom was utterly destroyed.

Amos is in 4 parts.
Part 1: Judgments on surrounding peoples.
Look at Amos 1: 6, 7, 10, 12:

6 This is what the LORD says:
"For three sins of Gaza,
even for four, I will not relent.
Because she took captive whole communities
  and sold them to Edom,
7 I will send fire on the walls of Gaza
  that will consume her fortresses.
10 I will send fire on the walls of Tyre
  that will consume her fortresses."
12 I will send fire on Teman
  that will consume the fortresses of Bozrah."

Wow! Fire on the wall! Wall is homah, a het word. If you remember from our first het book the letter het itself means fence or **wall**.

Part 2: Judgments on Judah and Israel. Fire is sent to destroy Judah, and there is judgment on Israel. Read 2: 5, 6:

5 I will send fire on Judah
that will consume the fortresses of Jerusalem."
6 This is what the LORD says:
"For three sins of Israel,
even for four, I will not relent.
They sell the innocent for silver,
  and the needy for a pair of sandals.

Part 3: Jehovah's controversy with the family of Jacob. Read 7:7-9:

7 This is what he showed me: The Lord was standing by a wall that had been built true to plumb, with a plumb line in his hand. **8** And the LORD asked me, "What do you see, Amos?"
"A plumb line," I replied.
Then the Lord said, "Look, I am setting a plumb line among my people Israel; I will spare them no longer.
9 "The high places of Isaac will be destroyed
and the sanctuaries of Israel will be ruined;
with my sword I will rise against the house of Jeroboam."

Look at verse 7 again. Did you notice where the Lord was standing? By a **wall**! What a wonderful link to our het letter's symbolic meaning. Now read 9: 9, 10:

⁹ "For I will give the command,
  and I will shake the people of Israel
  among all the nations
as grain is shaken in a sieve,
  and not a pebble will reach the ground.
¹⁰ All the sinners among my people
  will die by the sword,
all those who say,
  'Disaster will not overtake or meet us.'

God will not totally destroy the house of Jacob, but this does look pretty bleak. Not to fear, though, see part 4.

Part 4: Future kingdom blessing and restored Israel. Let's read it all: 9:11-15

¹¹ "In that day
  "I will restore David's fallen shelter—
I will repair its broken walls
and restore its ruins—
and will rebuild it as it used to be,
¹² so that they may possess the remnant of Edom
and all the nations that bear my name,"
    declares the LORD, who will do these things.
  ¹³ "The days are coming," declares the LORD,
    "when the reaper will be overtaken by the plowman
  and the planter by the one treading grapes.
New wine will drip from the mountains
  and flow from all the hills,
 ¹⁴ and I will bring my people Israel back from exile.
    "They will rebuild the ruined cities and live in them.
  They will plant vineyards and drink their wine;
  they will make gardens and eat their fruit.
¹⁵ I will plant Israel in their own land,
  never again to be uprooted
  from the land I have given them,"
    says the LORD your God.

Amos's single prophecy of future blessing was revealed above. The details are (1) the restoration of the Davidic dynasty (v. 11); (2) the conversion of the nations (v. 12); (3) the fruitfulness of the land (v. 13); (4) Israel's return from captivity (v. 14); (5) the rebuilding of the waste cities (v. 14); and (6) Israel's permanent settlement in the holy land.

As a het book Amos has some links back to Ruth and forward to 1st Thessalonians. In Ruth we saw the **wall** of warmth that surrounded Ruth in her relationship with family and in Amos we saw the fire on the **wall** and the Lord standing by it. I'll leave the rest of the links for the next section on 1ˢᵗ Thessalonians.

ח

Het + 1st Thessalonians

Remember that this Hebrew letter symbolically means fence or hedge. Its original pictographic form looked like two fence poles with two or three rails across.

Our third het book was written by St. Paul. It is the earliest of his letters. He wrote it shortly after he preached in the Thessalonian church for about a month. The young disciples in this church needed confirmation in the foundational truths and Paul gives it here. He also exhorts them to go on to holiness and he comforts them regarding those who had died.

All of the great and wonderful doctrines of the Christian faith can be found in this little letter. Let's look first at chapter 1 where we find the subjects of election, the Holy Spirit and assurance, the Trinity, conversion and also the second coming:

> 1 Paul, Silas and Timothy,
> To the church of the Thessalonians in God the Father and the Lord Jesus Christ:
> Grace and peace to you.
> 2 We always thank God for all of you and continually mention you in our prayers. 3 We remember before our God and Father your work produced by faith, your labor prompted by love, and your endurance inspired by hope in our Lord Jesus Christ.
> 4 For we know, brothers and sisters loved by God, that he has chosen you, 5 because our gospel came to you not simply with words but also with power, with the Holy Spirit and deep conviction. You know how we lived among you for your sake. 6 You became imitators of us and of the Lord, for you welcomed the message in the midst of severe suffering with the joy given by the Holy Spirit. 7 And so you became a model to all the believers in Macedonia and Achaia. 8 The Lord's message rang out from you not only in Macedonia and Achaia—your faith in God has become known everywhere. Therefore we do not need to say anything about it, 9 for they themselves report what kind of reception you gave us. They tell how you turned to God from idols to serve the living and true God, 10 and to wait for his Son from heaven, whom he raised from the dead—Jesus, who rescues us from the coming wrath.

Election: verse 4 – God has CHOSEN you.

Assurance: verse 5 – you don't just believe some words, but there is POWER with the HOLY SPIRIT and deep CONVICTION.

The Trinity: God, the Holy Spirit and Jesus are all mentioned in this passage.

Conversion: verse 9 – you "turned to God from idols". That is what conversion is all about.

The 2nd Coming: verse 10 – wait for his Son from heaven. Wow, Paul gives a whole sermon in a few short verses, doesn't he?

In the chapters following he covers the believer's walk and sanctification and hope. Please read and carefully study this letter. We'll look at just a couple of other things here. Read chapter 4: 13 – 18:

13 Brothers and sisters, we do not want you to be uninformed about those who sleep in death, so that you do not grieve like the rest of mankind, who have no hope. **14** For we believe that Jesus died and rose again, and so we believe that God will bring with Jesus those who have fallen asleep in him. **15** According to the Lord's word, we tell you that we who are still alive, who are left until the coming of the Lord, will certainly not precede those who have fallen asleep. **16** For the Lord himself will come down from heaven, with a loud command, with the voice of the archangel and with the trumpet call of God, and the dead in Christ will rise first. **17** After that, we who are still alive and are left will be caught up together with them in the clouds to meet the Lord in the air. And so we will be with the Lord forever. **18** Therefore encourage one another with these words.

These are the "rapture" verses. Opponents like to say that the word rapture doesn't occur in the Bible. So? That doesn't change the meaning of this passage one bit. Actually the Greek word in verse 17 for "caught up" is "harpazo" which means "to seize upon by force" or "snatch away". In Latin "harpazo" is "raptus". See where I'm going? "Raptus" became the English word "rapture."

Read the verses again. First of all there is comfort here – we do not need to grieve for our deceased Christian loved ones. They "sleep in death." This reminds me of the phrase in the 23rd Psalm about the "shadow of death." For us Christians, death is just like a shadow; it may cover us, but it can't hurt us. We have hope. Our loved ones "sleep in death," so, no, they are not looking down on us; no, they cannot hear our prayers; no, they are not leaving signs for us such as flickering light bulbs. We are missing them, but they are not missing us. We will all meet again. When? See verse 14: when Jesus returns He will have with Him those "who have fallen asleep in him." They will rise first at the voice of the archangel and the trumpet sound from God. Then what? This is the coolest part ever and I sometimes get a shot of adrenaline when I think hard about how wonderful it will be to "be caught up together with them in the clouds." If you are not encouraged by these words, why not?

Now let's look at 1st Thessalonians 5: 14 – 28:

14 And we urge you, brothers and sisters, warn those who are idle and disruptive, encourage the disheartened, help the weak, be patient with everyone. **15** Make sure that nobody pays back wrong for wrong, but always strive to do what is good for each other and for everyone else.

16 Rejoice always, **17** pray continually, **18** give thanks in all circumstances; for this is God's will for you in Christ Jesus.

19 Do not quench the Spirit. **20** Do not treat prophecies with contempt **21** but test them all; hold on to what is good, **22** reject every kind of evil.

23 May God himself, the God of peace, sanctify you through and through. May your whole spirit, soul and body be kept blameless at the coming of our Lord Jesus Christ. **24** The one who calls you is faithful, and he will do it.

25 Brothers and sisters, pray for us. **26** Greet all God's people with a holy kiss. **27** I charge you before the Lord to have this letter read to all the brothers and sisters.

28 The grace of our Lord Jesus Christ be with you.

Paul packs a lot into his final instructions. Sometimes it helps to just list things out for ourselves. What we have here are some do's and a couple of don'ts:
1. Warn people who are idle or disruptive.
2. Encourage those who need it.
3. Help the weak.
4. Be patient with everyone.
5. Remember the Golden Rule – yes, that's what verse 15 is saying.
6. Rejoice always.
7. Pray continually.
8. Always give thanks
9. Don't ignore the Holy Spirit's proddings. (Listen to that still, soft voice in your conscience.)
10. Do not treat prophecies with contempt.
11. Test the prophecies.
12. Reject evil.

Now we need to link up 1st Thessalonians to our Hebrew letter het. In 1st Thessalonians 2: 7 – 8, Paul writes tender endearing words (KJV):

7But we were gentle among you, even as a nurse cherisheth her children:
8So being affectionately desirous of you, we were willing to have imparted unto you, not the gospel of God only, but also our own souls, because ye were dear unto us.

The word here for "cherisheth" is the Greek word "thalpo" which literally means "to keep warm." Incidentally Thessalonica was originally an ancient town named Thermai, meaning "hot springs". 1st Thessalonians is also the ONLY book in the New Testament where the word "nurse" is used. Compare this warm imagery to our first het book of Ruth, chapter 4, verse 16 (KJV):

16And Naomi took the child, and laid it in her bosom, and became nurse unto it.

Isn't that interesting?
1st Thessalonians has another divine connection to the second het book, Amos. In Amos there is a promise to the wicked. Amos 5:18 (KJV):

18Woe unto you that desire the day of the LORD! to what end is it for you? the day of the LORD is darkness, and not light.

The Day of The Lord . . . Darkness . . . Light, hmm, let's look at 1st Thessalonians 5: 1 – 4 (KJV):

1But of the times and the seasons, brethren, ye have no need that I write unto you.
2For yourselves know perfectly that the day of the Lord so cometh as a thief in the night.

³For when they shall say, Peace and safety; then sudden destruction cometh upon them, as travail upon a woman with child; and they shall not escape.
⁴But ye, brethren, are not in darkness, that that day should overtake you as a thief.

We are NOT in Darkness!

Chapter 9 Tet

Aleph	1. Genesis	23. Isaiah		45. Romans	
Bet	2. Exodus	24. Jeremiah		46. 1st Corinthians	
Gimel	3. Leviticus	25. Lamentations		47. 2nd Corinthians	
Dalet	4. Numbers	26. Ezekiel		48. Galatians	
Hey	5. Deuteronomy	27. Daniel		49. Ephesians	
Vav	6. Joshua	28. Hosea		50. Philippians	
Zayin	7. Judges	29. Joel		51. Colossians	
Het	8. Ruth	30. Amos		52. 1st Thessalonians	
Tet	*9. 1st Samuel*	*31. Obadiah*		*53. 2nd Thessalonians*	
Yod	10. 2nd Samuel	32. Jonah		54. 1st Timothy	
Kaph	11. 1st Kings	33. Micah		55. 2nd Timothy	
Lamed	12. 2nd Kings	34. Nahum		56. Titus	
Mem	13. 1st Chronicles	35. Habakkuk		57. Philemon	
Nun	14. 2nd Chronicles	36. Zephaniah		58. Hebrews	
Samek	15. Ezra	37. Haggai		59. James	
Ayin	16. Nehemiah	38. Zechariah		60. 1st Peter	
Pey	17. Esther	39. Malachi		61. 2nd Peter	
Tzaddi	18. Job	40. Matthew		62. 1st John	
Quph	19. Psalms	41. Mark		63. 2nd John	
Resh	20. Proverbs	42. Luke		64. 3rd John	
Shin	21. Ecclesiastes	43. John		65. Jude	
Tav	22. Song of Songs	44. Acts		66. Revelation	

ט
Tet + 1st Samuel

The ninth Hebrew letter, tet, sounds like our letter T and literally means "twist" or "**serpent.**" Key tet T words are tov, which means good, as in "mazel tov" – what you hear at Jewish weddings, tahor (clean), tumah (dirty) and ta'am (taste).

Some alphabetic verses are (KJV):

Psalm 25:8 **Good** and upright is the LORD: therefore will he teach sinners in the way.
Psalm 112.5a A **good** man sheweth favour, and lendeth
Lamentations 3:27 It is **good** for a man that he bear the yoke in his youth.
Psalm 119:71 It is **good** for me that I have been afflicted; that I might learn thy statutes.
Lamentations 3.26 It is **good** that a man should both hope and quietly wait for the salvation of the LORD.
Psalm 119.68 Thou art **good**, and doest good; teach me thy statutes.
Psalm 119:66 Teach me **good** judgment and knowledge: for I have believed thy commandments.
Psalm 145.9 The LORD is **good** to all: and his tender mercies are over all his works.
Lamentations 3.25 The LORD is **good** unto them that wait for him, to the soul that seeketh him.

We don't know who wrote this book. It wasn't Samuel because, though he was the central character, he died before the end.

This book gives us a full account of Samuel's birth and reign as judge. The first two verses of chapter one get us into a most interesting story right away:

¹ There was a certain man from Ramathaim, a Zuphite from the hill country of Ephraim, whose name was Elkanah son of Jeroham, the son of Elihu, the son of Tohu, the son of Zuph, an Ephraimite. ² He had two wives; one was called Hannah and the other Peninnah. Peninnah had children, but Hannah had none.

Oh, can't you just imagine the problems in that household? Let's look at the names because they so often help us understand things. Ramathaim means "double high place"; Elkanah means "whom God possessed," Hannah means "gracious" and Peninnah means "coral" or "pearl." Now if you keep reading the story you'll find mentioned in the very next verse the sons of Eli. Now they didn't have to be named here, yet they are: Hophni (pugilist) and Phinehas (mouth of a serpent). Wait! I just sat up and took notice. What's our Hebrew letter that matches up to this book? Tet. And what does it mean? **Serpent**. Wow, already God throws in a connection. The story continues with Hannah making a vow that if she conceives a son she will dedicate him to the Lord for all the days of his life. She prayed so earnestly that unconsciously she was moving her lips and the priest, Eli, saw her and thought she was drunk. After she explains that she had not been drinking, but rather was pouring out her heart to God, Eli tells her to go in peace and may God grant her prayer. Hannah did conceive and bore a son. She named him Samuel, saying, "Because I asked the Lord for him." The name "Samuel" sounds like the Hebrew expression for "heard of God" or "asked of God."

Samuel is raised by the priest Eli and during that time the ark of the covenant is captured by the Philistines. Here is chapter 4:

1 And Samuel's word came to all Israel.

Now the Israelites went out to fight against the Philistines. The Israelites camped at Ebenezer, and the Philistines at Aphek. **2** The Philistines deployed their forces to meet Israel, and as the battle spread, Israel was defeated by the Philistines, who killed about four thousand of them on the battlefield. **3** When the soldiers returned to camp, the elders of Israel asked, "Why did the LORD bring defeat on us today before the Philistines? Let us bring the ark of the LORD's covenant from Shiloh, so that he may go with us and save us from the hand of our enemies."

4 So the people sent men to Shiloh, and they brought back the ark of the covenant of the LORD Almighty, who is enthroned between the cherubim. And Eli's two sons, Hophni and Phinehas, were there with the ark of the covenant of God.

5 When the ark of the LORD's covenant came into the camp, all Israel raised such a great shout that the ground shook. **6** Hearing the uproar, the Philistines asked, "What's all this shouting in the Hebrew camp?"

When they learned that the ark of the LORD had come into the camp, **7** the Philistines were afraid. "A god has come into the camp," they said. "Oh no! Nothing like this has happened before. **8** We're doomed! Who will deliver us from the hand of these mighty gods? They are the gods who struck the Egyptians with all kinds of plagues in the wilderness. **9** Be strong, Philistines! Be men, or you will be subject to the Hebrews, as they have been to you. Be men, and fight!"

10 So the Philistines fought, and the Israelites were defeated and every man fled to his tent. The slaughter was very great; Israel lost thirty thousand foot soldiers. **11** The ark of God was captured, and Eli's two sons, Hophni and Phinehas, died.

12 That same day a Benjamite ran from the battle line and went to Shiloh with his clothes torn and dust on his head. **13** When he arrived, there was Eli sitting on his chair by the side of the road, watching, because his heart feared for the ark of God. When the man entered the town and told what had happened, the whole town sent up a cry.

14 Eli heard the outcry and asked, "What is the meaning of this uproar?"

The man hurried over to Eli, **15** who was ninety-eight years old and whose eyes had failed so that he could not see. **16** He told Eli, "I have just come from the battle line; I fled from it this very day."

Eli asked, "What happened, my son?"

17 The man who brought the news replied, "Israel fled before the Philistines, and the army has suffered heavy losses. Also your two sons, Hophni and Phinehas, are dead, and the ark of God has been captured."

18 When he mentioned the ark of God, Eli fell backward off his chair by the side of the gate. His neck was broken and he died, for he was an old man, and he was heavy. He had led Israel forty years.

19 His daughter-in-law, the wife of Phinehas, was pregnant and near the time of delivery. When she heard the news that the ark of God had been captured and that her father-in-law and her husband were dead, she went into labor and gave birth, but was overcome by her labor pains. **20** As she was dying, the women attending her said, "Don't despair; you have given birth to a son." But she did not respond or pay any attention.

21 She named the boy Ichabod, saying, "The Glory has departed from Israel"—because of the capture of the ark of God and the deaths of her father-in-law and her husband. **22** She said, "The Glory has departed from Israel, for the ark of God has been captured."

You'll have to read the rest on your own to find out what else happens. We're moving on. Samuel is the judge and when he grew old he appointed his sons as judges, but they were dishonest, accepted bribes, and perverted justice so all the elders of Israel came to him and demanded that he appoint a king. He talks to God about it – you see, they don't need a king if they would just serve the Lord. But God says to warn them what will happen. No dice – they still want a king. Let's see who God picks. Samuel 9: 1, 2:

1 There was a Benjamite, a man of standing, whose name was Kish son of Abiel, the son of Zeror, the son of Bekorath, the son of Aphiah of Benjamin. **2** Kish had a son named Saul, as handsome a young man as could be found anywhere in Israel, and he was a head taller than anyone else.

Saul sounds pretty good, in fact, most translations say "a choice young man, and goodly". The actual word here in Hebrew is "tov" one of our key "tet" words. Saul is made king. Later Samuel makes a farewell speech. Here it is in chapter 12: 20 – 25:

20 "Do not be afraid," Samuel replied. "You have done all this evil; yet do not turn away from the LORD, but serve the LORD with all your heart. **21** Do not turn away after useless idols. They can do you no good, nor can they rescue you, because they are useless. **22** For the sake of his great name the LORD will not reject his people, because the LORD was pleased to make you his own. **23** As for me, far be it from me that I should sin against the LORD by failing to pray for you.

And I will teach you the way that is good and right. **24** But be sure to fear the LORD and serve him faithfully with all your heart; consider what great things he has done for you. **25** Yet if you persist in doing evil, both you and your king will perish."

Did you notice that he is going to teach what is **good** and right. Yes, that tet word "tov" comes up a lot. In fact, if you look at just the Old Testament History books (Joshua through Esther) and graph the times that the word "tov" appears, this is what you get:

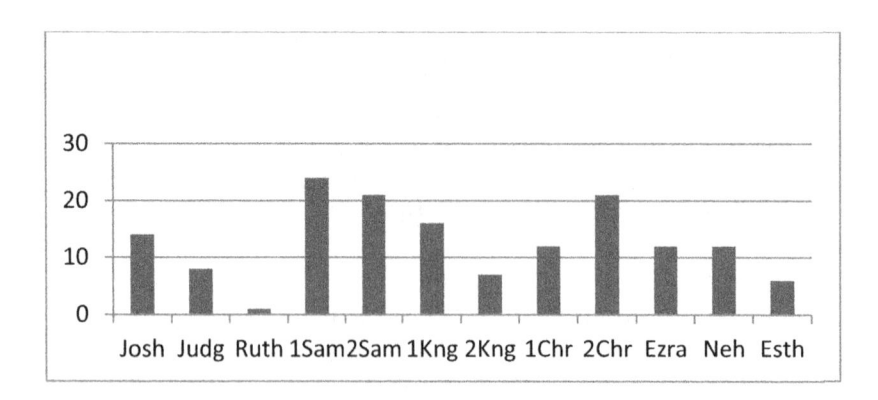

And 1st Samuel edges the rest out with more instances of the word **good**. I'm not surprised.

The choice of David, his struggles with Saul, Saul's ruin at last, and the opening of the way for David to the throne finish out this book.

The major themes of this book are the personal history of Samuel, a record of the last of the judges, the taking of the Ark of the Covenant, the reign of King Saul and the calling of David. Other things you'll find in 1st Samuel are the story of David and Goliath, David and Jonathan, and David sparing Saul's life.

ט
Tet + Obadiah

When we looked at our first tet book, 1st Samuel, we learned how the tet T word "tov" meaning "good" appeared multiple times in the alphabetic verses. Though this word appears over 770 times in the Bible it does not show up even once in the book of Obadiah.

Obadiah's name means "the servant of Yahweh."

Since Obadiah is such a short little prophetical book (the shortest book in the Old Testament) I am copying it all here with my notes in parenthesis referring to what I have underlined:

¹ The vision of Obadiah.
　　This is what the Sovereign LORD says about <u>Edom</u>— (Edom is identified with Islamic God Allah and West Bank Palestinians)
　　We have heard a message from the LORD:
An envoy was sent to the nations to say,
"Rise, let us go against her for battle"—
　　² "See, I will make you <u>small among the nations</u>; (Israel is certainly looked down on now by other nations)
　　you will be utterly <u>despised</u> (just read the newspapers to see how the neighboring countries hate Israel).
³ The pride of your heart has deceived you,
　　you who live in the clefts of the rocks
　　and make your home on the heights,
you who say to yourself,
　　'Who can bring me down to the ground?'
⁴ Though you soar like the <u>eagle</u> (the eagle is on the Palestinian emblem)
　　and make your nest among the <u>stars</u>, (possible reference to the United States)
　　from there I will bring you down,"
　　　　declares the LORD.
⁵ "If thieves came to you,
　　if robbers in the night—
oh, <u>what a disaster awaits you</u>!— (Obadiah seems empathetic)
　　would they not steal only as much as they wanted? (the obvious answer is yes)
If grape pickers came to you,
　　would they not leave a few grapes?
⁶ But <u>how Esau will be ransacked,</u> (Esau is equivalent of Edom – note how they will be cleaned out)
　<u>his hidden treasures pillaged</u>!
⁷ All your allies will force you to the border;
　　your friends will deceive and overpower you;
those who eat your bread will set a trap for you,
　　but you will not detect it.
　　⁸ "In that day," declares the LORD,
"will I not destroy the wise men of Edom,
those of understanding in the mountains of Esau?

⁹ Your warriors, <u>Teman</u>, will be terrified, (Teman means south and is associated with Medina, one of Islam's holy cities)
   and <u>everyone in Esau's mountains</u> (those trying to keep possession of the al Aqsa Mosque)
   will be cut down in the slaughter.
¹⁰ Because of the <u>violence against your brother Jacob,</u> (this is the way the Arabs have treated the Jews for years and
   you will be covered with shame; it is most interesting that the Hebrew word here is transliterated as Hamas)
   you will be destroyed forever.
¹¹ On the day you stood aloof
   while strangers carried off his wealth
and foreigners entered his gates
      and cast lots for Jerusalem,
   you were like one of them.
¹² You <u>should not gloat</u> over your brother ("should not" phrase is repeated in 13 and 14 as well hammering the fact of Palestinian pillaging)
   in the day of his misfortune,
<u>nor rejoice</u> over the people of Judah (and yet we find the Palestinians partying in the streets after terrorist attacks on Israel)
   in the day of their destruction,
nor boast so much
   in the day of their trouble.
¹³ You should not march through the gates of my people
   in the day of their disaster,
nor gloat over them in their calamity
   in the day of their disaster,
nor seize their wealth
   in the day of their disaster.
¹⁴ You should not wait at the crossroads
   to cut down their fugitives,
nor <u>hand over their survivors</u> (this was done in the 1930's and 1940's)
   <u>in the day of their trouble</u>.
    ¹⁵ "The day of the LORD is near
   <u>for all nations</u>.   (not just Islam)
As you have done, it will be done to you;
   your deeds will return upon your own head.
¹⁶ Just as you drank on my <u>holy hill</u>, (the Temple Mount)
   so all the nations will drink continually;
they will drink and drink
   and be <u>as if they had never been</u>. (this means total annihilation)
¹⁷ But on Mount Zion will be deliverance;
   it will be holy,
   and Jacob <u>will possess his inheritance</u>. (this is a promise to Israel)
¹⁸ <u>Jacob will be a fire</u>
   <u>and Joseph a flame</u>; (this is a blessing for Israel)
<u>Esau will be stubble</u>, (this is a curse for the Arabs)
   and they will set him on fire and destroy him.

There will be no survivors
  from Esau." (this is a prophetical curse on the Arabs)
       The LORD has spoken.
    ¹⁹ People from the Negev will occupy (Negev means dry, hence desert)
  the mountains of Esau,
and people from the foothills will possess (promise to Israel – 1)
  the land of the Philistines.
They will occupy the fields of Ephraim and Samaria, (promise to Israel – 2)
  and Benjamin will possess Gilead. (promise to Israel – 3)
²⁰ This company of Israelite exiles who are in Canaan
  will possess the land as far as Zarephath;   (promise to Israel – 4)
the exiles from Jerusalem who are in Sepharad
  will possess the towns of the Negev. (promise to Israel – 5)
²¹ Deliverers will go up on Mount Zion
  to govern the mountains of Esau. (promise to Israel – 6, this may mean the Dome of the Rock/Al Asqa Mosque)
  And the kingdom will be the LORD's.

    This is a tiny little book that doesn't get much attention and yet it seems to be very relevant to events in today's world.

ט
Tet + 2ⁿᵈ Thessalonians

Our third tet book is the second letter that Paul, Silas and Timothy together wrote to the Thessalonians. Paul and his friends had received some feedback after their first letter had reached the church in Thessalonica. It seemed that the Thessalonians still needed someone to teach them about certain things and had not understood some of what was in the first letter. This second letter clears up some stuff.

Because they now trust in the Lord Jesus, the Thessalonians must expect some persecution. However, God has a purpose and a plan in allowing them to suffer. He will reward them. Let's look at 2ⁿᵈ Thessalonians 1:5-10:

⁵ All this is evidence that God's judgment is right, and as a result you will be counted worthy of the kingdom of God, for which you are suffering. ⁶ God is just: He will pay back trouble to those who trouble you ⁷ and give relief to you who are troubled, and to us as well. This will happen when the Lord Jesus is revealed from heaven in blazing fire with his powerful angels. ⁸ He will punish those who do not know God and do not obey the gospel of our Lord Jesus. ⁹ They will be punished with everlasting destruction and shut out from the presence of the Lord and from the glory of his might ¹⁰ on the day he comes to be glorified in his holy people and to be marveled at among all those who have believed. This includes you, because you believed our testimony to you.

Paul, Silas and Timothy have written to give them strength and encouragement. Next we see that the Thessalonians must have had some weird ideas about the return of Christ. In fact, it seems that some said that the Lord had already come. Not so. Let's look at 2ⁿᵈ Thessalonians 2: 1-2:

¹ Concerning the coming of our Lord Jesus Christ and our being gathered to him, we ask you, brothers and sisters, ² not to become easily unsettled or alarmed by the teaching allegedly from us—whether by a prophecy or by word of mouth or by letter—asserting that the day of the Lord has already come.

Looks like some thought that the Lord would come at any moment. The return of the Lord **will** be sudden, but there are things that must happen preceding His return. Here's 2ⁿᵈ Thessalonians 2:3-12:

³ Don't let anyone deceive you in any way, for that day will not come until the rebellion occurs and the man of lawlessness is revealed, the man doomed to destruction. ⁴ He will oppose and will exalt himself over everything that is called God or is worshiped, so that he sets himself up in God's temple, proclaiming himself to be God.
⁵ Don't you remember that when I was with you I used to tell you these things? ⁶ And now you know what is holding him back, so that he may be revealed at the proper time. ⁷ For the secret power of lawlessness is already at work; but the one who now holds it back will continue to do so till he is taken out of the way. ⁸ And then the lawless one will be revealed, whom the Lord Jesus will overthrow with the breath of his mouth and destroy by the splendor

of his coming. **⁹** The coming of the lawless one will be in accordance with how Satan works. He will use all sorts of displays of power through signs and wonders that serve the lie, **¹⁰** and all the ways that wickedness deceives those who are perishing. They perish because they refused to love the truth and so be saved. **¹¹** For this reason God sends them a powerful delusion so that they will believe the lie **¹²** and so that all will be condemned who have not believed the truth but have delighted in wickedness.

Some of these Thessalonian Christians were, apparently, lazy. They had given up their jobs. They thought that Jesus' return was eminent and now they depended on their friends to keep them housed and fed. Paul had mentioned this in the first letter (1st Thessalonians 5:14) and now he tells them what they should do to these people who refuse to work. 2nd Thessalonians 3:6-13:

⁶ In the name of the Lord Jesus Christ, we command you, brothers and sisters, to keep away from every believer who is idle and disruptive and does not live according to the teaching you received from us. **⁷** For you yourselves know how you ought to follow our example. We were not idle when we were with you, **⁸** nor did we eat anyone's food without paying for it. On the contrary, we worked night and day, laboring and toiling so that we would not be a burden to any of you. **⁹** We did this, not because we do not have the right to such help, but in order to offer ourselves as a model for you to imitate. **¹⁰** For even when we were with you, we gave you this rule: "The one who is unwilling to work shall not eat."
¹¹ We hear that some among you are idle and disruptive. They are not busy; they are busybodies. **¹²** Such people we command and urge in the Lord Jesus Christ to settle down and earn the food they eat. **¹³** And as for you, brothers and sisters, never tire of doing what is good.

That's quite a warning against idleness! No work, no food. But at least it ends on a pleasant note: never tire of doing what is good. Good is a key tet word, "tov", so that matches up nicely with the divine ordering of the Holy Scriptures.

Chapter 10 Yod

Aleph	1. Genesis	23. Isaiah		45. Romans	
Bet	2. Exodus	24. Jeremiah		46. 1st Corinthians	
Gimel	3. Leviticus	25. Lamentations		47. 2nd Corinthians	
Dalet	4. Numbers	26. Ezekiel		48. Galatians	
Hey	5. Deuteronomy	27. Daniel		49. Ephesians	
Vav	6. Joshua	28. Hosea		50. Philippians	
Zayin	7. Judges	29. Joel		51. Colossians	
Het	8. Ruth	30. Amos		52. 1st Thessalonians	
Tet	9. 1st Samuel	31. Obadiah		53. 2nd Thessalonians	
Yod	*10. 2nd Samuel*	*32. Jonah*		*54. 1st Timothy*	
Kaph	11. 1st Kings	33. Micah		55. 2nd Timothy	
Lamed	12. 2nd Kings	34. Nahum		56. Titus	
Mem	13. 1st Chronicles	35. Habakkuk		57. Philemon	
Nun	14. 2nd Chronicles	36. Zephaniah		58. Hebrews	
Samek	15. Ezra	37. Haggai		59. James	
Ayin	16. Nehemiah	38. Zechariah		60. 1st Peter	
Pey	17. Esther	39. Malachi		61. 2nd Peter	
Tzaddi	18. Job	40. Matthew		62. 1st John	
Quph	19. Psalms	41. Mark		63. 2nd John	
Resh	20. Proverbs	42. Luke		64. 3rd John	
Shin	21. Ecclesiastes	43. John		65. Jude	
Tav	22. Song of Songs	44. Acts		66. Revelation	

י

Yod + 2nd Samuel

The 10th Hebrew letter is based on the word yad which means **hand**. The symbol of the hand represents power, might, ability and authority. Interestingly enough this letter is the smallest of all the Hebrew letters. Can you pick it out?

א ב ג ד ה ו ז ח ט י כ ל מ נ ס ע פ צ ק ר ש ת

Look closely – all the other letters have this little yod as part of their construction. Here are a few excerpts from the alphabetic verses:

Proverbs 31:19 – In her **hand** she holds the distaff . . .
Lamentations 1:10 – The enemy laid **hands** on all her treasures . . .
Lamentations 4:10 – With their own **hands** . . .
Psalms 119:73 – Your **hands** made me and formed me . . .

Obviously **hand** is a key word that starts with yod and is practically a homonym (yad). Other important words that start with this letter are yadah (praise), yada (know), yehudah (Judah), yahi (let there be), yashuvu (turn repent), and yareh (fear, awe or reverence). Also notice that it is the first letter in the names given to represent the Jewish people as well as the name of the sacred Jewish city. (Remember, Hebrew is read from right to left.)

יעקב = Jacob

ישראל = Israel

יהודה = Judah

ירושלים = Jerusalem

It is the first letter of Jesus' name:

ישוע = Yeshua

And the first letter of God's Holy Name: יהוה. This name is often called the Tetragrammaton and you may see it written in our alphabet as YHVH. It is considered by Orthodox Jews too sacred and holy to be pronounced and so when they are reading scripture they will substitute another name for God such as HaShem or Adonai. Now that we have reached the letter yod in this book I'd like to point out something that made me gasp as I was learning these letters and studying God's name. The symbolic meanings behind these 4 individual letters are HAND, BEHOLD, NAIL, BEHOLD. Right there in God's Holy Name have been clues to Jesus' crucifixion!

Yod gave rise to the Greek iota and the English jot. In Matthew 5: 18 it says:

¹⁸I tell you the truth, until heaven and earth disappear, not the smallest letter, not the least stroke of a pen, will by any means disappear from the Law until everything is accomplished.

The original Greek says "not one iota".
This little yod is also used grammatically to show possession. By placing it at the end of a word it means "my" because it's like you have grasped it with your hand. We know another of God's names is El (El Olam, Elohim, El shadai) and in Matthew 27:46 we read about the crucifixion:

About the ninth hour Jesus cried out with a loud voice, saying, "**ELI, ELI,** LAMA SABACHTHANI?" that is, "MY GOD, MY GOD, WHY HAVE YOU FORSAKEN ME?"

Our first yod book is 2ⁿᵈ Samuel written, perhaps, by the king's scribes. In this book Saul dies and David is anointed king over Judah and then Israel. The ark is brought to Jerusalem. In 2ⁿᵈ Samuel you'll find the story of David and Bathsheba in chapter 11. It is a story of lust, love, honor and dishonor and in the end Bathsheba marries David and bears him a son. But we're going to look at a different family story. Before you read 2ⁿᵈ Samuel 15: 1-12 there are a few things you need to know to understand this passage. There is a back story. Absalom, David's son, is angry with his father for how he dealt with an earlier situation. Because David had children with many different women there are some interesting, to say the least, family dynamics. Absalom had a sister, Tamar, who was quite beautiful. His half-brother, Amnon, lusted after her until he finally raped her (read all of chapter 13). King David, though furious, did nothing to Amnon. Absalom plotted for two years until finally he killed Amnon in revenge then fled and stayed away for three years, banished. When he finally was allowed to return he went back to his own house, but could not let David see his face. This went on for two years until Absalom did something that resulted in his father accepting him again. Then came his conspiracy:

¹ In the course of time, Absalom provided himself with a chariot and horses and with fifty men to run ahead of him. **²** He would get up early and stand by the side of the road leading to the city gate. Whenever anyone came with a complaint to be placed before the king for a decision, Absalom would call out to him, "What town are you from?" He would answer, "Your servant is from one of the tribes of Israel." **³** Then Absalom would say to him, "Look, your claims are valid and proper, but there is no representative of the king to hear you." **⁴** And Absalom would add, "If only I were appointed judge in the land! Then everyone who has a complaint or case could come to me and I would see that they receive justice."
⁵ Also, whenever anyone approached him to bow down before him, Absalom would reach out his hand, take hold of him and kiss him. **⁶** Absalom behaved in this way toward all the Israelites who came to the king asking for justice, and so he stole the hearts of the people of Israel.
⁷ At the end of four years, Absalom said to the king, "Let me go to Hebron and fulfill a vow I made to the LORD. **⁸** While your servant was living at Geshur in Aram, I made this vow: 'If the LORD takes me back to Jerusalem, I will worship the LORD in Hebron.'"

⁹ The king said to him, "Go in peace." So he went to Hebron.
¹⁰ Then Absalom sent secret messengers throughout the tribes of Israel to say, "As soon as you hear the sound of the trumpets, then say, 'Absalom is king in Hebron.'" ¹¹ Two hundred men from Jerusalem had accompanied Absalom. They had been invited as guests and went quite innocently, knowing nothing about the matter. ¹² While Absalom was offering sacrifices, he also sent for Ahithophel the Gilonite, David's counselor, to come from Giloh, his hometown. And so the conspiracy gained strength, and Absalom's following kept on increasing.

Notice the impression Absalom created in verse 1. Can you imagine 50 men running in front of someone riding in a chariot drawn by several horses? Then he positioned himself at the best possible spot and reached out to the troubled people. He took a personal interest in them. See in verse 2 how he asked each one where he was from. Then he showed sympathy for their complaints and in verse 3 made an indirect attack on the King by saying that there was no representative there to help them. Like a politician he made the claim that he would do better than that if he were judge.

Verse 5 gives us a hit on our letter yod (meaning hand) when we learn what Absalom would do if anyone tried to bow to him. In this way, offering his hand and kissing the person, Absalom stole the hearts of the King's subjects. Absalom patiently bides his time and when he is ready he tells the King that he is going to Hebron to fulfill a vow. David's last words to his son are "Go in peace." Unfortunately there won't be peace. Here's the rest of the story:

Absalom mounted an offensive and David and his troops fled. Through some subterfuge a plan was implemented that resulted in a massacre of Absalom's followers (20,000 casualties). Absalom, while riding on a mule, got caught up in some thick oak branches. The mule kept going and Absalom was left hanging by his head. One of the King's men, Joab, threw three javelins into his heart and ten more armor-bearers finished the kill. David, of course, was devastated. Remember, his last words to his son were to go in peace and that certainly didn't happen.

Besides recording David's sad words of grief over Absalom's death (18:33), the book of 2nd Samuel also records David's song of praise and his last words. The song of praise can be found in chapter 22. Notice these yod verses:

²¹ "The LORD has dealt with me according to my righteousness;
according to the cleanness of my **hands** he has rewarded me.

³⁵ He trains my **hands** for battle;
my arms can bend a bow of bronze.

And from his last words in chapter 23:
⁶ But evil men are all to be cast aside like thorns,
which are not gathered with the **hand**.

Yod + Jonah

The 10th Hebrew letter is yod and symbolizes the **hand**. Key words that start with this letter are fear, awe, reverence (yarah), turn, repent (yashuvu) and to know (yada). We'll see these appear quickly in Jonah.

The book of Jonah was probably written by Jonah though scholars seem to be divided on this. This book is read at the afternoon service of Yom Kippur, the Jewish holy day. It is considered the holiest day of the Jewish year; on this day Jews fast and say prayers of penitence.

Yes, this is the book with the story about Jonah and the whale. God sent Jonah to preach to Nineveh, a great but wicked city. Nineveh stood on the eastern bank of the Tigris River. It had walls that were a hundred feet high and fifty (!) feet thick. The main wall had fifteen gates. That sounds like a lot, but that wall was over seven and a half miles long. The population of Nineveh was about 600,000 people including those who lived in the "suburb" outside the city walls. That population estimate is based on a curious verse we'll look at last.

These residents were wicked idolaters who worshiped Asur and Ishtar, chief male and female deities. Most of the Assyrians worshiped them and since Assyria was a threat to Israel's security (see Hosea 11:5 and Amos 5:27) this was one reason Jonah didn't want to go to Nineveh. He was afraid that if the people did repent then God would not punish them and this did not sit well with his self-righteousness.

This is a short book, just four chapters and you can read it pretty quickly. Many people think this is a big mythical story and that no one could survive in the stomach of a "great fish" for three days. Stop right here and go read the story for yourself; it is just three and a half pages.

Here are some things I noticed as I studied this book: God told Jonah to go to Nineveh and Jonah ran away to Tarshish. Tarshish was about 2500 miles away. In fact, it was about as far away as you could go at that time. Of course, Jonah didn't get there. As soon as he was on the ship the Lord sent a violent storm and the sailors, a superstitious lot, decided that it was Jonah's fault. Jonah answered them saying that he feared (yarah) the God of heaven; it was indeed his fault and they should throw him over to calm the seas. At first they didn't want to, but as the storm grew worse they tossed Jonah over and instantly the raging sea quieted. What a witness to these pagans! And then they feared the Lord, offered a sacrifice and made vows to Him.

That's when the great fish swallowed Jonah. We have an account of Jonah's prayer from inside the whale. It's in chapter two and if you skipped out on reading the book here are a few verses that are incredibly convicting:

> 8 "Those who cling to worthless idols
> turn away from God's love for them.
> 9 But I, with shouts of grateful praise,

will sacrifice to you.
What I have vowed I will make good.
   I will say, 'Salvation comes from the LORD.'"

Many say that Jonah's three days in the whale are like Jesus' three days in the tomb. Definitely, even Jesus says that as we'll see in a minute. Jonah typifies Christ (the Sent One), raised from the dead, carrying salvation to the Gentiles.

And what happened next? God commanded the fish to vomit up Jonah onto dry land and it did. Jonah then received the same instructions to go preach to Nineveh and this time he went. The Ninevites believed, turned from their evil ways and God had compassion on them and did not destroy them. Jonah was angry. He had one more little altercation with God in chapter 4 from which we should get a pretty good picture of God's love and kindness for us sinners. As I mentioned earlier, the population was over half a million. Based on chapter 4, verse 11, we make that assumption:

11 And should I not have concern for the great city of Nineveh, in which there are more than a hundred and twenty thousand people who cannot tell their right hand from their left—and also many animals?"

The 120,000 people who don't know their left from their right are children, very little children. What a clever way to state something.

Jewish and Christian interpreters believed that the book of Jonah was historical fact and they continued to believe that until the rise of critical scholarship in modern times. Now for anyone who thinks that Jonah was a mythical character I'd like to point out that Jesus Christ Himself referred to Jonah as a historical person and to his experience as real. Matthew 12:38-41, 16:4; and Luke 11:29-32:

38 Then some of the Pharisees and teachers of the law said to him, "Teacher, we want to see a sign from you."
39 He answered, "A wicked and adulterous generation asks for a sign! But none will be given it except the sign of the prophet Jonah. **40** For as Jonah was three days and three nights in the belly of a huge fish, so the Son of Man will be three days and three nights in the heart of the earth. **41** The men of Nineveh will stand up at the judgment with this generation and condemn it; for they repented at the preaching of Jonah, and now something greater than Jonah is here.

4 A wicked and adulterous generation looks for a sign, but none will be given it except the sign of Jonah." Jesus then left them and went away.

29 As the crowds increased, Jesus said, "This is a wicked generation. It asks for a sign, but none will be given it except the sign of Jonah. **30** For as Jonah was a sign to the Ninevites, so also will the Son of Man be to this generation.

Jonah is the only Old Testament character with whom Jesus compared Himself directly, therefore I believe in the Jonah and the whale story.

Lastly, a final point with the yod word yashuvu (turn from) as it appears in the Nineveh king's decree (KJV Jonah 3:8b-10):

⁸yea, let them **turn** every one from his evil way, and from the violence that is in their hands.

⁹Who can tell if God will **turn** and repent, and **turn away** from his fierce anger, that we perish not?

¹⁰And God saw their works, that they **turned** from their evil way; and God repented of the evil, that he had said that he would do unto them; and he did it not.

Yod + 1st Timothy

Our third yod book is 1st Timothy, a letter written by St. Paul to Timothy to instruct him on how to deal with the growing problem of false teachers in Ephesus. There are only six chapters; in chapter 1 legalism and unsound doctrine are rebuked; chapter 2 deals with prayer and worship; chapter 3 gives the qualifications of elders and deacons; chapter 4 has instructions to Timothy; chapters 5 and 6 are full of advice for the work of the good minister of Jesus Christ.

Read chapter one. Paul tells us in chapter 1 that the law is made not for the righteous but for lawbreakers, rebels, the ungodly, murderers, adulterers, perverts (literally sodomites – think about it, it may make you uncomfortable because it is not "politically correct" to call gay people perverts, but you cannot argue with God), perjurers, slave traders and liars. Oh, and the unholy and irreligious. I think he covered all the sinners and if he didn't he added "whatever else is contrary to sound doctrine." Now if you think Paul sounds a bit arrogant, he goes on to say that he was once a blasphemer, a persecutor and a violent man, but that he acted in ignorance and unbelief. He claims that Jesus Christ came into the world to save sinners, among whom he is the worst. So he's not arrogant, but rather quite self-aware.

Here's chapter 2: 8-12:

8 Therefore I want the men everywhere to pray, lifting up holy hands without anger or disputing. **9** I also want the women to dress modestly, with decency and propriety, adorning themselves, not with elaborate hairstyles or gold or pearls or expensive clothes, **10** but with good deeds, appropriate for women who profess to worship God.

11 A woman should learn in quietness and full submission. **12** I do not permit a woman to teach or to assume authority over a man; she must be quiet.

Okay, ladies and gents, let's examine these verses carefully. Right away in verse 8 there is a reference to our 10th Hebrew letter that matches up to this book and means **hand**. We are to lift up "holy hands"; Young's Literal translation says "kind hands." Is this just for the men? No, because verse 9 actually starts in the original Greek with a word that means "in the same way" or "in like manner". So, women should lift up their hands, too, plus dress modestly and, to give it a modern interpretation, they should not look like they are vying for a cover shot on a magazine about Hollywood glamour. Nope, instead they should adorn themselves with good deeds – do something to make God proud. (Extra info: three 1st century writers, the poet Juvenal, the Roman historian Pliny the Elder, and Philo a Jewish Hellenistic philosopher, all wrote about the women of their time who dressed extravagantly. From prostitutes to the wife of Caligula, they describe the jewelry, clothing and makeup of these pagan women. Paul probably wanted to caution Christian women to avoid being mistaken for one of them and compromising their witness. Wearing jewelry, makeup and nice clothes is not prohibited anywhere in the Bible.)

All right, verse 11 brings out the women's libber in the majority of Americans. How do we deal with Paul's statement that a woman should learn in quietness and full submission? Well, first of all this is really pretty liberal in that he's saying that women <u>should</u> learn, up until then women didn't get much education, if any. Learning in quietness means just that. Full submission (or subjection, as some translators have used) does not mean that Christian women are not free and equal to their husbands – they are – but Paul is worried about the danger that a wife might usurp the husband's authority; that would not please the Lord because He has placed the man as head over the woman in the marital relationship. So ladies, don't get your feathers ruffled over these verses, there is a perfect order here and Paul is not relegating women to second class status anymore than the letter g is less important than the letter f just because it comes behind it in the order of the alphabet.

The problem with verse 12 is that the word "woman" is actually "wife" in the Greek and the word "teach" in this instance means "to teach continuously". Paul is saying that if the husband is present then the wife should not undermine his position in public; she should never encroach upon his role. When you understand the original intent of the language then you can avoid misunderstandings.

Now on to bishops and deacons. Chapter 3: 1-7:

1 Here is a trustworthy saying: Whoever aspires to be an overseer desires a noble task. **2** Now the overseer is to be above reproach, faithful to his wife, temperate, self-controlled, respectable, hospitable, able to teach, **3** not given to drunkenness, not violent but gentle, not quarrelsome, not a lover of money. **4** He must manage his own family well and see that his children obey him, and he must do so in a manner worthy of full respect. **5** (If anyone does not know how to manage his own family, how can he take care of God's church?) **6** He must not be a recent convert, or he may become conceited and fall under the same judgment as the devil. **7** He must also have a good reputation with outsiders, so that he will not fall into disgrace and into the devil's trap.

This translation uses "overseer", some say "bishop". The original Greek word is "episkope" which implies overseeing, observing, examining the state of affairs of something. If your church has bishops here is where you can see the criteria you should hold them to.

8 In the same way, deacons are to be worthy of respect, sincere, not indulging in much wine, and not pursuing dishonest gain. **9** They must keep hold of the deep truths of the faith with a clear conscience. **10** They must first be tested; and then if there is nothing against them, let them serve as deacons.
11 In the same way, the women are to be worthy of respect, not malicious talkers but temperate and trustworthy in everything.

12 A deacon must be faithful to his wife and must manage his children and his household well. **13** Those who have served well gain an excellent standing and great assurance in their faith in Christ Jesus.

Deacons can be men or women. Verse 11 indicates that women are included as candidates for this office (Phoebe is called a deacon in Romans 16:1). The high standards for both bishops and deacons are strict. The difference in these 2 offices seems to be that the overseer (bishop, elder) should be able to teach (vs.2). Both offices have a **hand** in the affairs of the church.

Remember our alphabetic verses for the 10th Hebrew letter yod (KJV):

Psalm 119:73 Thy **hands** have made me and fashioned me: give me understanding, that I may learn thy commandments.
Proverbs 31:19 She layeth her **hands** to the spindle, and her hands hold the distaff.
Lamentations 1:10 The adversary hath spread out his **hand** upon all her pleasant things:
Lamentations 4:10 The **hands** of the pitiful women have sodden their own children

The symbol of the hand naturally represents **power**, **might**, **ability**, and **authority** because with it we handle, control, possess, and manipulate (from the Latin manus = hand) everything in our world. In fact, **yad** is translated as **power** twelve times in the KJV and when God gave dominion over all creatures to Noah and his sons, he said "into your **hand** are they delivered." A ruling king has the land under the "power of his **hand**" and God freed the Jews from their Egyptian bondage "with **great power**, and with a **mighty hand**" (Exo 32:11).

We saw several instances of "hand" in our other two yod books, 2nd Samuel and Jonah. Now look at 1st Timothy 2:8: 4:14; and 5:22:

8 Therefore I want the men everywhere to pray, lifting up holy **hands** without anger or disputing.
14 Do not neglect your gift, which was given you through prophecy when the body of elders laid their **hands** on you.
22 Do not be hasty in the laying on of **hands**, and do not share in the sins of others. Keep yourself pure.

Chapter 11 Kaph

Aleph	1. Genesis	23. Isaiah		45. Romans	
Bet	2. Exodus	24. Jeremiah		46. 1st Corinthians	
Gimel	3. Leviticus	25. Lamentations		47. 2nd Corinthians	
Dalet	4. Numbers	26. Ezekiel		48. Galatians	
Hey	5. Deuteronomy	27. Daniel		49. Ephesians	
Vav	6. Joshua	28. Hosea		50. Philippians	
Zayin	7. Judges	29. Joel		51. Colossians	
Het	8. Ruth	30. Amos		52. 1st Thessalonians	
Tet	9. 1st Samuel	31. Obadiah		53. 2nd Thessalonians	
Yod	10. 2nd Samuel	32. Jonah		54. 1st Timothy	
Kaph	*11. 1st Kings*	*33. Micah*		*55. 2nd Timothy*	
Lamed	12. 2nd Kings	34. Nahum		56. Titus	
Mem	13. 1st Chronicles	35. Habakkuk		57. Philemon	
Nun	14. 2nd Chronicles	36. Zephaniah		58. Hebrews	
Samek	15. Ezra	37. Haggai		59. James	
Ayin	16. Nehemiah	38. Zechariah		60. 1st Peter	
Pey	17. Esther	39. Malachi		61. 2nd Peter	
Tzaddi	18. Job	40. Matthew		62. 1st John	
Quph	19. Psalms	41. Mark		63. 2nd John	
Resh	20. Proverbs	42. Luke		64. 3rd John	
Shin	21. Ecclesiastes	43. John		65. Jude	
Tav	22. Song of Songs	44. Acts		66. Revelation	

כ

Kaph + 1st Kings

The name of the eleventh letter, kaph , denotes the **palm of the hand** (or spoon or sole of the foot). It symbolizes the open, giving hand as well as the receiving hand as when we hold our hands open to God to receive His blessings. Compare the kaph to the yod – grammatically, yod is attached to nouns to mean "my" and kaph is attached to mean "your". Picture that in your mind: both letters symbolize an aspect of the hand, the yod closes the hand and grasps and the kaph opens up the hand and gives. The sound of the letter kaph is like a guttural "ch," like how the Germans pronounce "Bach." The letter Kaph is also a word meaning bent, like the shape of the letter and like a spoon, the cupping of the hand, the sole of the foot or palm branches. When kaph appears at the end of a word it takes on a different shape.

In the alphabetic verses we can see pretty clearly the difference in the yod and the kaph. Proverbs 31: 10 – 31 are the 22 aleph to tav acrostics. Look at verses 19 and 20:

> **19** In her hand she holds the distaff
> and grasps the spindle with her fingers.
> **20** She opens her arms to the poor
> and extends her hands to the needy.

Did you see the difference in what the hand is doing? Pretty cool, isn't it? There are several key words that start with kaph such as throne, atone, mercy seat, crown, finished, cherub/ cherubim, and glory. "Glory" is the kaph word in the alphabetic verse 11 of Psalm 145 and we'll see that glory graphically in 1st Kings.

In Hebrew the first book of Kings is "Mal-chim" which means "messengers" or "kings." According to the Jewish Talmud this book was written by the prophet Jeremiah. The major themes are the death of David, the reign of Solomon, the building of the temple, the death of Solomon, the division of the kingdom and the ministry of Elijah. 1st Kings establishes the typology of Christ sitting on the Throne of Glory (2 kaph words). See the graph below for the distribution of the word "throne" in the 12 Old Testament history books.

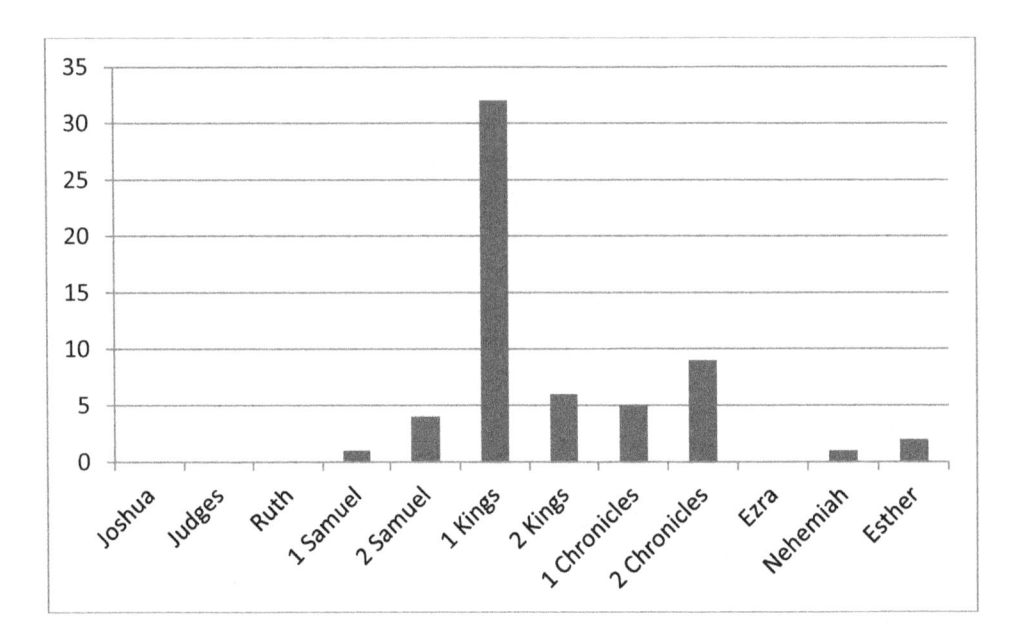

[Bar chart showing occurrences of the Hebrew word for throne across Old Testament historical books: Joshua 0, Judges 0, Ruth 0, 1 Samuel 1, 2 Samuel 4, 1 Kings 32, 2 Kings 6, 1 Chronicles 5, 2 Chronicles 9, Ezra 0, Nehemiah 1, Esther 2.]

The Hebrew word for throne appears 32 times!

Now let's look at the temple that King Solomon built. Read chapter 6, verses 1 – 6:

¹ In the four hundred and eightieth year after the Israelites came out of Egypt, in the fourth year of Solomon's reign over Israel, in the month of Ziv, the second month, he began to build the temple of the LORD.
² The temple that King Solomon built for the LORD was sixty cubits long, twenty wide and thirty high. **³** The portico at the front of the main hall of the temple extended the width of the temple, that is twenty cubits, and projected ten cubits from the front of the temple. **⁴** He made narrow windows high up in the temple walls. **⁵** Against the walls of the main hall and inner sanctuary he built a structure around the building, in which there were side rooms. **⁶** The lowest floor was five cubits wide, the middle floor six cubits and the third floor seven. He made offset ledges around the outside of the temple so that nothing would be inserted into the temple walls.

The temple sanctuary, which contained the Holy of Holies, was a rectangular building measuring about 90 feet long by 30 feet wide by 45 feet high. This assumes that the cubit is about 18 inches, though there is also the royal cubit from Egypt which is 20.5 inches making the measurements slightly larger. On the eastern side of the sanctuary was an enclosed porch that extended the width of the building. It projected about 15 feet from it and apparently formed a 180 foot high tower (you can cross reference 2nd Chronicles 3:4 if you want). Around the sanctuary building Solomon built a very curious honeycomb of rooms (maybe offices?). These rooms were arranged in three stories. Picture it: the lowest rooms were about 7.5 feet wide, the middle story rooms were about 9 feet wide and the upper rooms were about 10.5 feet wide.

In 1st Kings 6:6 we are told that Solomon built "offset ledges around the outside of the temple so that nothing would be inserted into the temple walls." This indicates that the sides of the sanctuary must have had a step-like or terraced appearance during construction. The upper story offices each projected one cubit (18 inches) further toward the sanctuary interior than the room below. There seems to be no doubt that the exterior façade would have concealed this stepped feature once the building was completed. Within the south facing side of the compound was a winding stairway, maybe circular, maybe squarish, that gave access to the upper floors. Now look at the next verse, 1st Kings 6:7:

7 In building the temple, only blocks dressed at the quarry were used, and no hammer, chisel or any other iron tool was heard at the temple site while it was being built.

Wow! Think about that . . . every stone was cut and polished and prepared for its exact position far away from the building site. Who does that? God does. This is just like how He is preparing us for how we will fit into His heavenly kingdom some day. As a matter of fact, the comparison goes pretty deep since Christians are referred to as "living stones" in 1st Peter 2:5 and we will be brought together into a "spiritual temple" according to 1st Corinthians 3:16.

More about the Solomon's temple from verses 8 – 10:

8 The entrance to the lowest floor was on the south side of the temple; a stairway led up to the middle level and from there to the third. **9** So he built the temple and completed it, roofing it with beams and cedar planks. **10** And he built the side rooms all along the temple. The height of each was five cubits, and they were attached to the temple by beams of cedar.

This must have been kind of lodge-like with all the cedar planks and beams. Then God gives a promise:

11 The word of the LORD came to Solomon: **12** "As for this temple you are building, if you follow my decrees, observe my laws and keep all my commands and obey them, I will fulfill through you the promise I gave to David your father. **13** And I will live among the Israelites and will not abandon my people Israel."

What a wonderful promise that is for God's chosen people. Now, really try to imagine the inside of the temple:

14 So Solomon built the temple and completed it. **15** He lined its interior walls with cedar boards, paneling them from the floor of the temple to the ceiling, and covered the floor of the temple with planks of juniper. **16** He partitioned off twenty cubits at the rear of the temple with cedar boards from floor to ceiling to form within the temple an inner sanctuary, the Most Holy Place. **17** The main hall in front of this room was forty cubits long. **18** The inside of the temple was cedar, carved with gourds and open flowers. Everything was cedar; no stone was to be seen.

I live in a full log home so I know how comforting it is to be in this kind of a warm, woodsy interior. Even the stone is covered by the cedar, but for the inner sanctuary God has Solomon use all that wealth that God blessed him with to decorate:

19 He prepared the inner sanctuary within the temple to set the ark of the covenant of the LORD there. **20** The inner sanctuary was twenty cubits long, twenty wide and twenty high. He overlaid the inside with **pure gold**, and he also overlaid the altar of cedar. **21** Solomon covered the inside of the temple with **pure gold**, and he extended **gold chains** across the front of the inner sanctuary, which was **overlaid with gold**. **22** So he overlaid the whole interior with **gold**. He also overlaid with **gold** the altar that belonged to the inner sanctuary.
23 For the inner sanctuary he made a pair of cherubim out of olive wood, each ten cubits high. **24** One wing of the first cherub was five cubits long, and the other wing five cubits—ten cubits from wing tip to wing tip. **25** The second cherub also measured ten cubits, for the two cherubim were identical in size and shape. **26** The height of each cherub was ten cubits. **27** He placed the cherubim inside the innermost room of the temple, with their wings spread out. The wing of one cherub touched one wall, while the wing of the other touched the other wall, and their wings touched each other in the middle of the room. **28** He overlaid the cherubim with **gold**.
29 On the walls all around the temple, in both the inner and outer rooms, he carved cherubim, palm trees and open flowers. **30** He also covered the floors of both the inner and outer rooms of the temple with **gold**.

Now you may have noticed the verses that explain the carving, size and overlaying in gold of the cherubim. Remember, cherub and cherubim, are key kaph words. In case you ever wondered, adding "im" is how you make a noun plural in Hebrew – one cherub, two cherubim. Let's finish the temple now with verses 31 – 38:

31 For the entrance to the inner sanctuary he made doors out of olive wood that were one fifth of the width of the sanctuary. **32** And on the two olive-wood doors he carved cherubim, palm trees and open flowers, and overlaid the cherubim and palm trees with hammered gold. **33** In the same way, for the entrance to the main hall he made doorframes out of olive wood that were one fourth of the width of the hall. **34** He also made two doors out of juniper wood, each having two leaves that turned in sockets. **35** He carved cherubim, palm trees and open flowers on them and overlaid them with gold hammered evenly over the carvings.
36 And he built the inner courtyard of three courses of dressed stone and one course of trimmed cedar beams.
37 The foundation of the temple of the LORD was laid in the fourth year, in the month of Ziv. **38** In the eleventh year in the month of Bul, the eighth month, the temple was finished in all its details according to its specifications. He had spent seven years building it.

Seven years! Most scholars think that was a long time for the building itself and so they think that the majority of the time spent must have been spent on all the carvings and the gold overlay. Though you can do a search on the internet and find lots of pictures of drawings and models, I don't think you can imagine how magnificent and beautiful this temple must have been. Solomon dedicated the temple and said this in verse 23 of chapter 8:

"LORD, the God of Israel, there is no God like you in heaven above or on earth below—you who keep your covenant of love with your servants who continue wholeheartedly in your way."

There is no God like our God.

כ
Kaph + Micah

The Hebrew letter kaph k symbolizes the open, giving **hand**. The second kaph book is Micah. The name means "who is like God?" The prophet Micah was a contemporary of Isaiah and he spoke out strongly against immorality, social injustices and the oppression of the poor by the rich. Let's look first at chapter 1 verse 2:

> ² Hear, you peoples, all of you,
> listen, earth and all who live in it,
> that the Sovereign LORD may bear witness against you,
> the Lord from his holy temple.

So is this prophecy for you? Appears so. And it looks like the Lord is going to bear witness against us.

What did we do? Hmm, the usual . . . See here in 2: 1-2 man's plans:

> ¹ Woe to those who plan iniquity,
> to those who plot evil on their beds!
> At morning's light they carry it out
> because it is in their power to do it.
> ² They covet fields and seize them,
> and houses, and take them.
> They defraud people of their homes,
> they rob them of their inheritance.

Iniquity, evil, fraud, covetousness, theft . . . sounds like a pretty thorough assessment of mankind. But not only that, this passage directly relates back to chapter 21 of 1st Kings (our first kaph book) and the story about Naboth's vineyard and how Jezebel urges Ahab to seize that coveted field.

Those are man's plans. What are God's? 2: 3-4:

> ³ Therefore, the LORD says:
> "I am planning disaster against this people,
> from which you cannot save yourselves.
> You will no longer walk proudly,
> for it will be a time of calamity.
> ⁴ In that day people will ridicule you;
> they will taunt you with this mournful song:
> 'We are utterly ruined;
> my people's possession is divided up.
> He takes it from me!
> He assigns our fields to traitors.'"

A disaster. A time of calamity. Ridicule and taunting. Chapter 2 goes on with a warning against false prophets (boy, that comes up a lot), but deliverance is promised along with a glimpse of the Messiah king, 2:12-13:

¹² "I will surely gather all of you, Jacob;
   I will surely bring together the remnant of Israel.
I will bring them together like sheep in a pen,
   like a flock in its pasture;
   the place will throng with people.
¹³ The One who breaks open the way will go up before them;
   they will break through the gate and go out.
Their King will pass through before them,
   the LORD at their head."

In chapter 3 God blames Israel's leaders and in chapter 4 there are some end times prophecies (my comments are in parentheses):

¹ In the last days
   the mountain of the LORD's temple will be established   (the mountain is a symbol of a great earth power)
   as the highest of the mountains; (a supreme kingdom)
it will be exalted above the hills, (the hills are lesser powers or nations)
   and peoples will stream to it.
   ² Many nations will come and say,
      "Come, let us go up to the mountain of the LORD, (a universal kingdom)
   to the temple of the God of Jacob.
He will teach us his ways,   ("He" who will teach us is Jesus)
   so that we may walk in his paths."
The law will go out from Zion,
   the word of the LORD from Jerusalem.
³ He will judge between many peoples
   and will settle disputes for strong nations far and wide. (it will be a peaceful kingdom)
They will beat their swords into plowshares
   and their spears into pruning hooks.
Nation will not take up sword against nation,
   nor will they train for war anymore.
⁴ Everyone will sit under their own vine (having your own vine and fig tree illustrates universal prosperity)
   and under their own fig tree,
and no one will make them afraid,
   for the LORD Almighty has spoken.
⁵ All the nations may walk
   in the name of their gods, ("gods" is the Hebrew word "elohim")
but we will walk in the name of the LORD
   our God for ever and ever. ("God" here is also the Hebrew word "Elohim" referring to Jehovah)

The LORD's Plan
⁶ "In that day," declares the LORD,
  "I will gather the lame;
I will assemble the exiles
and those I have brought to grief.
⁷ I will make the lame my remnant,
  those driven away a strong nation.
The LORD will rule over them in Mount Zion   (Israel is regathered – this is the tribulation time)
  from that day and forever.
⁸ As for you, watchtower of the flock,
  stronghold of Daughter Zion,
the former dominion will be restored to you;
  kingship will come to Daughter Jerusalem."
    ⁹ Why do you now cry aloud— (intervening time period of Babylonian captivity)
  have you no king?
Has your ruler perished,
  that pain seizes you like that of a woman in labor?
¹⁰ Writhe in agony, Daughter Zion,
  like a woman in labor,

for now you must leave the city
  to camp in the open field.
You will go to Babylon;
  there you will be rescued.
There the LORD will redeem you
  out of the hand of your enemies.
    ¹¹ But now many nations
  are gathered against you.
They say, "Let her be defiled,
  let our eyes gloat over Zion!"
¹² But they do not know
  the thoughts of the LORD;
they do not understand his plan,
  that he has gathered them like sheaves to the threshing floor.
¹³ "Rise and thresh, Daughter Zion,
  for I will give you horns of iron; (this is the time of Armageddon)
I will give you hooves of bronze,
  and you will break to pieces many nations."
You will devote their ill-gotten gains to the LORD,
  their wealth to the Lord of all the earth.

   Pretty heavy stuff and I would recommend that you do your own research and study to better understand it.
   One verse from chapter 5:

> ² "But you, Bethlehem Ephrathah,
>   though you are small among the clans of Judah,
> out of you will come for me
>   one who will be ruler over Israel,
> whose origins are from of old,
>   from ancient times."

Has this prophecy been fulfilled? Yes, Jesus was born in Bethlehem.

In chapter 6 the writer asks about coming before the Lord with burnt offerings. He even asks if he should offer his firstborn for his transgressions. What does God answer? Read 6:8:

> ⁸ He has shown you, O mortal, what is good.
>   And what does the LORD require of you?
> To act justly and to love mercy
>   and to walk humbly with your God.

So, God DOES NOT require sacrifices. He's going to take care of that for us. Final thoughts – read 7: 18-20:

> ¹⁸ Who is a God like you,
>   who pardons sin and forgives the transgression
>   of the remnant of his inheritance?
> You do not stay angry forever
>   but delight to show mercy.
> ¹⁹ You will again have compassion on us;
>   you will tread our sins underfoot
>   and hurl all our iniquities into the depths of the sea.
> ²⁰ You will be faithful to Jacob,
>   and show love to Abraham,
> as you pledged on oath to our ancestors
>   in days long ago.

If I were a Jew I would be clinging to these verses for sure – such hope and mercy and love.

כ

Kaph + 2nd Timothy

Our third kaph book was written by St. Paul shortly before he was martyred. This letter to his beloved friend has to do with the personal walk and testimony of a true servant of Christ. Let's see how Paul encourages Timothy in the opening verses of the second chapter:

1 You then, my son, be strong in the grace that is in Christ Jesus. **2** And the things you have heard me say in the presence of many witnesses entrust to reliable people who will also be qualified to teach others.

He tells him to "be strong" and the implication here from the Greek is to be strong in mind. He encourages him to teach others to be teachers. There is a huge difference between teaching your subject matter and teaching someone else how to teach your subject matter. I spent over thirty years teaching and the experience of having a student-teacher to train was incredibly difficult yet enriching and like Paul says, you need that future teacher to be reliable.

3 Join with me in suffering, like a good soldier of Christ Jesus. **4** No one serving as a soldier gets entangled in civilian affairs, but rather tries to please his commanding officer. **5** Similarly, anyone who competes as an athlete does not receive the victor's crown except by competing according to the rules. **6** The hardworking farmer should be the first to receive a share of the crops. **7** Reflect on what I am saying, for the Lord will give you insight into all this.

The soldier analogy is perfect because, unfortunately, every generation can relate to the comparisons. Paul likens Christians to soldiers so we must be at war. Look again at verse 4. The commanding officer is Christ. Do you want to please Him?

Paul likes to use athletic analogies. Some of the qualities he is inferring are effort, setting a goal, being self-sacrificing and following rules. The athlete parallel and the farmer comparison are forever current. The soldier and the athlete are in it for the victory and the crown. What does the farmer get? Ah, yes, the first fruits. First fruits are the blessings.

1 In the presence of God and of Christ Jesus, who will judge the living and the dead, and in view of his appearing and his kingdom, I give you this charge: **2** Preach the word; be prepared in season and out of season; correct, rebuke and encourage—with great patience and careful instruction. **3** For the time will come when people will not put up with sound doctrine. Instead, to suit their own desires, they will gather around them a great number of teachers to say what their itching ears want to hear. **4** They will turn their ears away from the truth and turn aside to myths. **5** But you, keep your head in all situations, endure hardship, do the work of an evangelist, discharge all the duties of your ministry.

⁶ For I am already being poured out like a drink offering, and the time for my departure is near. **⁷** I have fought the good fight, I have finished the race, I have kept the faith. **⁸** Now there is in store for me the crown of righteousness, which the Lord, the righteous Judge, will award to me on that day—and not only to me, but also to all who have longed for his appearing.

The time will come when people will not put up with correct doctrine. And that time seems to be right now as many reject portions of the Bible as being old-fashioned, narrow minded or misinterpreted. Look what verses 3 and 4 say they will do: they will surround themselves with people who tell them what they want to hear. They will turn from the truth and accept myths. Myths? You mean like horoscopes, witchcraft, paranormal stuff, extra-terrestrials, vampires, scientology, drugs, global warming, yoga meditation and myriad superstitions? Yup. I like the phrase "itching ears." What does that mean to you?

In verse 6 the Greek phrase that is translated "being poured out like a drink offering" is an allusion to an Old Testament sacrifice mentioned 32 times in Numbers 15. What do you think Paul means?

Paul finishes by keeping his soldier, athlete and farmer images in order: I have fought the good fight (soldier), I have finished the race (athlete), I have kept the faith (farmer).

Chapter 12 Lamed

Aleph	1. Genesis	23. Isaiah	45. Romans
Bet	2. Exodus	24. Jeremiah	46. 1st Corinthians
Gimel	3. Leviticus	25. Lamentations	47. 2nd Corinthians
Dalet	4. Numbers	26. Ezekiel	48. Galatians
Hey	5. Deuteronomy	27. Daniel	49. Ephesians
Vav	6. Joshua	28. Hosea	50. Philippians
Zayin	7. Judges	29. Joel	51. Colossians
Het	8. Ruth	30. Amos	52. 1st Thessalonians
Tet	9. 1st Samuel	31. Obadiah	53. 2nd Thessalonians
Yod	10. 2nd Samuel	32. Jonah	54. 1st Timothy
Kaph	11. 1st Kings	33. Micah	55. 2nd Timothy
Lamed	*12. 2nd Kings*	*34. Nahum*	*56. Titus*
Mem	13. 1st Chronicles	35. Habakkuk	57. Philemon
Nun	14. 2nd Chronicles	36. Zephaniah	58. Hebrews
Samek	15. Ezra	37. Haggai	59. James
Ayin	16. Nehemiah	38. Zechariah	60. 1st Peter
Pey	17. Esther	39. Malachi	61. 2nd Peter
Tzaddi	18. Job	40. Matthew	62. 1st John
Quph	19. Psalms	41. Mark	63. 2nd John
Resh	20. Proverbs	42. Luke	64. 3rd John
Shin	21. Ecclesiastes	43. John	65. Jude
Tav	22. Song of Songs	44. Acts	66. Revelation

ל

Lamed + 2ⁿᵈ Kings
The 12th Hebrew letter pictures a shepherd's staff or an ox goad. As a verb "lamad" means **teach**, learn, point, prick or goad.

In 2ⁿᵈ Kings we find the prophet Elijah at the end of his life. We'll take a close look at chapter 2. Here is 2ⁿᵈ Kings 2: 1-18:

¹ When the LORD was about to take Elijah up to heaven in a whirlwind, Elijah and Elisha were on their way from Gilgal. ² Elijah said to Elisha, "Stay here; the LORD has sent me to Bethel."

But Elisha said, "As surely as the LORD lives and as you live, I will not leave you." So they went down to Bethel.

³ The company of the prophets at Bethel came out to Elisha and asked, "Do you know that the LORD is going to take your master from you today?"

"Yes, I know," Elisha replied, "but do not speak of it."

⁴ Then Elijah said to him, "Stay here, Elisha; the LORD has sent me to Jericho."

And he replied, "As surely as the LORD lives and as you live, I will not leave you." So they went to Jericho.

⁵ The company of the prophets at Jericho went up to Elisha and asked him, "Do you know that the LORD is going to take your master from you today?"

"Yes, I know," he replied, "but do not speak of it."

⁶ Then Elijah said to him, "Stay here; the LORD has sent me to the Jordan."

And he replied, "As surely as the LORD lives and as you live, I will not leave you." So the two of them walked on.

⁷ Fifty men of the company of the prophets went and stood at a distance, facing the place where Elijah and Elisha had stopped at the Jordan. ⁸ Elijah took his cloak, rolled it up and struck the water with it. The water divided to the right and to the left, and the two of them crossed over on dry ground.

⁹ When they had crossed, Elijah said to Elisha, "Tell me, what can I do for you before I am taken from you?"

"Let me inherit a double portion of your spirit," Elisha replied.

¹⁰ "You have asked a difficult thing," Elijah said, "yet if you see me when I am taken from you, it will be yours—otherwise not."

¹¹ As they were walking along and talking together, suddenly a chariot of fire and horses of fire appeared and separated the two of them, and Elijah went up to heaven in a whirlwind. ¹² Elisha saw this and cried out, "My father! My father! The chariots and horsemen of Israel!" And Elisha saw him no more. Then he took hold of his own clothes and tore them apart.

¹³ He picked up the cloak that had fallen from Elijah and went back and stood on the bank of the Jordan. ¹⁴ Then he took the cloak that had fallen from him and struck the water with it. "Where now is the LORD, the God of Elijah?" he asked. When he struck the water, it divided to the right and to the left, and he crossed over.

¹⁵ The company of the prophets from Jericho, who were watching, said, "The spirit of Elijah is resting on Elisha." And they went to meet him and bowed to the ground before him. ¹⁶ "Look," they said, "we your servants have fifty able men. Let them go and look for your master. Perhaps the Spirit of the LORD has picked him up and set him down on some

mountain or in some valley."

"No," Elisha replied, "do not send them."

17 But they persisted until he was too ashamed to refuse. So he said, "Send them." And they sent fifty men, who searched for three days but did not find him. **18** When they returned to Elisha, who was staying in Jericho, he said to them, "Didn't I tell you not to go?"

Did you notice that Elijah told Elisha to "Stay here" three different times? When something comes up in Scripture three times God is really trying to get your attention. Each time the Lord sent Elijah somewhere new, Bethel, Jericho and the Jordan, Elisha proclaimed that as long as the Lord lived and Elijah lived that he, Elisha, would not leave Elijah. A company of 50 prophets came out at each place and told Elisha that the Lord was going to take Elijah that very day. It is interesting that Elisha said, in each instance, "Yes, I know, but don't speak of it." (This reminds me of the messianic prophecies and how Jesus told even a demon to keep quiet about who He was, as in Luke 4:35.)

Elijah performs a miracle at the Jordan by striking the water with his cloak and causing the waters to divide so they could cross on dry ground. Elisha asks for a double portion of Elijah's spirit, in other words, he wants the first born son's inheritance, which Elijah warns is a difficult thing, but not too hard for God, of course. "If you see me when I am taken from you, it will be yours – otherwise, not," he tells him.

Next is the scene that many people misconstrue: read verses 1 and 11 again and if you thought that Elijah was carried away on that chariot (swing low, sweet chariot) you'll see that the fiery chariot and horses merely separated Elijah and Elisha before Elijah went up to heaven in a whirlwind. Well, Elisha saw this so now he'll get that double portion of spirit (power, authority). First, though, he tore his clothes apart. Compare this to Mark 15: 38 and how the curtain of the temple was torn in two when Jesus died. By the way, Elisha cried out the very phrase that would be spoken by King Jehoash when the king weeps about Elisha's death years later (2nd Kings 2:12 & 2nd Kings 13:14). Think about that!

Elisha picked up Elijah's cloak and performed the same miracle of parting the Jordan while the company of prophets from Jericho watched. These prophets knew that the Lord would take Elijah. They saw Elijah go up in the whirlwind, they saw Elisha take over with power and authority from God, yet what do they say? They want to go looking for Elijah, maybe he's on a mountain or in a valley, they say. Such unbelief can only be likened to the continual denying of Jesus by the Jews who knew of the messianic prophecies, saw the miracles and fulfillment of Scripture yet are still looking. Did you notice how long the 50 prophets looked for Elijah? 3 days.

ל
Lamed + Nahum

The 12th Hebrew letter, lamed pictures a shepherd's staff or an ox goad. As a verb it means **teach**, learn, point, prick or goad.

The book of Nahum was written by Nahum, a prophet who was a contemporary of Jeremiah. It had been about 150 years since Jonah was sent to Ninevah. Ninevah had repented, but now the people are turning away from God. (What else is new?) Nahum's name means consolation or comfort. In fact, the word is used in the 23rd Psalm: "thy rod and thy staff, they **comfort** me." See the connections?

Nahum 3:7:

"And it shall come to pass, that all they that look upon thee shall flee from thee, and say, Nineveh is laid waste: who will bemoan her? Whence shall I seek **comforters** for thee?"

Read the opening of the book of Nahum: chapter 1, verses 1 – 6:

¹ A prophecy concerning Nineveh. The book of the vision of Nahum the Elkoshite.
² The LORD is a jealous and avenging God;
  the LORD takes vengeance and is filled with wrath.
The LORD takes vengeance on his foes
  and vents his wrath against his enemies.
³ The LORD is slow to anger but great in power;
  the LORD will not leave the guilty unpunished.
His way is in the whirlwind and the storm,
  and clouds are the dust of his feet.
⁴ He rebukes the sea and dries it up;
  he makes all the rivers run dry.
Bashan and Carmel wither
  and the blossoms of Lebanon fade.
⁵ The mountains quake before him
  and the hills melt away.
The earth trembles at his presence,
  the world and all who live in it.
⁶ Who can withstand his indignation?
  Who can endure his fierce anger?
His wrath is poured out like fire;
  the rocks are shattered before him.

We are 22 books past the book of 2nd Kings where Elijah was carried up in a whirlwind, where the Jordon was dried up, where the chariot and horses of fire separated Elijah and Elisha. Did you see these three things again in these verses? Isn't it amazing how there are links between the books that match up with the same Hebrew letter?

In fact, back in 2nd Kings chapters 15, 18 and 19 you can find the story, the fulfillment of the prophesy found here in Nahum, chapter 1, verses 7 -14. Pull out your Bible and work this one out for yourself.

ל

Lamed + Titus

The 12th Hebrew letter ל pictures a shepherd's staff or an ox goad. As a verb "lamad" means **teach**, learn, point, prick or goad. You'd expect to see the word **teach** show up a lot in this little book and, in fact, it does by a rate of about 10 times more (per 1000 words) than any other book.

What does Paul's letter to Titus tell us? See chapter 2 in Titus for a list of what should be taught. Here's my summary:

1. Teach older men temperance, to be respectable, to be self-controlled and to be sound in faith, love and endurance.
2. Teach older women to be reverent, not to be slanderers, not to be addicted to alcohol and to be teachers of what is good.
3. Older women are to train younger women to love their husbands and children, to be self-controlled and pure, to be busy at home and to be subject to their husbands.
4. Young men are to be encouraged to be self-controlled and to do what is good, to show integrity, seriousness and soundness of speech that cannot be condemned.

But wait, there's more. Slaves are to be taught, too. Here it would be helpful to substitute employees for slaves (some would argue they are the same thing nowadays).

5. Slaves/employees are to be subject to their masters/bosses in everything, to please them, not to talk back, not to steal from them and to show trustworthiness.

Think about these things from a boss's perspective. How pleased would he be to have such an employee?

The end of chapter 2 tells us to say no to ungodliness and worldly passions and to live self-controlled, upright and godly lives.

Read Chapter 3 for more – we are to be subject to rulers and authorities, to be obedient, to be ready to do whatever is good. We are to slander no one, to be peaceable and considerate and to show true humility toward all men. Some synonyms for humility are humbleness, modesty and meekness.

Can you see how well our Hebrew letter, lamed, relates? Throughout this epistle I envision Paul holding a staff and teaching, exhorting, explaining, and pointing with it. There is plenty to learn in this short book; take some time now and study it.

Chapter 13 Mem

Aleph	1. Genesis		23. Isaiah		45. Romans
Bet	2. Exodus		24. Jeremiah		46. 1st Corinthians
Gimel	3. Leviticus		25. Lamentations		47. 2nd Corinthians
Dalet	4. Numbers		26. Ezekiel		48. Galatians
Hey	5. Deuteronomy		27. Daniel		49. Ephesians
Vav	6. Joshua		28. Hosea		50. Philippians
Zayin	7. Judges		29. Joel		51. Colossians
Het	8. Ruth		30. Amos		52. 1st Thessalonians
Tet	9. 1st Samuel		31. Obadiah		53. 2nd Thessalonians
Yod	10. 2nd Samuel		32. Jonah		54. 1st Timothy
Kaph	11. 1st Kings		33. Micah		55. 2nd Timothy
Lamed	12. 2nd Kings		34. Nahum		56. Titus
Mem	*13. 1st Chronicles*		*35. Habakkuk*		*57. Philemon*
Nun	14. 2nd Chronicles		36. Zephaniah		58. Hebrews
Samek	15. Ezra		37. Haggai		59. James
Ayin	16. Nehemiah		38. Zechariah		60. 1st Peter
Pey	17. Esther		39. Malachi		61. 2nd Peter
Tzaddi	18. Job		40. Matthew		62. 1st John
Quph	19. Psalms		41. Mark		63. 2nd John
Resh	20. Proverbs		42. Luke		64. 3rd John
Shin	21. Ecclesiastes		43. John		65. Jude
Tav	22. Song of Songs		44. Acts		66. Revelation

מ ם
Mem + 1st Chronicles
The letter Mem represents **water**. The pictograph was drawn as a wavy line depicting waves of water. When mem is the last letter of a word it is written more squarish, like calm water. There are many words starting with this letter that have to do with water like bath (miqveh), fountain or spring, source or origin (maqor or ma'ayin), rain (matar), the flood of Noah (mabul) and baptized or immersed (mutbal). Other keywords that start with mem are king, kingdom and bowels (yes, I know, sounds gross – many translations use the word heart instead).

In the Hebrew Bible 1st and 2nd Chronicles are one book called Divrei Ha-Yamim which means "words of the days," hence the English word "chronicles." These books were probably written by Ezra.

The first 9 chapters of 1st Chronicles are dedicated to lists and genealogies. More lists and genealogies are scattered throughout the rest of the book. In between it records David's ascension to the throne and his actions from then on. The book ends with David's son Solomon becoming King of Israel. Since it starts with all these genealogies we think the book is dry, uninteresting, and we skip over it, but the genealogies remind us that God knows each of His children personally, even down to the number of hairs on our heads (Matthew 10:30). This is the largest genealogical list in the Bible (44% of the book) and since our mem letter signifies water and has the additional meaning of source or origin, this synchronizes wonderfully. In Isaiah 48:1 God speaks of His people as coming "out of the waters of Judah", some critics prefer the translation to be "out of the bowels of". In fact, in Isaiah 49:1 we find "The Lord hath called me from the womb; from the bowels of my mother hath he made mention of my name." We see the parallel and overlap in the meaning. A mother's womb is definitely watery.

The lessons of Chronicles are that obedience to God brings blessing and disobedience brings disaster and defeat.

We're going to look specifically at chapter 17 (this section can be found nearly word for word in 2nd Samuel 7). Here are the first 15 verses from the NIV translation:

¹ After David was settled in his palace, he said to Nathan the prophet, "Here I am, living in a palace of cedar, while the ark of the covenant of the LORD is under a tent."
² Nathan replied to David, "Whatever you have in mind, do it, for God is with you."
³ That night the word of God came to Nathan, saying:
⁴ "Go and tell my servant David, 'This is what the LORD says: You are not the one to build me a house to dwell in. ⁵ I have not dwelt in a house from the day I brought Israel up out of Egypt to this day. I have moved from one tent site to another, from one dwelling place to another. ⁶ Wherever I have moved with all the Israelites, did I ever say to any of their leaders whom I commanded to shepherd my people, "Why have you not built me a house of cedar?" '
⁷ "Now then, tell my servant David, 'This is what the LORD Almighty says: I took you from the pasture and from following the flock, to be ruler over my people Israel. ⁸ I have

been with you wherever you have gone, and I have cut off all your enemies from before you. Now <u>I will make your name like the names of the greatest men of the earth</u>. ⁹ And <u>I will provide a place for my people Israel and will plant them so that they can have a home of their own and no longer be disturbed</u>. Wicked people will not oppress them anymore, as they did at the beginning ¹⁰ and have done ever since the time I appointed leaders over my people Israel. <u>I will also subdue all your enemies</u>.

" 'I declare to you that <u>the LORD will build a house for you</u>: ¹¹ When your days are over and you go to be with your fathers, <u>I will raise up your offspring to succeed you, one of your own sons, and I will establish his kingdom</u>. ¹² He is the one who will build a house for me, and I will establish his throne forever. ¹³ I will be his father, and he will be my son. I will never take my love away from him, as I took it away from your predecessor. ¹⁴ I will set him over my house and my kingdom forever; his throne will be established forever.' "

¹⁵ Nathan reported to David all the words of this entire revelation.

Do you see all of the promises? I underlined them. We had quite a bit of discussion in Bible Study about just who the son was in verses 12 through 14. Some said Solomon, some said Jesus. I think that if you look at this passage from the perspective of a Jew then it looks pretty obvious that it's Solomon. Later, in chapter 28, King David says:

⁶ He said to me: 'Solomon your son is the one who will build my house and my courts, for I have chosen him to be my son, and I will be his father. ⁷ I will establish his kingdom forever if he is unswerving in carrying out my commands and laws, as is being done at this time.'

Looks like David believed it would be Solomon, and maybe it was for a while, until Solomon "swerved" and built a high place for Chemosh and Molech, gods of the Moabs and the Ammonites (see 1st Kings 11). God then said that He would "tear the kingdom away" from Solomon. Now look again at verse 14 of 1st Chronicles 17 where it says that God will set his son over His house and His kingdom FOREVER and that his throne will be established FOREVER. I believe that takes Solomon out of the picture. Christians know that the One whom God will put on the throne FOREVER is Jesus. And let's look a little bit deeper – God will set him over His **house**. Christians are God's house as it says in Hebrews 3: 6:

⁶But Christ is faithful as a son over God's house. And we are his house, if we hold on to our courage and the hope of which we boast.

Read also Ephesians 3:19:

¹⁹Consequently, you are no longer foreigners and aliens, but fellow citizens with God's people and members of God's household,

and 1st Corinthians 3:16:

¹⁶Don't you know that you yourselves are God's temple and that God's Spirit lives in you?

מ ח

Mem + Habakkuk

Habakkuk is a small, but important book in the Old Testament. This little book was written by the prophet Habakkuk, whose name means either "the embracer" or "the wrestler." Interestingly, Habakkuk <u>wrestled</u> with the question of why God would let evil go unpunished and why God would bring tragedy and misfortune on His own people. But at the same time he <u>embraced</u> salvation by faith.

Let's read Habakkuk's 1st complaint in chapter 1, verses 2 through 4 (New International version):

> ² How long, O LORD, must I call for help,
> but you do not listen?
> Or cry out to you, "Violence!"
> but you do not save?
> ³ Why do you make me look at injustice?
> Why do you tolerate wrong?
> Destruction and violence are before me;
> there is strife, and conflict abounds.
> ⁴ Therefore the law is paralyzed,
> and justice never prevails.
> The wicked hem in the righteous,
> so that justice is perverted.

Well, people just don't seem to follow God's rules and Habakkuk doesn't seem to understand why God allows this to go on. The law is paralyzed and justice doesn't prevail. The evildoers are surrounding the righteous and justice is perverted. This sounds pretty current to me. Think about it. Here are the same verses in a really modern translation (The Message):

> ¹⁻⁴ The problem as God gave Habakkuk to see it: God, how long do I have to cry out for help
>   before you listen?
> How many times do I have to yell, "Help! Murder! Police!"
>   before you come to the rescue?
> Why do you force me to look at evil,
>   stare trouble in the face day after day?
> Anarchy and violence break out,
>   quarrels and fights all over the place.
> Law and order fall to pieces.
>   Justice is a joke.
> The wicked have the righteous hamstrung
>   and stand justice on its head.

We find God's answer in verses 5 – 11 and essentially God says He is going to use the Babylonians to punish Israel.

What's Habakkuk's next complaint? He cannot believe that the most Holy God would look at, let alone use, the evil Babylonians to punish Israel. Habakkuk is incredulous and waits for the Lord to answer him.

In Chapter 2 God gives his answer. He points out the 5 things bad people (bad nations) do: thievery (verse 6), dishonesty (verse 9), murder (verse 12), drunkenness (verse 15) and idolatry (verse 18). There's a sermon in each one of these. Babylon is guilty of these things and God will eventually punish them, too. He says that someone will destroy Babylon. In verse 5 we read, 'wine will destroy Babylon'. Read the book of Daniel and you'll find out that this really happened, about 70 years later.

God may use bad people, but be in no doubt that He makes sure that they will get their punishment at some point. It always happens because God is in control.

Chapter 3 is Habakkuk's prayer or psalm, complete with musical direction as you can read in verses 1 and 19. I especially like verse 2 (NIV):

> ² LORD, I have heard of your fame;
> I stand in awe of your deeds, O LORD.
> Renew them in our day,
> in our time make them known;
> in wrath remember mercy.

Habakkuk expresses a strong faith in God despite the adverse situation. In the rest of the chapter he sings of the great events of 800 years before when God led them out of Egypt. He remembers the plagues and pestilences that God used to punish the Egyptians. I think he has grasped the concept, which is that God will do what God reasons to be righteous and just at the exact time that He, in His infinite wisdom, deems to be the right time.

Finally, Habakkuk sees that, although he (and we) may question God's actions and timing, he (and we) must be patient and, in all things, praise God. If things are bad for us (verse 17) we should still rejoice in the Lord and be joyful in God, or, as written in verse 18 of The Message translation:

> I'm singing joyful praise to God.
> I'm turning cartwheels of joy to my Savior God.
> Counting on God's Rule to prevail

Amen.

But wait, there's more. What about our mem letter? We learned earlier that mem m represents **water**. Did we see water in Habakkuk? Yes, of course. Check out these verses (KJV):

Habakkuk 1:14 And makest men as the fishes of the **sea** ...

Habakkuk 2:14 For the earth shall be filled with the knowledge of the glory of the LORD, as the **waters** cover the **sea**.

Habakkuk 3:8 Was the LORD displeased against the **rivers**? was thine anger against the **rivers**? was thy wrath against the **sea**?

Habakkuk 3:9 ... Thou didst cleave the earth with **rivers**.

Habakkuk 3:10 The mountains saw thee, and they trembled: **the overflowing of the water** passed by: the **deep** uttered his voice, and lifted up his hands on high.

Habakkuk 3:15 Thou didst walk through the **sea** with thine horses, through the heap of **great waters**.

מ ם
Mem + Philemon

Paul opens his letter to Philemon by identifying himself as "a prisoner of Christ Jesus". He uses the same phrase in his letter to the Ephesians where he adds "for the sake of the Gentiles". I like that he reveals the "prisoner" status as he was, at that time, writing from prison. I think he is stating that although he is incarcerated he knows that this is the best place for him to be of service to Christ.

He writes to Philemon (and Apphia, Archippus and the church that meets in their home) and uses a greeting in verse 3 of "grace" and "peace". In the original Greek the word here for "grace" has the connotations of that which causes joy, pleasure and gratification. "Peace" means quietness and rest.

Our mem word "bowels" comes into play three times throughout this letter where your translation may use "heart" (verses 7, 12 and 20). Three times is a high occurrence considering how short this letter is.

Paul appeals to Philemon for mercy on behalf of Philemon's escaped slave, Onesimus. Onesimus has made himself useful to Paul in prison and, as a matter of fact, the name actually means "useful". Paul is going against Old Testament tradition and is sending Onesimus back. In Deuteronomy 23: 15, 16 there is a law which says:

15 If a slave has taken refuge with you, do not hand him over to his master. **16** Let him live among you wherever he likes and in whatever town he chooses. Do not oppress him.

Of course, Paul can break this law as he is no longer bound to the law, but set free through faith in Jesus. Paul sends him back with this letter that contains subtle suggestions to influence Philemon. Read verses 13 through 18 with that in mind:

13 I would have liked to keep him with me so that he could take your place in helping me while I am in chains for the gospel. **14** But I did not want to do anything without your consent, so that any favor you do will be spontaneous and not forced. **15** Perhaps the reason he was separated from you for a little while was that you might have him back for good— **16** no longer as a slave, but better than a slave, as a dear brother. He is very dear to me but even dearer to you, both as a man and as a brother in the Lord.

17 So if you consider me a partner, welcome him as you would welcome me. **18** If he has done you any wrong or owes you anything, charge it to me.

Boy, Paul is really steering things in a certain direction, isn't he? We know he didn't always write his own letters and it was probably Tertius (see Romans 16:22) who was writing this for him, except for verse 19 when he mentions that he is writing this part. This is undoubtedly to give more strength to his offer to pay Onesimus's debts. This is a picture of Christ paying for our sins. Paul prods Philemon's conscience two more times in verses 21 and 22:

21Confident of your obedience, I write to you, knowing that you will do even more than I ask.

22And one thing more: Prepare a guest room for me, because I hope to be restored to you in answer to your prayers.

This Onesimus may be the same person who, years later, became the Bishop of Ephesus, mentioned by Ignatius, Bishop of Antioch, in a letter to Ephesus.

Chapter 14 Nun

Aleph	1. Genesis	23. Isaiah	45. Romans
Bet	2. Exodus	24. Jeremiah	46. 1st Corinthians
Gimel	3. Leviticus	25. Lamentations	47. 2nd Corinthians
Dalet	4. Numbers	26. Ezekiel	48. Galatians
Hey	5. Deuteronomy	27. Daniel	49. Ephesians
Vav	6. Joshua	28. Hosea	50. Philippians
Zayin	7. Judges	29. Joel	51. Colossians
Het	8. Ruth	30. Amos	52. 1st Thessalonians
Tet	9. 1st Samuel	31. Obadiah	53. 2nd Thessalonians
Yod	10. 2nd Samuel	32. Jonah	54. 1st Timothy
Kaph	11. 1st Kings	33. Micah	55. 2nd Timothy
Lamed	12. 2nd Kings	34. Nahum	56. Titus
Mem	13. 1st Chronicles	35. Habakkuk	57. Philemon
Nun	*14. 2nd Chronicles*	*36. Zephaniah*	*58. Hebrews*
Samek	15. Ezra	37. Haggai	59. James
Ayin	16. Nehemiah	38. Zechariah	60. 1st Peter
Pey	17. Esther	39. Malachi	61. 2nd Peter
Tzaddi	18. Job	40. Matthew	62. 1st John
Quph	19. Psalms	41. Mark	63. 2nd John
Resh	20. Proverbs	42. Luke	64. 3rd John
Shin	21. Ecclesiastes	43. John	65. Jude
Tav	22. Song of Songs	44. Acts	66. Revelation

Nun + 2nd Chronicles

Symbolically, this letter means fish, but also can mean continue, propagate, increase, or flourish. Fish are prolific and symbolize this idea. As a noun nun means perpetuity and posterity and its basic symbolic meaning is **heir**. Why are there two very different symbolic meanings for the same letter? I don't know, perhaps because this letter has two forms. When it comes at the end of a word its form is elongated and denotes continuity. One Key nun word is nehehman (faithful) from which comes our word amen. Nun also starts the word neshamah (soul) which is called ner (candle). Proverbs 20:27 reads:

> ²⁷ The lamp of the LORD searches the spirit of a man ;
> it searches out his inmost being.

Lamp was translated from the original Hebrew word ner, candle. God uses this candle to probe the nooks and crannies of our souls. The soul, when housed in our earthly bodies, is like the bent nun, but when released by death it returns to its full magnificence. When this letter is attached to the end of a Hebrew word it gives the word a habitual or eternal quality, i.e. a trait that has become its possessor's second nature.

Let's read Psalm 119: 105 – 112, the acrostic verses for nun:

> ¹⁰⁵ Your word is a **lamp** to my feet
> and a light for my path.
> ¹⁰⁶ I have taken an oath and confirmed it,
> that I will follow your righteous laws.
> ¹⁰⁷ I have suffered much;
> preserve my life, O LORD, according to your word.
> ¹⁰⁸ Accept, O LORD, the willing praise of my mouth,
> and teach me your laws.
> ¹⁰⁹ Though I constantly take my **life** in my hands,
> I will not forget your law.
> ¹¹⁰ The wicked have set a snare for me,
> but I have not strayed from your precepts.
> ¹¹¹ Your statutes are my **heritage** forever;
> they are the joy of my heart.
> ¹¹² My heart is set on keeping your decrees
> to the very end.

Among the nun words in these verses are: ner (candle), nephesh (soul), and nachal (heritage). You can see that in the above NIV version ner was translated as lamp and nephesh was translated as life.

2nd Chronicles was written by Ezra. This book continues the history from 1st Chronicles, telling about the reign of King Solomon and how he built the temple. Then it records the rule of Jeroboam and Rehoboam and the growing apostasy once again of

Israel. The kingdom was split into two parts as two tribes accepted Rehoboam (Solomon's son) as their king and they became known as Judah. The other 10 tribes refused to accept him and were known as the kingdom of Israel. The information in 1st and 2nd Chronicles covers the same history as 1st and 2nd Kings, but focuses more on Solomon and the kings of Judah. The kings of Israel are only talked about when they have some impact on Judah. There are periods of revival, but every time there was a king who was righteous he was succeeded by a son who became an idolater. It is also interesting to note that in parallel verses from Kings and Chronicles, Chronicles adds many references to the priests and Levites. We will see a link to another nun book, Hebrews, because of this, and we will look at the priest connection when we get to Hebrews.

In 2nd Chronicles we have again the building of the temple by King Solomon. Since we previously examined the building of the temple in 1st Kings, we'll look now at the dedication of the Temple. First, in chapter 6, Solomon gives a lengthy prayer of dedication.

> **14** He said:
> "O LORD, God of Israel, there is no God like you in heaven or on earth—you who keep your covenant of love with your servants who continue wholeheartedly in your way. **15** You have kept your promise to your servant David my father; with your mouth you have promised and with your hand you have fulfilled it—as it is today.
> **16** "Now LORD, God of Israel, keep for your servant David my father the promises you made to him when you said, 'You shall never fail to have a man to sit before me on the throne of Israel, if only your sons are careful in all they do to walk before me according to my law, as you have done.' **17** And now, O LORD, God of Israel, let your word that you promised your servant David come true.
> **18** "But will God really dwell on earth with men? The heavens, even the highest heavens, cannot contain you. How much less this temple I have built! **19** Yet give attention to your servant's prayer and his plea for mercy, O LORD my God. Hear the cry and the prayer that your servant is praying in your presence. **20** May your eyes be open toward this temple day and night, this place of which you said you would put your Name there. May you hear the prayer your servant prays toward this place. **21** Hear the supplications of your servant and of your people Israel when they pray toward this place. Hear from heaven, your dwelling place; and when you hear, forgive.

The prayer goes on to give 7 problems that may happen with a request for God to solve the situation: (22-23) that God judge legal problems, (24-25) that God forgive the sin of Israel, (26-27) that God send rain, (28-31) that God hear and forgive His people through disasters and diseases, (32-33) that God hear foreigners' prayers, (34-35) that God uphold His people in war, and (36-39) that God forgive His people if they are exiled because of sin, but have a change of heart and repent.

Read the end of the prayer in verses 41 – 42 and then chapter 7:1-3:

> **41** "Now arise, O LORD God, and come to your resting place,
> you and the ark of your might.

May your priests, O LORD God, be clothed with salvation,
may your saints rejoice in your goodness.
42 O LORD God, do not reject your anointed one.
Remember the great love promised to David your servant."
1 When Solomon finished praying, fire came down from heaven and consumed the burnt offering and the sacrifices, and the glory of the LORD filled the temple. **2** The priests could not enter the temple of the LORD because the glory of the LORD filled it. **3** When all the Israelites saw the fire coming down and the glory of the LORD above the temple, they knelt on the pavement with their faces to the ground, and they worshiped and gave thanks to the LORD, saying,
"He is good;
his love endures forever."

Wow! Imagine that. Solomon finished praying and FIRE came down from heaven and the glory of the LORD filled the temple! Wow, wow, wow! Then the Lord appeared to Solomon that night:

11 When Solomon had finished the temple of the LORD and the royal palace, and had succeeded in carrying out all he had in mind to do in the temple of the LORD and in his own palace, **12** the LORD appeared to him at night and said:
"I have heard your prayer and have chosen this place for myself as a temple for sacrifices.
13 "When I shut up the heavens so that there is no rain, or command locusts to devour the land or send a plague among my people, **14 if** my people, who are called by my name, will humble themselves and pray and seek my face and turn from their wicked ways, **then** will I hear from heaven and will forgive their sin and will heal their land. **15** Now my eyes will be open and my ears attentive to the prayers offered in this place. **16** I have chosen and consecrated this temple so that my Name may be there forever. My eyes and my heart will always be there.
17 "As for you, **if** you walk before me as David your father did, and do all I command, and observe my decrees and laws, **18 I will** establish your royal throne, as I covenanted with David your father when I said, 'You shall never fail to have a man to rule over Israel.'
19 "But **if** you turn away and forsake the decrees and commands I have given you and go off to serve other gods and worship them, **20 then** I will uproot Israel from my land, which I have given them, and will reject this temple I have consecrated for my Name. I will make it a byword and an object of ridicule among all peoples. **21** And though this temple is now so imposing, all who pass by will be appalled and say, 'Why has the LORD done such a thing to this land and to this temple?' **22** People will answer, 'Because they have forsaken the LORD, the God of their fathers, who brought them out of Egypt, and have embraced other gods, worshiping and serving them—that is why he brought all this disaster on them.' "

Look at the "if, then" statements of verses 14, 17 and 19, which I put in bold print. God is looking for 4 things in verse 14: humility, prayer, seeking Him, and repentance. First, when we humble ourselves before Him, we are admitting that we have no faith in our own inability. Humility may be a very difficult thing to aim for because as soon as we think we're humble our pride surges up. So let's concentrate on keeping pride down. If we recognize and smother pride that would be great. The evidences of pride in a life can be seen in the following ways: A proud person refuses to listen and often interrupts others. A proud person likes to talk about himself all the time. A proud person has an intense desire to be noticed. He believes that he deserves everything he gets. He is not thankful. A proud person cannot be corrected. He does not like to follow instructions. A proud person exalts himself in the presence of others; he brags. He criticizes and tries to makes himself look better by putting others down. A proud person thinks of his own needs first. Think on these and see if you agree.

Second, the people of God are challenged to pray. When we call on His name in prayer, we are proclaiming our faith in His ability. Prayerlessness is the first cousin to pride. Prayerlessness says, "*I do not need to call on the Lord, I can make it just fine without His aid.*" Prayerlessness does not say, "*He is all I need*"; but "*I am all I need.*" Prayerlessness relies on self and the resources self can produce and refuses to lean on Jesus alone. Prayerlessness is the enemy of revival!

Third, seek God: God's people are told to "*seek His face*". The word "*seek*" means "*to search out by any method; especially by worship and prayer.*" The word "*face*" refers to "*the countenance; to turn toward His direction.*" This little phrase is a call for God's people to stop looking for help and purpose in every other thing in life. They are called upon to make God their primary focus and their first priority.

And finally, fourth, turn away from wicked ways or repent. Wicked ways could be interpreted as idols. Possible idols in our lives are money, position, status, hobbies, habits, lust, TV, sports, on and on. There are an unlimited number of things that you and I put before God in our lives!

So, God has declared that he would forgive the Israelites' sin and heal the land if they would do those 4 things. Then in verse 17 he makes another if, then statement. Study that one and see if you can see the 3 things after the **if** and the promise after the **then**.

Verses 19 and 20 give the big "**but if**" and the consequences. Judging by how things turned out, I think you can guess what happened.

Read for yourself in 2nd Chronicles about Solomon's other activities, building and rebuilding, his visit with the Queen of Sheba and his death. The rest of 2nd Chronicles records the division of the kingdom into Israel and Judah and the various kings that ruled Judah. When Solomon died, he left to his son, Rehoboam, a kingdom that was filled with splendor, power and the presence of God. Unlike his father, Rehoboam was a very foolish and wicked man. He listened to the advice of young men rather than the elders and, as a result, ten of the tribes rebelled against him and Israel was divided into two kingdoms with the 10 tribes forming the Northern Kingdom. They chose a man named Jeroboam to be their king and the Northern Kingdom left the worship of Jehovah and fell into idolatry. The priests and the Levites left the Northern Kingdom and moved to Judah to serve the Lord (2 Chron. 11:13-17). Throughout 2nd Chronicles in various parallel passages to Kings there are references to the priests and Levites that are missing from the Kings verses (compare 1st Kings 8:10-11 to 2nd Chronicles 5:11-14, 1st Kings 8: 63-64 to 2nd Chronicles 7:5-7, 2nd Kings 11:5-7 to 2nd Chronicles 23:4-7 and 2nd Kings 23:22-23 to 2nd Chronicles

35:18-19). Why do you think that is? (Think of the nun key word "faithful." More on this when we get to the 3rd nun book, Hebrews.)

נ ן

Nun + Zephaniah

Our second nun book is **Zephaniah.** It was written by Zephaniah, whose name means "God has secreted" or "Jehovah hides." He was of royal lineage as is revealed in the first verse.

Though he prophesied in a time of revival, the coming captivity was imminent and Zephaniah points out that the revival is superficial. He foretells the coming invasion of Nebuchadnezzar, judgment on certain peoples, the moral state of Israel and the judgment of the nations followed by kingdom blessing under Messiah.

Read Zephaniah 1:1-13:

[1] The word of the LORD that came to Zephaniah son of Cushi, the son of Gedaliah, the son of Amariah, the son of Hezekiah, during the reign of Josiah son of Amon king of Judah:

[2] "I will sweep away everything from the face of the earth," declares the LORD.

[3] "I will sweep away both men and animals; I will sweep away the birds of the air and the fish of the sea. The wicked will have only heaps of rubble when I cut off man from the face of the earth," declares the LORD.

[4] "I will stretch out my hand against Judah and against all who live in Jerusalem. I will cut off from this place every remnant of Baal, the names of the pagan and the idolatrous priests-

[5] those who bow down on the roofs to worship the starry host, those who bow down and swear by the LORD and who also swear by Molech,

[6] those who turn back from following the LORD and neither seek the LORD nor inquire of him.

[7] Be silent before the Sovereign LORD, for the day of the LORD is near. The LORD has prepared a sacrifice; he has consecrated those he has invited.

[8] On the day of the LORD's sacrifice I will punish the princes and the king's sons and all those clad in foreign clothes.

[9] On that day I will punish all who avoid stepping on the threshold, who fill the temple of their gods with violence and deceit.

[10] "On that day," declares the LORD, "a cry will go up from the Fish Gate, wailing from the New Quarter, and a loud crash from the hills.

[11] Wail, you who live in the market district; all your merchants will be wiped out, all who trade with silver will be ruined.

[12] At that time I will search Jerusalem with lamps and punish those who are complacent, who are like wine left on its dregs, who think, 'The LORD will do nothing, either good or bad.'

[13] Their wealth will be plundered, their houses demolished. They will build houses but not live in them; they will plant vineyards but not drink the wine.

Did you notice how angry God is in verses 2 and 3? In Genesis we read the creation account and learned that God created the fish then the birds then the animals and then man. Now here we have God sweeping everything from the face of the earth and in the reverse order: men, then animals then birds then fish. Despite the awfulness of these verses I can't help but be amazed at God's order. For those who like to say that the God of the Old Testament seems vengeful, angry and bloodthirsty and that their God is kind and loving, I'd like to point out that God is both loving and just. Of course He is going to get angry. When will man honor, worship, love and obey only Him?

There were 7 types of people that God will "cut off" according to the above verses. They are pagans (vs.4), astrologers (vs.5), worshipers of other gods (vs.5), those who reject God (vs.6), those who side with the heathen (vs. 8), idol worshipers (vs. 9) and those who presume that God is indifferent to them (vs.12). What do these 7 groups of people have in common? They are all breaking the first commandment.

I'd like to offer a little insight into a couple of verses that may seem confusing. In verse 8 God says he will punish those "clad in foreign clothes". Strange, huh? It means that when you act and dress like those of another belief then you are siding with them and rejecting your own. We do judge by appearances, don't we? Think of teens who like to dress as "Goths", get piercing, tattoos, etc., and distance themselves from their parents' beliefs and values. Nothing new under the sun.

In verse 9 God will punish "all who avoid stepping on the threshold". See the story in 1st Samuel 5: 1 – 5:

¹ After the Philistines had captured the ark of God, they took it from Ebenezer to Ashdod. ² Then they carried the ark into Dagon's temple and set it beside Dagon. ³ When the people of Ashdod rose early the next day, there was Dagon, fallen on his face on the ground before the ark of the LORD! They took Dagon and put him back in his place. ⁴ But the following morning when they rose, there was Dagon, fallen on his face on the ground before the ark of the LORD! His head and hands had been broken off and were lying on the threshold; only his body remained. ⁵ That is why to this day neither the priests of Dagon nor any others who enter Dagon's temple at Ashdod step on the threshold.

So, that's why I listed idol worshipers among the 7 types of people God will cut off. The Bible is so rich. Open one little verse and it's like opening a treasure chest that keeps overflowing.

Is Jesus in Zephaniah? Look at verse 7: "The Lord has prepared a sacrifice" and I believe He means Jesus.

Since this is a nun n book I expect to find the symbolic meaning of nun n or some of its alphabetic words in this book. Look at verse 10: Fish Gate (nun means **fish**) and verse 12: God will search with lamps – the original word is ner which means candle and is a nun key word.

Next Zephaniah prophesies about the Great Day of the Lord in Zephaniah 1:14-18. I've put in bold print the words that show the complete devastation of what will happen:

¹⁴ "The great day of the LORD is near—
near and coming quickly.
Listen! The cry on the day of the LORD will be bitter,
the shouting of the warrior there.

15 That day will be a day of **wrath**,
a day of **distress** and **anguish**,
a day of **trouble** and **ruin**,
a day of **darkness** and **gloom**,
a day of **clouds** and **blackness**,
16 a day of trumpet and battle cry
against the fortified cities
and against the corner towers.
17 I will bring **distress** on the people
and they will **walk like blind men**,
because they have sinned against the LORD.
Their **blood will be poured out like dust**
and **their entrails like filth**.
18 Neither their silver nor their gold
will be able to save them
on the day of the LORD's wrath.
In the fire of his jealousy
the **whole world will be consumed**,
for he will make a **sudden end**
of all who live in the earth."

Yikes! Hurry. Hurry and gather together (Zephaniah 2: 1-3):

1 Gather together, gather together,
O shameful nation,
2 before the appointed time arrives
and that day sweeps on like chaff,
before the fierce anger of the LORD comes upon you,
before the day of the LORD's wrath comes upon you.
3 Seek the LORD, all you **humble** of the land,
you who do what he commands.
Seek righteousness, seek humility;
perhaps you will **be sheltered**
on the day of the LORD's anger.

Well, verse 3 seems to link us right back to the first nun book, 2nd Chronicles. Remember 2nd Chronicles 7:13?

14 if my people, who are called by my name, will **humble** themselves and **pray** and **seek my face** and **turn from their wicked ways,** then will I hear from heaven and will forgive their sin and will heal their land.

We have the same thing here about humility and seeking God. Also note that the phrase "be sheltered" is a play on Zephaniah's name which could be translated as "Jehovah shelters" or "hides."

The rest of chapter 2 tells what will happen to the west of Israel (vs. 4 – 7), to the east (vs. 8 – 11), to the south (vs. 12) and to the north vs. 13 – 15).
Zephaniah 3: 1 – 4:

¹ Woe to the city of oppressors,
rebellious and defiled!
² She obeys no one,
she accepts no correction.
She does not trust in the LORD,
she does not draw near to her God.
³ Her officials are roaring lions,
her rulers are evening wolves,
who leave nothing for the morning.
⁴ Her prophets are arrogant;
they are treacherous men.
Her priests profane the sanctuary
and do violence to the law.

We see that Jerusalem is spiritually bankrupt. Notice the pride evident in verse 2, something that we covered in the chapter on 2nd Chronicles. In the rest of Zephaniah 3 the Lord says to wait for him, he will restore His remnant, purify them for the purpose of service to Him in fellowship with others, regather them for the purpose of worship, humble and forgive them. For a description of the remnant, read chapter 3: 12 – 13:

¹² But I will leave within you
the meek and humble,
who trust in the name of the LORD.
¹³ The remnant of Israel will do no wrong;
they will speak no lies,
nor will deceit be found in their mouths.
They will eat and lie down
and no one will make them afraid."

Notice the humility? The remnant will be righteous and honest. They will find provision, rest and security. Finally there are 6 blessings which are sovereign acts of the Lord in verses 18 – 20:

¹⁸ "The sorrows for the appointed feasts
I will remove from you;
they are a burden and a reproach to you.
¹⁹ At that time I will deal
with all who oppressed you;
I will rescue the lame
and gather those who have been scattered.

> I will give them praise and honor
> in every land where they were put to shame.
> **20** At that time I will gather you;
> at that time I will bring you home.
> I will give you honor and praise
> among all the peoples of the earth
> when I restore your fortunes
> before your very eyes,"
> says the LORD.

The Lord will 1) remove sorrows, 2) punish oppressors, 3) rescue the lame, 4) gather the scattered, 5) bestow honor and praise and 6) restore their fortunes. The Day of the LORD is characterized by both judgment and blessing.

Nun + Hebrews

Our third nun n book is **Hebrews** which was written by . . . we don't know, though some believe that Paul is the author. Martin Luther thought it was Apollos, Tertulian thought it was Barnabas, others thought it might have been Priscilla or Philip.

There seems to be a double intent in this book: first to confirm Jewish Christians by showing that the Jewish age had ended by the fulfillment of the Law through Christ and, second, that there is an urgency to be strong in the faith and not lapse back into Judaism or fall short in faith in Jesus.

First let's read Hebrews 1: 1-5:

¹In the past God spoke to our forefathers through the prophets at many times and in various ways, ²but in these last days he has spoken to us by his Son, whom he appointed heir of all things, and through whom he made the universe. ³The Son is the radiance of God's glory and the exact representation of his being, sustaining all things by his powerful word. After he had provided purification for sins, he sat down at the right hand of the Majesty in heaven. ⁴So he became as much superior to the angels as the name he has inherited is superior to theirs.

⁵For to which of the angels did God ever say,
"You are my Son;
today I have become your Father"? Or again,
"I will be his Father,
and he will be my Son"?

Remember when we looked at 1st Chronicles 17:13 (p. 95)? If there was any doubt that the reference was to Jesus in Chronicles, I think that the writer of Hebrews has cleared things up.

Chapters 1 and 2 show Jesus, son of God, is greater than all. He is greater than the prophets, angels, and Moses.

Look at Hebrews 3:1-6:

¹Therefore, holy brothers, who share in the heavenly calling, fix your thoughts on Jesus, the apostle and high priest whom we confess. ²He was faithful to the one who appointed him, just as Moses was faithful in all God's house. ³Jesus has been found worthy of greater honor than Moses, just as the builder of a house has greater honor than the house itself. ⁴For every house is built by someone, but God is the builder of everything. ⁵Moses was faithful as a servant in all God's house, testifying to what would be said in the future. ⁶But Christ is faithful

as a son over God's house. And **we are his house**, if we hold on to our courage and the hope of which we boast.

I put "house" in bold because it's important that we remember that **we** are His house. Now look at Hebrews 4:14-16:

¹⁴Therefore, since we have a great high priest who has gone through the heavens, Jesus the Son of God, let us hold firmly to the faith we profess. ¹⁵For we do not have a high priest who is unable to sympathize with our weaknesses, but we have one who has been tempted in every way, just as we are—yet was without sin. ¹⁶Let us then approach the throne of grace with confidence, so that we may receive mercy and find grace to help us in our time of need.

Jesus is the great high priest. I think this links back to 2ⁿᵈ Chronicles in an interesting way. Remember that in Chronicles the kingdom was divided into the northern region of Israel (10 tribes) and the southern kingdom of Judah (2 tribes). The priests and Levites left the northern region because of the idolatry. Where there were parallel accounts in Chronicles to historical events recorded in Kings, Chronicles always had many more references to the priests and Levites. Here, in Hebrews, we have the ultimate priest. Read Hebrews 5:1-10:

¹Every high priest is selected from among men and is appointed to represent them in matters related to God, to offer gifts and sacrifices for sins. ²He is able to deal gently with those who are ignorant and are going astray, since he himself is subject to weakness. ³This is why he has to offer sacrifices for his own sins, as well as for the sins of the people.
⁴No one takes this honor upon himself; he must be called by God, just as Aaron was. ⁵So Christ also did not take upon himself the glory of becoming a high priest. But God said to him,
"You are my Son;
today I have become your Father." ⁶And he says in another place,
"You are a priest forever,
in the order of Melchizedek."
⁷During the days of Jesus' life on earth, he offered up prayers and petitions with loud cries and tears to the one who could save him from death, and he was heard because of his reverent submission. ⁸Although he was a son, he learned obedience from what he suffered ⁹and, once made perfect, he became the source of eternal salvation for all who obey him ¹⁰and was designated by God to be high priest in the order of Melchizedek.

An important part to clarify is in verse 9. The translation here says "once made perfect", which sounds like He wasn't always perfect. The original Greek meaning, however, is "having been made perfect", implying that Jesus was made perfect originally. Jesus was sinless and perfect.

More about His priesthood is revealed in Hebrews 7: 1-4:

¹This Melchizedek was king of Salem and priest of God Most High. He met Abraham returning from the defeat of the kings and blessed him, ²and Abraham gave him a tenth of everything. First, his name means "king of righteousness"; then also, "king of Salem" means

"king of peace." **³**Without father or mother, without genealogy, without beginning of days or end of life, like the Son of God he remains a priest forever.

⁴Just think how great he was: Even the patriarch Abraham gave him a tenth of the plunder!

Look at how Melchizedik was a type of Christ figure: king of righteousness, king of peace, no earthly parents, no beginning of days or end of life, a priest forever.

I have put in bold print below some things you can ponder from Hebrews 7:11-22:

¹¹If perfection could have been attained through the Levitical priesthood (for on the basis of it the law was given to the people), **why was there still need for another priest to come—one in the order of Melchizedek, not in the order of Aaron?** **¹²**For when there is a change of the priesthood, there must also be a change of the law. **¹³**He of whom these things are said belonged to a different tribe, and no one from that tribe has ever served at the altar. **¹⁴**For it is clear that our Lord descended from Judah, and in regard to that tribe Moses said nothing about priests. **¹⁵**And what we have said is even more clear if another priest like Melchizedek appears, **¹⁶one who has become a priest not on the basis of a regulation as to his ancestry but on the basis of the power of an indestructible life**. **¹⁷**For it is declared:

"You are a priest forever,
   in the order of Melchizedek."

¹⁸The former regulation is set aside because it was weak and useless ¹⁹(for the law made nothing perfect), and a better hope is introduced, by which we draw near to God.
²⁰And it was not without an oath! Others became priests without any oath, **²¹**but he became a priest with an oath when God said to him:

"The Lord has sworn
   and will not change his mind:
'You are a priest forever.' " **²²Because of this oath, Jesus has become the guarantee of a better covenant**.

Other cool stuff can be found in Hebrews. For example, when someone says something about a past life or "in my next life I'm going to . . ." or makes some reference to **reincarnation** you can direct them to Hebrews 9: 27-28:

²⁷Just as man is destined to die once, and after that to face judgment, **²⁸**so Christ was sacrificed once to take away the sins of many people; and he will appear a second time, not to bear sin, but to bring salvation to those who are waiting for him.

See? There is no reincarnation. You live, you die and then there are consequences. Read Hebrews 11:1 for a **definition of faith**:

¹Now faith is being sure of what we hope for and certain of what we do not see.

A word about marriage in Hebrews 13: 4:

⁴Marriage should be honored by all, and the marriage bed kept pure, for God will judge the adulterer and all the sexually immoral.

All the sexually immoral! "Whoremongers" is the word used in the King James Version. (Aren't you glad you're covered by the blood of Jesus?)

One last favorite verse, 13:8:

⁸Jesus Christ is the same yesterday and today and forever.

Praise the Lord!
Lastly, since this was our third nun book we should look carefully for links back to the other two nun books. Indeed, Hebrews 11:28 says:

²⁸By faith he kept the **Passover** and the **sprinkling** of **blood**, so that the destroyer of the firstborn would not touch the firstborn of Israel.

And 2nd Chronicles 35:11 says:

¹¹ The **Passover** lambs were slaughtered, and the priests **sprinkled** the **blood** handed to them, while the Levites skinned the animals.

Does Hebrews link to Zephaniah? Of course. Compare these two verses. Hebrews 10:25:

²⁵Let us not give up **meeting together**, as some are in the habit of doing, but let us encourage one another—and all the more **as you see the Day approaching**.

And Zephaniah 2:1 – 2:

¹ **Gather together, gather together**,
O shameful nation,
² **before** the appointed time arrives
and that day sweeps on like chaff,
before the fierce anger of the LORD comes upon you,
before the day of the LORD's wrath comes upon you.

Chapter 15 Samek

Aleph	1. Genesis		23. Isaiah		45. Romans
Bet	2. Exodus		24. Jeremiah		46. 1st Corinthians
Gimel	3. Leviticus		25. Lamentations		47. 2nd Corinthians
Dalet	4. Numbers		26. Ezekiel		48. Galatians
Hey	5. Deuteronomy		27. Daniel		49. Ephesians
Vav	6. Joshua		28. Hosea		50. Philippians
Zayin	7. Judges		29. Joel		51. Colossians
Het	8. Ruth		30. Amos		52. 1st Thessalonians
Tet	9. 1st Samuel		31. Obadiah		53. 2nd Thessalonians
Yod	10. 2nd Samuel		32. Jonah		54. 1st Timothy
Kaph	11. 1st Kings		33. Micah		55. 2nd Timothy
Lamed	12. 2nd Kings		34. Nahum		56. Titus
Mem	13. 1st Chronicles		35. Habakkuk		57. Philemon
Nun	14. 2nd Chronicles		36. Zephaniah		58. Hebrews
Samek	*15. Ezra*		*37. Haggai*		*59. James*
Ayin	16. Nehemiah		38. Zechariah		60. 1st Peter
Pey	17. Esther		39. Malachi		61. 2nd Peter
Tzaddi	18. Job		40. Matthew		62. 1st John
Quph	19. Psalms		41. Mark		63. 2nd John
Resh	20. Proverbs		42. Luke		64. 3rd John
Shin	21. Ecclesiastes		43. John		65. Jude
Tav	22. Song of Songs		44. Acts		66. Revelation

ס

Samech (or Samek) + **Ezra**

Samech means **support** or **uphold** and has also been translated as **sustain**, **establish** and **stand fast**. In ancient Hebrew script it was drawn as a pillar supporting 3 beams. In the alphabetic verse of Psalm 145:14 and Psalm 119:116,117 we find it doubly evident:

[14] The Lord **upholds** all those who fall and **lifts up** all who are bowed down.
[116] **Sustain** me according to your promise, and I will live;
do not let my hopes be dashed.
[117] **Uphold** me, and I will be delivered;
I will always have regard for your decrees.

The Jews explain that this letter, samech, as a closed rounded letter, symbolizes the idea of Divine support with God as the perimeter of the shape and Israel as the interior. The center is an allusion to the Tabernacle and the outside line of the letter represents the camps of Israel surrounding the Sanctuary. I mention this because you will see the rebuilding of the Temple in our first samech book, Ezra.

Ezra was written by Ezra whose name means "aid" or "help" as in "**support**," our corresponding letter's meaning.

Ezra records the return to Palestine under Zerubbabel of a Jewish remnant that laid the temple foundations (536 BC). The Scriptures record the return of three groups of exiles to Jerusalem from Babylon. The first group came in 536 BC, the second in 457 BC under Ezra and the third in 444 BC under Nehemiah. The book of Ezra tells of the first two groups. Read Ezra 1: 1-4 then look at the last 2 verses of 2nd Chronicles – this is why scholars conclude that Ezra wrote 2nd Chronicles. At the time of the writing, for historical perspective, Confucius and Buddha were alive and within a century Sophocles and Socrates would live. Here's all of chapter 1:

[1] In the first year of Cyrus king of Persia, in order to fulfill the word of the LORD spoken by Jeremiah, the LORD moved the heart of Cyrus king of Persia to make a proclamation throughout his realm and also to put it in writing:
[2] "This is what Cyrus king of Persia says:
"'The LORD, the God of heaven, has given me all the kingdoms of the earth and he has appointed me to build a temple for him at Jerusalem in Judah. [3] Any of his people among you may go up to Jerusalem in Judah and build the temple of the LORD, the God of Israel, the God who is in Jerusalem, and may their God be with them. [4] And in any locality where survivors may now be living, the people are to provide them with silver and gold, with goods and livestock, and with freewill offerings for the temple of God in Jerusalem.'"
[5] Then the family heads of Judah and Benjamin, and the priests and Levites—everyone whose heart God had moved—prepared to go up and build the house of the LORD in Jerusalem. [6] All their neighbors assisted them with articles of silver and gold, with goods and livestock, and with valuable gifts, in addition to all the freewill offerings.

7 Moreover, King Cyrus brought out the articles belonging to the temple of the LORD, which Nebuchadnezzar had carried away from Jerusalem and had placed in the temple of his god. **8** Cyrus king of Persia had them brought by Mithredath the treasurer, who counted them out to Sheshbazzar the prince of Judah.
  9 This was the inventory:
   gold dishes 30
   silver dishes 1,000
   silver pans 29
  10 gold bowls 30
   matching silver bowls 410
   other articles 1,000
11 In all, there were 5,400 articles of gold and of silver. Sheshbazzar brought all these along with the exiles when they came up from Babylon to Jerusalem.

In verse 2 you see that King Cyrus gives God credit for his success, but he was a respecter of all religions and was just covering his back. God used him, though.

Note the inventory in verses 9 -11 of the thousands of items that God kept safe all those years until they could be returned to their rightful place.

The Books of Ezra and Nehemiah are two parts of the same story. They tell us about the time when the Jews returned from Babylonia to their own country, Judah. The journey between Babylonia and Judah took about 4 months to walk. The Babylonians had defeated the people from Judah. They had forced most of the Jews to go to Babylonia and to live there. After many years, the Persians defeated the Babylonians. Then Cyrus, the king of Persia, allowed the Jews to return to Judah.

The Book of Ezra tells us about the first two groups of Jews who returned to Judah. This happened about 70 years after the Babylonians had taken the Jews into exile. The book also explains how the Jews built their temple again.

Glance at chapter 2 and note that the people are listed as leaders, families, towns, priests, Levites, temple servants, descendants of the servants of Solomon and those who couldn't verify their genealogy. All in all, God is telling us that He knows His people personally and that the common people were important to this rebuilding and also that they were still keeping track of racial purity. Chapter 3 tells us that they began rebuilding the altar first and then the temple. They started in the 7th month because that is the month with 3 Jewish feasts including the Feast of Tabernacles. They gathered together, worshiped together, celebrated together and worked together, and sang and praised God together. Look at 3:11-13:

11 With praise and thanksgiving they sang to the LORD:
   "He is good;
  his love toward Israel endures forever."
   And all the people gave a great shout of praise to the LORD, because the foundation of the house of the LORD was laid. **12** But many of the older priests and Levites and family heads, who had seen the former temple, wept aloud when they saw the foundation of this temple being laid, while many others shouted for joy. **13** No one could distinguish the sound of

the shouts of joy from the sound of weeping, because the people made so much noise. And the sound was heard far away.

Imagine the noise! Some shouted praise while the older priests and Levites wept aloud. Why? Why would they weep? For one thing, the foundation was smaller than the previous temple. These older people who are weeping were children before the exile, children who saw the glory and wonder and lavish splendor of King Solomon's temple. They are upset that the new one is not as awesome. (In our second samech book, Haggai, which was written at this same time, God assures them that the glory of this house will be greater than the former. Haggai 2:9.)

So, the foundation is laid but there's a setback: opposition. In chapter 4 the enemies of Judah and Benjamin step in. Read 4: 1-5:

[1] When the enemies of Judah and Benjamin heard that the exiles were building a temple for the LORD, the God of Israel, [2] they came to Zerubbabel and to the heads of the families and said, "Let us help you build because, like you, we seek your God and have been sacrificing to him since the time of Esarhaddon king of Assyria, who brought us here."
[3] But Zerubbabel, Joshua and the rest of the heads of the families of Israel answered, "You have no part with us in building a temple to our God. We alone will build it for the LORD, the God of Israel, as King Cyrus, the king of Persia, commanded us."
[4] Then the peoples around them set out to discourage the people of Judah and make them afraid to go on building. [5] They bribed officials to work against them and frustrate their plans during the entire reign of Cyrus king of Persia and down to the reign of Darius king of Persia.

These evil men went on a letter writing campaign and you can read the letter they sent to King Artaxerxes in chapter 4. They claim the Jews are rebellious and wicked and they assert that the Jews won't be paying taxes and tributes if they're allowed to build their city. They end their letter by asking the King to check the archives for verification that the Jews have been rebellious and troublesome. The King writes back that he checked, he agrees and he issues a "stop work" order. Read 4: 23, 24:

[23] As soon as the copy of the letter of King Artaxerxes was read to Rehum and Shimshai the secretary and their associates, they went immediately to the Jews in Jerusalem and compelled them by force to stop.
[24] Thus the work on the house of God in Jerusalem came to a standstill until the second year of the reign of Darius king of Persia.

The work stoppage lasted 16 years.
If you take a look at the beginning of chapter 5 you find out that the prophet Haggai makes some prophecies at this time. Consider that Haggai, 22 books beyond this one (our 2nd samech book) could be inserted right here. You may want to jump ahead and read about the prophecies now before continuing with Ezra.

When they start up work again in chapter 5 the governor of Trans-Euphrates and his associates butt in and say "who authorized this?". We get to read the letter which includes the Jews' explanation that King Cyrus had issued a decree to rebuild the house of God and the governor's request of King Darius to find out if indeed there was such a decree.

Chapter 6 contains King Darius's response wherein he affirms that they have the right to rebuild and furthermore, he commands the governor to pay the expenses out of the royal treasury so the work doesn't stop again. Interesting how God uses nonbelievers to get His work done and even more interesting that this chapter records the **Decree of Support** for the rebuilding of the Temple. This is the 15th book and corresponds to the 15th Hebrew letter which means **support** and is written by Ezra whose name also means **support**. The temple is completed and a dedication takes place. It is not as lavish as the original dedication we read about in 2nd Chronicles, though.

Now the book jumps ahead 60 years and Ezra is on the scene. He was a man devoted to the study and observance of the Law of the Lord and to teaching its decrees and laws in Israel (7:10). He receives a letter from King Artaxerxes decreeing that any Israelites who wish to go with Ezra back to Jerusalem may go. Chapter 8 lists all of the Family Heads who returned with Ezra. The journey probably took about 4 months. They arrived safe and sound with all of the silver, gold and sacred articles accounted for. However, there's a big problem. Read chapter 9: 1-2 and 10:10,11:

> **1** After these things had been done, the leaders came to me and said, "The people of Israel, including the priests and the Levites, have not kept themselves separate from the neighboring peoples with their detestable practices, like those of the Canaanites, Hittites, Perizzites, Jebusites, Ammonites, Moabites, Egyptians and Amorites. **2** They have taken some of their daughters as wives for themselves and their sons, and have mingled the holy race with the peoples around them. And the leaders and officials have led the way in this unfaithfulness."
> **10** Then Ezra the priest stood up and said to them, "You have been unfaithful; you have married foreign women, adding to Israel's guilt. **11** Now honor the LORD, the God of your ancestors, and do his will. Separate yourselves from the peoples around you and from your foreign wives."

Chapter 10 lists over a hundred men who had married foreign women. This is a small number compared to the thousands of Jews in all, but God is purifying them nonetheless. The last verse, 44, packs a punch as to how devastating this must have been.

> **44** All these had married foreign women, and some of them had children by these wives.

Since the wives were probably sent back to their homelands, the children would have gone with them. How devastating for these families, yet they were obedient unto the Lord.

ס
Samech + Haggai

Our 2nd samech book is Haggai. Remember that samech represents **support**. We will see in Haggai how the Lord withdrew His support from the Israelites until they got back to work on the temple. Then the Lord gave them support by using their opponents to supply all the moneys needed for their expenses. Haggai lines up exactly with the first samech book, Ezra. In fact, go back to Ezra 5:1 and you'll see that the prophet Haggai's prophecies were made at that point in history.

Haggai's name means "festive" or "festival" and it is awesome to learn that his second message (2:1–9) was delivered on the last day of the Feast of Tabernacles, an important Jewish festival. He was a prophet who most likely was born before the first Temple was destroyed in 586 BC. Perhaps he remembers the glory of the amazing Temple. He is an old man when he prophesies and we know exactly when he made each of his prophecies, right down to the exact date.

To begin, there are 4 prophecies and according to chapter 1, verse 1, the first one is made on the first day of the sixth month of the second year of King Darius, which was August 29, 520 BC. The Lord is angry with the people for stopping their work on the Temple and focusing on their own homes instead of His. Read Haggai 1: 7 – 11:

> **7** This is what the LORD Almighty says: "Give careful thought to your ways. **8** Go up into the mountains and bring down timber and build my house, so that I may take pleasure in it and be honored," says the LORD. **9** "You expected much, but see, it turned out to be little. What you brought home, I blew away. Why?" declares the LORD Almighty. "Because of my house, which remains a ruin, while each of you is busy with your own house. **10** Therefore, because of you the heavens have withheld their dew and the earth its crops. **11** I called for a drought on the fields and the mountains, on the grain, the new wine, the olive oil and everything else the ground produces, on people and livestock, and on all the labor of your hands."

They have obviously mixed-up their priorities, but when we study the history and look back at the book of Ezra we see that they got right with the Lord and became obedient. (They finished the Temple on the 3rd day of the month of Adar in the 6th year of the reign of King Darius or 515 BC.) Remember, this book fits hand in glove with the book of Ezra.

In chapter 2 we have the second prophecy given almost two months later on October 17, 520 BC. Read verses 6 – 9:

> **6** "This is what the LORD Almighty says: 'In a little while I will once more shake the heavens and the earth, the sea and the dry land. **7** I will shake all nations, and what is desired by all nations will come, and I will fill this house with glory,' says the LORD Almighty. **8** 'The silver is mine and the gold is mine,' declares the LORD Almighty. **9** 'The glory of this present house will be greater than the glory of the former house,' says the LORD Almighty. 'And in this place I will grant peace,' declares the LORD Almighty."

When the Lord said He would "shake all nations" we can interpret this to mean world-wide judgment. If you remember, the old people had wept when they saw the new foundations (Ezra 3:12) probably because they remembered the glory of Solomon's Temple and this new one was not measuring up. Yet God says through Haggai that the glory of His new house will be greater than the glory of the former one and that in this place He will grant peace. How can the glory be greater? Some scholars believe He's referring to the fact that Jesus will teach in that Temple. His glory is greater than all of King Solomon's silver and gold. But since He will "shake all nations" first, I think that perhaps the house being referred to is the final Heavenly Tabernacle. " 'In this place I will grant peace,' declares the Lord Almighty."

Verse 10 of chapter 2 gives the date of the 3rd prophecy as December 18, 520 BC. Read 10 – 19:

> **10** On the twenty-fourth day of the ninth month, in the second year of Darius, the word of the LORD came to the prophet Haggai: **11** "This is what the LORD Almighty says: 'Ask the priests what the law says: **12** If someone carries consecrated meat in the fold of their garment, and that fold touches some bread or stew, some wine, olive oil or other food, does it become consecrated?'"
>
> The priests answered, "No."
>
> **13** Then Haggai said, "If a person defiled by contact with a dead body touches one of these things, does it become defiled?"
>
> "Yes," the priests replied, "it becomes defiled."
>
> **14** Then Haggai said, "'So it is with this people and this nation in my sight,' declares the LORD. 'Whatever they do and whatever they offer there is defiled.
>
> **15** "'Now give careful thought to this from this day on—consider how things were before one stone was laid on another in the LORD's temple. **16** When anyone came to a heap of twenty measures, there were only ten. When anyone went to a wine vat to draw fifty measures, there were only twenty. **17** I struck all the work of your hands with blight, mildew and hail, yet you did not return to me,' declares the LORD. **18** 'From this day on, from this twenty-fourth day of the ninth month, give careful thought to the day when the foundation of the LORD's temple was laid. Give careful thought: **19** Is there yet any seed left in the barn? Until now, the vine and the fig tree, the pomegranate and the olive tree have not borne fruit.
>
> "'From this day on I will bless you.'"

This may seem like a confusing prophecy, but Haggai now asks the people a question which the priests are supposed to answer: If a priest is carrying something holy and he touches something unholy, like a corpse, does that make the corpse holy? The priests answer no. If the person who is unclean touches the priest, does that make the priest unclean? The priests answer yes. What is the point of this? It sounds like one bad apple spoils the bunch, doesn't it? The point is that holiness does not come by contact. It is not transferable. But contact with unholiness (ungodliness, sin) does defile a person. If a healthy person kisses a person with a communicable disease, the healthy person doesn't cure the sick one, but the sick one will infect the healthy one. This is a big reminder that sin contaminates.

Finally, at the end of verse 19 we read that from that day on God will bless them. Finishing the chapter we have a final word, or 4th prophecy, given on the same day as the 3rd prophecy. The people are given hope for the future by hearing that God was going to destroy their enemies and establish His kingdom with them, His chosen people. The fact that Zerubbabel is compared to a signet ring means that he is a symbol of authority. The previous 3 prophecies were given to Zerubbabel, governor of Judah, and to the people, but this one is just to Zerubbabel. The distant future is envisioned, when heaven and earth will be shaken and the Gentile nations destroyed. This will be the time of Christ's return and many scholars feel that the title "Zerubbabel My Servant" (2:23) is referring to Jesus. Also, Haggai's promise to the governor foresees the restoration of the Davidic dynasty.

All right, this is getting a little deep. We need some background on Zerubbabel. He was in the direct line of King David and thus should have been qualified to be king, but if you check the story in Jeremiah (22: 24 – 27) you find that his great grandfather was cursed and none of his descendants would be allowed to sit on the throne.

> **24** "As surely as I live," declares the LORD, "even if you, Jehoiachin son of Jehoiakim king of Judah, were a **signet ring** on my right hand, I would still pull you off. **25** I will hand you over to those who seek your life, those you fear—to Nebuchadnezzar king of Babylon and to the Babylonians. **26** I will hurl you and the mother who gave you birth into another country, where neither of you was born, and there you both will die. **27** You will never come back to the land you long to return to."

By calling Zerubbabel His "servant" and "chosen" one, God has reversed the curse and given him the same status that David had. The people must have been jubilant that the Gentile kingdoms would be destroyed and Zerubbabel would be exalted to rule! However, this prophecy has not yet been fulfilled. It is an end time prophecy.

ס
Samech + James

Our third samech book is James. It is generally believed that this James was the half-brother of Jesus. He writes to the twelve tribes which are scattered so it is assumed that he is writing to Christian Jews who had dispersed after the persecution. James' theme is that religious service is the expression and proof of faith, that is, faith produces works. Faith is shown by the outward acts of obedience and righteousness.

Remember, since samech means **support** we should be able to find some connection to this word in the book of James.

Let's start with chapter 1: 1 – 8:

¹ James, a servant of God and of the Lord Jesus Christ, To the twelve tribes scattered among the nations: Greetings.
² Consider it pure joy, my brothers and sisters, whenever you face trials of many kinds, ³ because you know that the testing of your faith produces perseverance. ⁴ Let perseverance finish its work so that you may be mature and complete, not lacking anything. ⁵ If any of you lacks wisdom, you should ask God, who gives generously to all without finding fault, and it will be given to you. ⁶ But when you ask, you must believe and not doubt, because the one who doubts is like a wave of the sea, blown and tossed by the wind. ⁷ That person should not expect to receive anything from the Lord. ⁸ Such a person is double-minded and unstable in all they do.

James writes to the 12 tribes, the Jews, who were scattered; hence they are Christian Jews, who fled after the Dispersion. Read 1: 13 – 15:

¹³ When tempted, no one should say, "God is tempting me." For God cannot be tempted by evil, nor does he tempt anyone; ¹⁴ but each person is tempted when they are dragged away by their own evil desire and enticed. ¹⁵ Then, after desire has conceived, it gives birth to sin; and sin, when it is full-grown, gives birth to death.

This is interesting since we pray the Lord's praying asking Him not to lead us into temptation. Here James says that God does not tempt anyone. How do we reconcile the two verses? In Matthew 6:13 we pray that God not lead us into "peirasmos", the Greek word we translate as temptation. It is a state of experiencing adversity or affliction that we endure and in which we should be able to trust God and prove our faith as well as our confidence in the Lord. (Would you rather say *Lead us not into temptation* or *Lead us not into a state of experiencing adversity or affliction that we endure and in which we should be able to trust you and prove our faith as well as our confidence in you?*)

James 1: 19 – 21 says:

¹⁹ My dear brothers and sisters, take note of this: Everyone should be quick to listen, slow to speak and slow to become angry, ²⁰ because human anger does not produce the

righteousness that God desires. **²¹** Therefore, get rid of all moral filth and the evil that is so prevalent and humbly accept the word planted in you, which can save you.

Read that again: Everyone should be **quick to listen, slow to speak and slow to become angry.** Now look at verses 26 – 27:

²⁶ Those who consider themselves religious and yet do not keep a tight rein on their tongues deceive themselves, and their religion is worthless. **²⁷** Religion that God our Father accepts as pure and faultless is this: to look after orphans and widows in their distress and to keep oneself from being polluted by the world.

We will get a closer look at reining in the tongue in chapter 3, but examine the last part of the above quotation and see if you agree with me that **support**, our samech letter's meaning, is evident here. I interpret looking after orphans and widows as supporting them. Likewise, keeping yourself from being polluted by the world would require you to support all of the Lord's teachings.

Are there other links to our Hebrew letter samech which means support? Well, in James 2: 14 – 17 there is a clear implied command to support our Christian brothers:

¹⁴ What good is it, my brothers and sisters, if someone claims to have faith but has no deeds? Can such faith save them? **¹⁵** Suppose a brother or a sister is without clothes and daily food. **¹⁶** If one of you says to them, "Go in peace; keep warm and well fed," but does nothing about their physical needs, what good is it? **¹⁷** In the same way, faith by itself, if it is not accompanied by action, is dead.

These verses also show that faith needs the support of works in order to be vital. Chapter 3 is all about taming the tongue. Read verses 9 and 10:

⁹ With the tongue we praise our Lord and Father, and with it we curse human beings, who have been made in God's likeness. **¹⁰** Out of the same mouth come praise and cursing. My brothers and sisters, this should not be.

Really meditate on this. In fact, read the whole chapter in your own Bible and underline the parts that apply to you. If you have trouble with your speech, that is, bad words flow readily out of your mouth, you can at least take comfort in the fact that "no man can tame the tongue", so you're not alone. However, the tongue is "a restless evil, full of deadly poison" and you would be wise to ask the Lord for help.

Now read chapter 4: 1 – 10:

¹ What causes fights and quarrels among you? Don't they come from your desires that battle within you? **²** You desire but do not have, so you kill. You covet but you cannot get what you want, so you quarrel and fight. You do not have because you do not ask God. **³** When you ask, you do not receive, because you ask with wrong motives, that you may spend what you get on your pleasures.

4 You adulterous people, don't you know that friendship with the world means enmity against God? Therefore, anyone who chooses to be a friend of the world becomes an enemy of God. **5** Or do you think Scripture says without reason that he jealously longs for the spirit he has caused to dwell in us? **6** But he gives us more grace. That is why Scripture says:

"God opposes the proud
but shows favor to the humble."

7 Submit yourselves, then, to God. Resist the devil, and he will flee from you. **8** Come near to God and he will come near to you. Wash your hands, you sinners, and purify your hearts, you double-minded. **9** Grieve, mourn and wail. Change your laughter to mourning and your joy to gloom. **10** Humble yourselves before the Lord, and he will lift you up.

That last phrase "he will lift you up" is a match for our Hebrew letter samech which means support.

Have you heard people say I'll do this or that "Lord willing"? See chapter 4 verse 15 and you'll see why Christians say this.

Chapter 5 gives a strong warning to the rich oppressors then goes on to encourage us to be patient until the Lord's coming. We also learn in verse 12 **not to swear** by heaven or earth or anything. Finally, James ends his letter with encouragement to us to pray for one another and to confess our sins to one another. Isn't that interesting? It doesn't say confess to a priest.

Chapter 16 Ayin

Aleph	1. Genesis	23. Isaiah	45. Romans
Bet	2. Exodus	24. Jeremiah	46. 1st Corinthians
Gimel	3. Leviticus	25. Lamentations	47. 2nd Corinthians
Dalet	4. Numbers	26. Ezekiel	48. Galatians
Hey	5. Deuteronomy	27. Daniel	49. Ephesians
Vav	6. Joshua	28. Hosea	50. Philippians
Zayin	7. Judges	29. Joel	51. Colossians
Het	8. Ruth	30. Amos	52. 1st Thessalonians
Tet	9. 1st Samuel	31. Obadiah	53. 2nd Thessalonians
Yod	10. 2nd Samuel	32. Jonah	54. 1st Timothy
Kaph	11. 1st Kings	33. Micah	55. 2nd Timothy
Lamed	12. 2nd Kings	34. Nahum	56. Titus
Mem	13. 1st Chronicles	35. Habakkuk	57. Philemon
Nun	14. 2nd Chronicles	36. Zephaniah	58. Hebrews
Samek	15. Ezra	37. Haggai	59. James
Ayin	*16. Nehemiah*	*38. Zechariah*	*60. 1st Peter*
Pey	17. Esther	39. Malachi	61. 2nd Peter
Tzaddi	18. Job	40. Matthew	62. 1st John
Quph	19. Psalms	41. Mark	63. 2nd John
Resh	20. Proverbs	42. Luke	64. 3rd John
Shin	21. Ecclesiastes	43. John	65. Jude
Tav	22. Song of Songs	44. Acts	66. Revelation

ע

Ayin + Nehemiah
The 16th Hebrew letter is ayin. The ancient script for this letter was a sideways oval, like an eye. In fact, the symbolic representation is **eye**. This was one of the easiest letters for me to learn because saying ayin sounds like "eye in." Let's go straight to the alphabetic verses to look for eyes.

Lamentations 3: 48 says "Streams of tears flow from my **eyes** because my people are destroyed."
Psalm 119: 123 says "My **eyes** fail, looking for your salvation, looking for your righteous promise."
Psalm 25:15 says "My **eyes** are ever on the Lord, for only he will release my feet from the snare."
Psalm 34:15 says "The **eyes** of the Lord are on the righteous and his ears are attentive to their cry;"
Psalm 145:15 says "The **eyes** of all look to you, and you give them their food at the proper time."

(If you noticed that these verses are the 15th verse instead of the 16th, it's because two letters were used in one verse. For example in the 145th Psalm mem and nun are covered in a long 13th verse and this chapter ends up having 21 total verses instead of 22.)

In addition to **eyes**, there are several words that start with this letter, ayin, which are emphasized by their recurrent use in other alphabetic verses. For example, in the 8 ayin verses in Psalm 119 we find "servant" three times. The Hebrew word for **servant** is ebed which begins with ayin (reading right to left).

The 16th book of the Bible is Nehemiah, so named because the main character is Nehemiah (his name means "Jehovah comforts"). Fourteen years after Ezra came back to Jerusalem with a group of the returning exiles, Nehemiah brought another bunch back and restored the walls and the civil authority. Originally, the books of Ezra and Nehemiah were in one volume. Scholars are divided on the authorship, some say Ezra, some say Nehemiah, some say both. The majority believe Nehemiah was the author.

Read Chapter 1:

[1] The words of Nehemiah son of Hakaliah:
In the month of Kislev in the twentieth year, while I was in the citadel of Susa, [2] Hanani, one of my brothers, came from Judah with some other men, and I questioned them about the Jewish remnant that had survived the exile, and also about Jerusalem.
[3] They said to me, "Those who survived the exile and are back in the province are in great trouble and disgrace. The wall of Jerusalem is broken down, and its gates have been burned with fire."
[4] When I heard these things, I sat down and wept. For some days I mourned and fasted and prayed before the God of heaven. [5] Then I said:

"LORD, the God of heaven, the great and awesome God, who keeps his covenant of love with those who love him and keep his commandments, **6** let your ear be attentive and your eyes open to hear the prayer your servant is praying before you day and night for your servants, the people of Israel. I confess the sins we Israelites, including myself and my father's family, have committed against you. **7** We have acted very wickedly toward you. We have not obeyed the commands, decrees and laws you gave your servant Moses.

8 "Remember the instruction you gave your servant Moses, saying, 'If you are unfaithful, I will scatter you among the nations, **9** but if you return to me and obey my commands, then even if your exiled people are at the farthest horizon, I will gather them from there and bring them to the place I have chosen as a dwelling for my Name.'

10 "They are your servants and your people, whom you redeemed by your great strength and your mighty hand. **11** Lord, let your ear be attentive to the prayer of this your servant and to the prayer of your servants who delight in revering your name. Give your servant success today by granting him favor in the presence of this man."

I was cupbearer to the king.

It ends with Nehemiah stating that he was cupbearer to the king. This says a lot. He had a position of great trust. He would taste the king's drink to guard against poisoning. Since anyone could be coerced by having his family threatened, the cupbearer was usually a eunuch. Notice again verse 6: "let your ear be attentive and your **eyes** open to hear the prayer your servant is praying". This is an example of the Hebrew letter ayin and its meaning of eyes. Frankly, I see no reason for Nehemiah to mention eyes since he is asking the Lord to "hear" the prayer, and yet, since this is the 16th book and related to the 16th letter which means **eye**, then it makes perfect sense. Additionally, this chapter has the word servant (ebed) no fewer than 8 times in reference to Nehemiah, Moses and the people.

In Chapter 2 Nehemiah brings the wine to King Artaxerxes who notices how sad Nehemiah's face is. "What is it you want?" the king asks him. Now look closely at verse 4 and what do you see? Nehemiah prays before answering. He prays to the God of Heaven then asks the king to send him to Jerusalem so he can rebuild it. He also asks for letters to the governors of Trans-Euphrates so he can have safe passage and a letter to the keeper of the king's forest so he can have timber for building. Verse 8 says "And because the gracious hand of my God was upon me, the king granted my requests." God uses unbelievers like Artaxerxes and look, Nehemiah got what he asked for and more, for the king also sent army officers and cavalry with him. Unfortunately this whole thing didn't go well with the officials. They were disturbed that someone was coming to "promote the welfare of the Israelites", because the rebuilding would eliminate Samaria as the political center of Judea. These officials, Sanballat and Tobiah, mocked and ridiculed Nehemiah, but Nehemiah had faith. He says in verse 20: "The God of heaven will give us success."

The next few chapters are a pretty clear reading of events. As the Jews worked on rebuilding the walls of the city, they had to work with one hand and hold a weapon in the other. There was quite a bit of opposition to the building, but the work got done in 52 days. Their enemies "were afraid and lost their self-confidence, because they realized that this work had been done with the help of our God." (6:16)

Chapter 7 gives a list of the exiles who returned, then in chapter 8 Ezra reads the Law of Moses to the people. The people were used to speaking Aramaic and not Hebrew so the Levites had quite a time instructing the people in the law and making it clear.

The Israelites confess their sins and make some promises. Let's look at chapter 10: 30 – 39. What are the 10 things that they promise? (1. Not to intermarry; 2. Not to buy on the Sabbath or any holy day; 3. Not to work the land on the 7th year; 4. To cancel debts; 5. To give a third of a shekel each year for the service of the house of God; 6. To contribute wood to burn on the altar; 7. To bring the firstfruits each year; 8. To bring the firstborn to the priests; 9. To bring to the storerooms the first of the produce; 10. To tithe.)

There's a big party and dedication of the wall of Jerusalem, but then there's trouble once more as the Israelites get off track. They never seem to learn and they break their promise not to work on the Sabbath and then they marry foreign women from Ashdod, Ammon and Moab, thus breaking the promise not to intermarry as well. If you read chapter 13 you'll see how angry Nehemiah gets. Read 13: 15 – 18:

15 In those days I saw people in Judah treading winepresses on the Sabbath and bringing in grain and loading it on donkeys, together with wine, grapes, figs and all other kinds of loads. And they were bringing all this into Jerusalem on the Sabbath. Therefore I warned them against selling food on that day. **16** People from Tyre who lived in Jerusalem were bringing in fish and all kinds of merchandise and selling them in Jerusalem on the Sabbath to the people of Judah. **17** I rebuked the nobles of Judah and said to them, "What is this wicked thing you are doing—desecrating the Sabbath day? **18** Didn't your ancestors do the same things, so that our God brought all this calamity on us and on this city? Now you are stirring up more wrath against Israel by desecrating the Sabbath."

Here's Zechariah's reaction: 19 – 22:

19 When evening shadows fell on the gates of Jerusalem before the Sabbath, I ordered the doors to be shut and not opened until the Sabbath was over. I stationed some of my own men at the gates so that no load could be brought in on the Sabbath day. **20** Once or twice the merchants and sellers of all kinds of goods spent the night outside Jerusalem. **21** But I warned them and said, "Why do you spend the night by the wall? If you do this again, I will arrest you." From that time on they no longer came on the Sabbath. **22** Then I commanded the Levites to purify themselves and go and guard the gates in order to keep the Sabbath day holy. Remember me for this also, my God, and show mercy to me according to your great love.

But there's more: 23 – 31:

23 Moreover, in those days I saw men of Judah who had married women from Ashdod, Ammon and Moab. **24** Half of their children spoke the language of Ashdod or the language of one of the other peoples, and did not know how to speak the language of Judah. **25** I rebuked them and called curses down on them. I beat some of the men and pulled out their hair. I made them take an oath in God's name and said: "You are not to give your daughters in marriage to their sons, nor are you to take their daughters in marriage for your sons or for yourselves. **26** Was it not because of marriages like these that Solomon king of Israel sinned? Among the many nations there was no king like him. He was loved by his God, and God made him king over all Israel, but even he was led into sin by foreign women. **27** Must we hear now that you too are doing all this terrible wickedness and are being unfaithful to our God by marrying foreign women?"

28 One of the sons of Joiada son of Eliashib the high priest was son-in-law to Sanballat the Horonite. And I drove him away from me.

29 Remember them, my God, because they defiled the priestly office and the covenant of the priesthood and of the Levites.

30 So I purified the priests and the Levites of everything foreign, and assigned them duties, each to his own task. **31** I also made provision for contributions of wood at designated times, and for the firstfruits.

Remember me with favor, my God.

He even drove away one man who married Sanballat's daughter; Sanballat was the ruler mentioned at the beginning of the book.

Now look closely at the ending of the book of Nehemiah. The final words are: "Remember me" which in Hebrew is "Zakrah Li." This is an anagram (change the letters around) for "LiZechariah" which means "to Zechariah." Well, isn't it interesting that our next ayin book is Zechariah?

ע

Ayin + Zechariah

If you're looking for it, and if you know Hebrew, you can find Nehemiah's name in the first chapter of Zechariah. (Hint: it's in verse 17.) First of all, Zechariah means "God has remembered." The first ayin book ended with Nehemiah stating "remember me" and now our second ayin book is named "God has remembered." Very cool. This book has more Messianic prophecy than all of the other Minor Prophets combined and is second only to Isaiah in the number of references to Christ. Additionally the New Testament refers to Zechariah more than 40 times. Zechariah is sometimes called the "Book of Revelation" of the Old Testament. The theme of the book is apparent in the opening verse which names Zechariah, his father, Berekiah, and Berekiah's father, Iddo. The Hebrew meanings of these names are "whom the Lord remembers" "the Lord blesses" "at the appointed time". God raised up Zechariah to proclaim that God remembers His chosen people and that He will bless them in His appointed time.

Zechariah's ministry began right between Haggai's second and third message. Haggai was talking about rebuilding the temple and Zechariah writes about the same thing. He comforted and encouraged the returned remnant to repent of their evil ways, to return to the Lord and to rebuild the temple. Zechariah's message focused on the future and declared that God would send the Messiah to set up His Kingdom through the annihilation of the Gentile empires and the salvation of Israel.

Chapters 1 through 6 give an amazing visual prophecy. Most of them start with "I lift up mine eyes" though your translation may be "I looked up". Remember, this is an ayin (**eye**) book and there is great beauty and intricacy in the original Hebrew. (As a matter of fact, in the other books of the 12 minor prophets the word **ayin** appears 16 times total as compared to Zechariah where it appears **20 times in this one book**!) Before summarizing the visions let me tell you that these are rich in interpretation and deserve a more thorough examination than space allows me here.

Vision number 1 (Zechariah 1:8 – 11) is of a horse patrol; four horses of varying colors go throughout the earth and report back that the whole earth is at rest and in peace. Sounds calm, but that phrase has bad connotations. In verse 15 the Lord says "I am very angry with the nations that feel secure." The Lord adds that He will return to Jerusalem with mercy and rebuild His house. The people are encouraged by this.

Vision number 2 (1: 18 – 21) is of four horns and four craftsmen. Horns usually signify military might. The four horns are Babylon, Medo-Persia, Greece and Rome, the four Gentile nations which plundered Judah and scattered its people. The four craftsmen are the succeeding Gentile nations which in turn clashed with each of the above "horns".

Vision number 3 (2:1 – 13) is of a man with a measuring line who sees how wide and long Jerusalem is. The prophecy states that Jerusalem will be a city without walls. Since it has always had walls, scholars believe that this is yet to be fulfilled in the millennium. However, this is still an encouraging word to the people Zechariah is speaking to. Remember they are working on rebuilding.

Vision number 4 (3:1 – 10) is about clean garments for the high priest, Joshua. This signifies purifying the nation, their sins forgiven. (You'll find the ayin word "eyes" as well as "servant" here.)

The next four prophecies match up, in reverse order, with the first four. The fifth vision (4: 1 – 14) is of a gold lampstand and two olive trees. The lampstand symbolizes the presence of God and the two olive trees are Zerubbabel and Joshua. The priest with clean garments from vision 4 can now work on the Lord's house. See verse 9:

"The hands of Zerubbabel have laid the foundation of this temple; his hands will also complete it. Then you will know that the Lord Almighty has sent me to you." (The 7 **eyes** of the Lord are mentioned in this section.)

In vision number 6 (5:1 – 4) Zechariah sees a flying scroll which is explained to be a curse to wipe out those who sin against man (every thief) and those who sin against God (everyone who swears falsely by my name). This matches up with the third vision in which a prosperous, peaceful Jerusalem without walls is foreseen. The flying scroll has eliminated those who would destroy that peaceful city.

The woman in the basket in vision 7 (5:5 – 11) is wickedness personified. Two other women take her to Babylon where a house will be built for her. When I match this up with vision 2 which started with the first of the four horns being Babylon, I am amazed at the symmetry.

The last vision (6:1 – 8) is the four horses, as in vision 1, out on patrol again. Remember they found the earth at rest the first time. This time they are out for judgment. I'm sure that Zechariah's audience was pleased with this and comforted.

After these 8 visions Zechariah is told by the Lord to make a crown for Joshua and also that people from far away will come to help build the Temple.

Now the book jumps ahead two years and there are rebukes and reminders before Israel can be restored. In chapter 7 the Lord rebukes the people for fasting and mourning for themselves instead of for the Lord. He reminds them to administer justice, show mercy and compassion, not to oppress widows, the fatherless, foreigners or the poor and not to think evil of each other. He reminds them that they did not do these things and as a result they suffered condemnation.

Chapter 8 outlines the restoration and that God will save His people and bring them back to live in Jerusalem. God will take them from poverty to productivity, from cursing to blessing, from fear to strength and power, and from fasting to feasting.

Next we have oracles and your Bible may have the print set up to look like poetry. The first oracle looks forward to the Good Shepherd's rejection and the people's acceptance of the anti-Christ. Look at 9:9:

"Rejoice greatly O Daughter of Zion! Shout, Daughter of Jerusalem! See, your king comes to you, righteous and having salvation, gentle and riding on a donkey, on a colt, the foal of a donkey."

Who is he talking about? Jesus rode into Jerusalem on a donkey! Chapter 10 sadly says in verse 2 that the "people wander like sheep oppressed for lack of a shepherd". Too bad, Israel, that you will fail to see Christ as the Messiah.

The second oracle describes the penalty for the nations who oppose Israel as well as the repentance of Israel. This means that they will finally realize that they had rejected the Messiah; someday they will repent and accept Him. There are plenty of references to the Lord's return in the end time prophecies here. Look at 14: 4:

"On that day his feet will stand on the Mount of Olives, east of Jerusalem, and the Mount of Olives will be split in two from east to west, forming a great valley, with half of the mountain moving north and half moving south."

This oracle looks forward to the Day of the Lord when the nations will finally be destroyed, the Israelites will be delivered and David's line will be re-instated as the kingdom is established.

The message of Zechariah (his name means "whom the Lord remembers") is that God remembers His covenant and will eventually fulfill all the promises. This is a message of hope for the returning exiles of that time and to us.

One final thing that relates to Zechariah being an ayin book: There is a strong relationship between the word for eye in Hebrew (עין) (actually the final nun letter would be elongated, but I don't want to get technical here) and the word for sheep (עןא). Remember that the aleph א is symbolic for God, the Alpha and Omega, and here in the word for sheep you have the **eye** continually facing and looking towards God. (And God is looking after the sheep, too!) Now look at the section about the two shepherds: Zechariah 11:4 – 13:

4 This is what the LORD my God says: "Shepherd the flock marked for slaughter. **5** Their buyers slaughter them and go unpunished. Those who sell them say, 'Praise the LORD, I am rich!' Their own shepherds do not spare them. **6** For I will no longer have pity on the people of the land," declares the LORD. "I will give everyone into the hands of their neighbors and their king. They will devastate the land, and I will not rescue anyone from their hands."
7 So I shepherded the flock marked for slaughter, particularly the oppressed of the flock. Then I took two staffs and called one Favor and the other Union, and I shepherded the flock. **8** In one month I got rid of the three shepherds.

The flock detested me, and I grew weary of them **9** and said, "I will not be your shepherd. Let the dying die, and the perishing perish. Let those who are left eat one another's flesh."
10 Then I took my staff called Favor and broke it, revoking the covenant I had made with all the nations. **11** It was revoked on that day, and so the oppressed of the flock who were watching me knew it was the word of the LORD.
12 I told them, "If you think it best, give me my pay; but if not, keep it." So they paid me thirty pieces of silver.

¹³ And the LORD said to me, "Throw it to the potter"—the handsome price at which they valued me! So I took the thirty pieces of silver and threw them to the potter at the house of the LORD.

Thirty pieces of silver! Judas betrayed Jesus for just that amount and when he regretted what he had done he gave the money back and it was used to buy **a potter's field!** Continuing on with verses 14 – 17:

¹⁴ Then I broke my second staff called Union, breaking the family bond between Judah and Israel.
¹⁵ Then the LORD said to me, "Take again the equipment of a foolish shepherd. ¹⁶ For I am going to raise up a shepherd over the land who will not care for the lost, or seek the young, or heal the injured, or feed the healthy, but will eat the meat of the choice sheep, tearing off their hooves.
¹⁷ "Woe to the worthless shepherd,
  who deserts the flock!
May the sword strike his arm and his right eye!
  May his arm be completely withered,
  his right eye totally blinded!"

Woe to the worthless shepherd. False teachers beware. Did you notice what happens to the right eye?

ע

Ayin + 1st Peter

Our 3rd ayin o book is 1st Peter, written by Peter about 30 years after Jesus' ascension. Peter encourages Christians who are suffering for Christ. Although Christians might suffer in this life, they will not suffer forever. This world is not our real home; we must keep our **eye** on heaven which is our real home. Peter also speaks to the grace of God. He wants every Christian to know what God has done for them and that when a person becomes a Christian his life changes. He tells us how to live a good Christian life.

1st Peter has a special relationship to the Hebrew letter ayin and to the word **shepherd**.

Let's start at the beginning by reading 1st Peter 1:1,2:

¹ Peter, an apostle of Jesus Christ,
 To God's **elect, exiles scattered** throughout the provinces of Pontus, Galatia, Cappadocia, Asia and Bithynia, ² who have been chosen according to the **foreknowledge** of God the Father, through the sanctifying work of the Spirit, to be obedient to Jesus Christ and sprinkled with his blood:
 Grace and peace be yours in abundance.

Jesus died for EVERYONE. We are pre-destined for salvation, but only if we accept Jesus. The **elect** are the believers. They (we) are strangers in the world, that is, Christian citizenship is in Heaven. Peter writes to the **scattered** because at that time there was a great dispersion due to persecution. The provinces he mentions are pretty much around the area now known as Turkey. I like that he refers to those to whom he is writing as **exiles** because this matches up beautifully with the other ayin books, Nehemiah and Zechariah, which speak to the returning Jewish exiles. The word **foreknowledge** that Peter uses means that God had knowledge beforehand of their faith.

Read 3 – 9:

³ Praise be to the God and Father of our Lord Jesus Christ! In his great mercy he has given us new birth into a living hope through the resurrection of Jesus Christ from the dead, ⁴ and into **an inheritance that can never perish**, spoil or fade. This inheritance is kept in heaven for you, ⁵ who through faith are shielded by God's power until the coming of the salvation that is ready to be revealed in the last time. ⁶ In all this you greatly rejoice, though now for a little while you may have had to suffer grief in all kinds of trials. ⁷ These have come so that the proven genuineness of your faith—of greater worth than gold, which perishes even though refined by fire—may result in praise, glory and honor when Jesus Christ is revealed. ⁸ Though you have not seen him, you love him; and even though you do not see him now, you believe in him and are filled with an inexpressible and glorious joy, ⁹ for you are receiving the end result of your faith, the salvation of your souls.

In this passage Peter is looking forward at the hope we have even in the face of death. Jesus has given us new birth into a living hope and **an inheritance that can never**

perish. (This is one of many arguments against those who think you can lose your salvation.) Verses 10 – 12 look backward:

¹⁰ Concerning this salvation, the prophets, who spoke of the grace that was to come to you, searched intently and with the greatest care, ¹¹ trying to find out the time and circumstances to which the Spirit of Christ in them was pointing when he predicted the sufferings of the Messiah and the glories that would follow. ¹² It was revealed to them that they were not serving themselves but you, when they spoke of the things that have now been told you by those who have preached the gospel to you by the Holy Spirit sent from heaven. Even angels long to look into these things.

Does that last line not grab you? **Even angels long (wish for, desire, yearn, crave) to look into these things!** This makes me want to study the Bible all the more.
Now read 13 – 16:

¹³ Therefore, with minds that are alert and fully sober, set your hope on the grace to be brought to you when Jesus Christ is revealed at his coming. ¹⁴ As obedient children, do not conform to the evil desires you had when you lived in ignorance. ¹⁵ But just as he who called you is holy, so be holy in all you do; ¹⁶ for it is written: "Be holy, because I am holy."

What words would you put in bold print? Look at the verse above again and underline, circle or highlight the parts that speak to you.
We're going to skip to chapter 2 and read verses 1 – 3:

¹ Therefore, rid yourselves of all malice and all deceit, hypocrisy, envy, and slander of every kind. ² Like newborn babies, crave pure spiritual milk, so that by it you may grow up in your salvation, ³ now that you have tasted that the Lord is good.

Now, think of someone you think should learn these verses and live by them. Is there someone who needs to rid himself/herself of malice (hatred, spite, meanness, nastiness, cruelty)? Who needs to get rid of deceit (dishonesty, pretense, cheating)? Who is involved in hypocrisy (insincerity, double standards, two-facedness)? And how about envy? Slander? I find that whenever I can think of someone else who should "hear that sermon", "read a certain book", or "learn these verses", it usually means that I'm that someone.
Here are verses 9 – 12. I had to put some parts in bold right away so Gentiles can see how they are included:

⁹ But you are a chosen people, a royal priesthood, a holy nation, God's special possession, that you may declare the praises of him who called you out of darkness into his wonderful light. ¹⁰ **Once you were not a people, but now you are the people of God**; once you had not received mercy, but now you have received mercy.
¹¹ Dear friends, I urge you, as foreigners and exiles, to abstain from sinful desires, which wage war against your soul. ¹² Live such good lives among the pagans that, though they accuse you of doing wrong, they may see your good deeds and glorify God on the day he visits us.

The rest of the chapter tells us how to live rightly by submission and ends with a reference to sheep. Here is the literal translation of verse 25:

²⁵for ye were as sheep going astray, but ye turned back now to the shepherd and overseer of your souls. *Young's Literal Translation* (YLT)

Some translations use "bishop" instead of overseer, but overseer is the accurate translation of the word here and relates exactly to our ayin word **eye**, for you need eyes to oversee; furthermore we see a link here between **shepherd** and overseer that corresponds to the Hebrew symbolism explained at the end of the section on Zechariah.

Chapter 3 contains the oft-quoted verse that wives should submit to their husbands. You can read it in your own Bible (1 – 6) and think about it. Then be sure to read 7:

⁷ Husbands, in the same way be considerate as you live with your wives, and treat them with respect as the weaker partner and as heirs with you of the gracious gift of life, so that nothing will hinder your prayers.

Our three ayin books, Nehemiah, Zechariah and 1st Peter, have some interesting links. For example, all three make reference to scattering in their first chapter: Nehemiah 1: 8: "I will scatter you among the nations", Zechariah 1:19: "These are the horns that scattered Judah, Israel and Jerusalem" and 1st Peter 1:1: "To God's elect, strangers in the world, scattered throughout." Additionally Zechariah says "the sheep shall be scattered" (13:7).

Another association among the three books is about gold. In Nehemiah (3:8) a goldsmith is mentioned as repairing a section of the Jerusalem wall and in both Zechariah (13:9) and 1st Peter (1:7) gold is mentioned as being refined and tried by fire. The gold in Zechariah symbolizes God's people and in 1st Peter the gold is faith.

Chapter 17 Pey

Aleph	1. Genesis		23. Isaiah		45. Romans
Bet	2. Exodus		24. Jeremiah		46. 1st Corinthians
Gimel	3. Leviticus		25. Lamentations		47. 2nd Corinthians
Dalet	4. Numbers		26. Ezekiel		48. Galatians
Hey	5. Deuteronomy		27. Daniel		49. Ephesians
Vav	6. Joshua		28. Hosea		50. Philippians
Zayin	7. Judges		29. Joel		51. Colossians
Het	8. Ruth		30. Amos		52. 1st Thessalonians
Tet	9. 1st Samuel		31. Obadiah		53. 2nd Thessalonians
Yod	10. 2nd Samuel		32. Jonah		54. 1st Timothy
Kaph	11. 1st Kings		33. Micah		55. 2nd Timothy
Lamed	12. 2nd Kings		34. Nahum		56. Titus
Mem	13. 1st Chronicles		35. Habakkuk		57. Philemon
Nun	14. 2nd Chronicles		36. Zephaniah		58. Hebrews
Samek	15. Ezra		37. Haggai		59. James
Ayin	16. Nehemiah		38. Zechariah		60. 1st Peter
Pey	*17. Esther*		*39. Malachi*		*61. 2nd Peter*
Tzaddi	18. Job		40. Matthew		62. 1st John
Quph	19. Psalms		41. Mark		63. 2nd John
Resh	20. Proverbs		42. Luke		64. 3rd John
Shin	21. Ecclesiastes		43. John		65. Jude
Tav	22. Song of Songs		44. Acts		66. Revelation

פ ף

Pey + Esther
The letter pey is one of the five Hebrew letters which have different forms if they come at the end of a word. Pey means **mouth**. Let's look at some acrostic verses to see pey in action:

Psalm 119: 131 - I open my **mouth** and pant,
longing for your commands.
Psalm 135: 16, 17 - They have **mouths**, but cannot speak, eyes, but cannot see.
Psalm 66: 17 - I cried out to him with my **mouth**;
his praise was on my tongue.
Proverbs 31:26 - She opens her **mouth** with wisdom, and on her tongue is the law of kindness.
Lamentations 3:46 - All our enemies have opened their **mouths** against us.

Our first pey book is Esther. We don't know who wrote it, but it is generally thought to be written by Mordecai, Esther's cousin, who plays a major role in the story.

We've just covered the prophecies of Haggai and Zechariah in the previous chapters during the period of the return from Exile. Now it is the time of rebuilding Jerusalem. Esther becomes queen and saves the Jews from extermination. Though the name of God does not occur even once in this book, His providence is evident as well as His protection of His people. Esther is spelled in Hebrew with the same letters as "I will be hid." Isn't that cool? It seems like God loves anagrams, codes and puzzles. Me, too. God is hidden in the book of Esther.

The events of Esther fit chronologically between chapters 6 and 7 of Ezra and tell us that anti-Jewish hostility is intolerable to God. First there is the story of queen Vashti. Esther 1: 10-12, and 19 give the highlights:

10 On the seventh day, when King Xerxes was in high spirits from wine, he commanded the seven eunuchs who served him—Mehuman, Biztha, Harbona, Bigtha, Abagtha, Zethar and Karkas— **11** to bring before him Queen Vashti, wearing her royal crown, in order to display her beauty to the people and nobles, for she was lovely to look at. **12** But when the attendants delivered the king's command, Queen Vashti refused to come. Then the king became furious and burned with anger.
19 "Therefore, if it pleases the king, let him issue a royal decree and let it be written in the laws of Persia and Media, which cannot be repealed, that Vashti is never again to enter the presence of King Xerxes. Also let the king give her royal position to someone else who is better than she.

Look again at verse 11. The implication is that she was summoned to appear wearing nothing but the crown! Yes, sir, naked. No wonder she refused to come.

Nevertheless, Vashti is out, banished, and now this Persian king needs a new queen. It took a while to round up the "many virgins" who would receive special baths, beauty treatments, clothing and accessories. Chapter 2 tells us that they completed 12 months of beauty treatments before spending a night with the king. Each girl was then one of his concubines, but would not get another night with him unless she pleased him. Then Esther (whose Hebrew name was Hadassah, meaning myrtle or joy) gets a turn. Her Jewish heritage is hidden from the king (2:10) who is very much attracted to her. She wins his favor and he crowns her as his queen.

Meanwhile, there is a conspiracy by a man named Haman to annihilate the Jews (3: 1-7):

> **1** After these events, King Xerxes honored Haman son of Hammedatha, the Agagite, elevating him and giving him a seat of honor higher than that of all the other nobles. **2** All the royal officials at the king's gate knelt down and paid honor to Haman, for the king had commanded this concerning him. But Mordecai would not kneel down or pay him honor.
> **3** Then the royal officials at the king's gate asked Mordecai, "Why do you disobey the king's command?" **4** Day after day they spoke to him but he refused to comply. Therefore they told Haman about it to see whether Mordecai's behavior would be tolerated, for he had told them he was a Jew.
> **5** When Haman saw that Mordecai would not kneel down or pay him honor, he was enraged. **6** Yet having learned who Mordecai's people were, he scorned the idea of killing only Mordecai. Instead Haman looked for a way to destroy all Mordecai's people, the Jews, throughout the whole kingdom of Xerxes.
> **7** In the twelfth year of King Xerxes, in the first month, the month of Nisan, the *pur* (that is, the lot) was cast in the presence of Haman to select a day and month. And the lot fell on the twelfth month, the month of Adar.

We need to clarify some things here. King Xerxes may be identified as King Ahasuerus in your translation. Actually, Ahasuerus is the Hebrew translation for his Persian name and Xerxes is the Greek translation, the one he is better known by in history. Do you want to know his Persian name? Don't ask me how to pronounce this: Khshayarsha. He was the Persian king who ruled an empire that ran from India to Ethiopia. Haman was one of his counselors, a wicked one at that. In fact, since he is identified in verse 1 as the son of Hammedatha, the Agagite, some scholars think this implies that he was a contemptible, hateful man because Agagite literally means "fiery one". We see in the passage above that Haman really got ticked when Mordecai (who had raised Esther) refused to kowtow to him. Hence he seeks revenge.

Haman cast the lot—*pur* is the Persian word for "lot"—to determine the day most favorable to wipe out the Jews. (3:7-11) In the pagan world of the time it was unimaginable to make such big plans without astrological guidance. The lot was supposed to disclose the most favorable day for this act. The official casting of lots happened during the first month of each year to determine the most suitable days for important events. Haman cast lots in the first month and the lot fell on the 12th month, hence there was almost a year for preparation. God controlled the lot-casting (Prov. 16:33). Archaeologists have found quadrangular prism type dice at Susa which may be what they used. It is also thought that they may have used broken pieces of pottery.

Meanwhile, lots of stuff happens: Mordecai learns of the evil plan and asks Esther for her help. Haman, still ticked at Mordecai, builds a gallows to hang him. The king, sleepless, reads the chronicles and discovers that Mordecai had done a great service to the king and had not been rewarded. Esther plots to set Haman up by inviting him and the King to her own banquet.

Results? Esther thwarts Haman's plans. Here's chapter 7:

¹ So the king and Haman went to Queen Esther's banquet, ² and as they were drinking wine on the second day, the king again asked, "Queen Esther, what is your petition? It will be given you. What is your request? Even up to half the kingdom, it will be granted."

³ Then Queen Esther answered, "If I have found favor with you, Your Majesty, and if it pleases you, grant me my life—this is my petition. And spare my people—this is my request. ⁴ For I and my people have been sold to be destroyed, killed and annihilated. If we had merely been sold as male and female slaves, I would have kept quiet, because no such distress would justify disturbing the king."

⁵ King Xerxes asked Queen Esther, "Who is he? Where is he—the man who has dared to do such a thing?"

⁶ Esther said, "An adversary and enemy! This vile Haman!"

Then Haman was terrified before the king and queen. ⁷ The king got up in a rage, left his wine and went out into the palace garden. But Haman, realizing that the king had already decided his fate, stayed behind to beg Queen Esther for his life.

⁸ Just as the king returned from the palace garden to the banquet hall, Haman was falling on the couch where Esther was reclining.

The king exclaimed, "Will he even molest the queen while she is with me in the house?"

As soon as the word left the king's mouth, they covered Haman's face. ⁹ Then Harbona, one of the eunuchs attending the king, said, "A pole reaching to a height of fifty cubits stands by Haman's house. He had it set up for Mordecai, who spoke up to help the king."

The king said, "Impale him on it!" ¹⁰ So they impaled Haman on the pole he had set up for Mordecai. Then the king's fury subsided.

פ

The Jews are saved and the feast of Purim is instituted (remember, pur means "lot", so purim is the plural, essentially the feast is named for the lots cast that never came to fruition). (9:17-22). Modern Jews celebrate Purim on the evening of Adar 14 (in March). It is their most festive and popular holiday.

Here's a little something extra: All three pey books, Esther, Malachi and 2nd Peter, have evidence of a chiastic structure, a literary pattern where concepts or ideas are placed in a symmetrical order to emphasize them (like what we saw on p. 125). A chiasm can be a crossing or intersecting of two things. You can see it clearly here:

 A Opening and background (chapter 1)
  B The king's first decree (chapters 2—3)
   C The clash between Haman and Mordecai (chapters 4—5)
    D "On the night the king could not sleep" (6:1)
   C' Mordecai's triumph over Haman (chapters 6—7)
  B' The king's second decree (chapters 8—9)
 A' Epilogue (chapter 10)

Joyce Baldwin believed that the writer of **Esther** composed the book in a chiastic structure that focuses on the providence of God in the king's sleepless night. (Baldwin, Joyce G. *Esther*. Tyndale Old Testament Commentaries series. Downers Grove, Ill.: InterVarsity Press, 1984. P. 30)

פ Pey + Malachi

Malachi ("my messenger") was written by Malachi. This book is the last of the Minor Prophets and fits in our timeline just after Esther, the first pey book, and the institution of the feast of Purim. Since Malachi addressed many of the same matters that Nehemiah tried to reform, it is thought that we can date Malachi during Nehemiah's governorship. Both Malachi and Nehemiah dealt with priestly laxity (Mal. 1:6; Neh. 13:4-9), neglect of tithes (Mal. 3:7-12; Neh. 13:10-13), and inter-marriage between Israelites and foreigners (Mal. 2:10-16; Neh. 13:23-28). When will they learn?

Let's start by reading chapter 1.

¹ A prophecy: The word of the LORD to Israel through Malachi.

² "I have loved you," says the LORD.

"But you ask, 'How have you loved us?'

"Was not Esau Jacob's brother?" declares the LORD. "Yet I have loved Jacob, ³ but Esau I have hated, and I have turned his hill country into a wasteland and left his inheritance to the desert jackals."

⁴ Edom may say, "Though we have been crushed, we will rebuild the ruins."

But this is what the LORD Almighty says: "They may build, but I will demolish. They will be called the Wicked Land, a people always under the wrath of the LORD. ⁵ You will see it with your own eyes and say, 'Great is the LORD—even beyond the borders of Israel!'

⁶ "A son honors his father, and a slave his master. If I am a father, where is the honor due me? If I am a master, where is the respect due me?" says the LORD Almighty.

"It is you priests who show contempt for my name.

"But you ask, 'How have we shown contempt for your name?'

⁷ "By offering defiled food on my altar.

"But you ask, 'How have we defiled you?'

"By saying that the LORD's table is contemptible. ⁸ When you offer blind animals for sacrifice, is that not wrong? When you sacrifice lame or diseased animals, is that not wrong? Try offering them to your governor! Would he be pleased with you? Would he accept you?" says the LORD Almighty.

⁹ "Now plead with God to be gracious to us. With such offerings from your hands, will he accept you?"—says the LORD Almighty.

¹⁰ "Oh, that one of you would shut the temple doors, so that you would not light useless fires on my altar! I am not pleased with you," says the LORD Almighty, "and I will accept no offering from your hands. ¹¹ My name will be great among the nations, from where the sun rises to where it sets. In every place incense and pure offerings will be brought to me, because my name will be great among the nations," says the LORD Almighty.

¹² "But you profane it by saying, 'The Lord's table is defiled,' and, 'Its food is contemptible.' ¹³ And you say, 'What a burden!' and you sniff at it contemptuously," says the LORD Almighty.

"When you bring injured, lame or diseased animals and offer them as sacrifices, should I accept them from your hands?" says the LORD. ¹⁴ "Cursed is the cheat who has an acceptable male in his flock and vows to give it, but then sacrifices a blemished animal to the

Lord. For I am a great king," says the LORD Almighty, "and my name is to be feared among the nations.

What is the Lord saying? Should we give Him our very best? Reread verses 8 and 14. Kind of hits me between the eyes. How can I give the Lord anything less than my best?

Read 2: 1-9 and notice the pey words for **mouth**:

¹ "And now, you priests, this warning is for you. ² If you do not listen, and if you do not resolve to honor my name," says the LORD Almighty, "I will send a curse on you, and I will curse your blessings. Yes, I have already cursed them, because you have not resolved to honor me.
³ "Because of you I will rebuke your descendants; I will smear on your faces the dung from your festival sacrifices, and you will be carried off with it. ⁴ And you will know that I have sent you this warning so that my covenant with Levi may continue," says the LORD Almighty. ⁵ "My covenant was with him, a covenant of life and peace, and I gave them to him; this called for reverence and he revered me and stood in awe of my name. ⁶ True instruction was in his mouth and nothing false was found on his lips. He walked with me in peace and uprightness, and turned many from sin.
⁷ "For the lips of a priest ought to preserve knowledge, because he is the messenger of the LORD Almighty and people seek instruction from his mouth. ⁸ But you have turned from the way and by your teaching have caused many to stumble; you have violated the covenant with Levi," says the LORD Almighty. ⁹ "So I have caused you to be despised and humiliated before all the people, because you have not followed my ways but have shown partiality in matters of the law."

Skip to chapter 3 and watch for John the Baptist and Jesus in verse 1:

¹ "I will send my messenger, who will prepare the way before me. Then suddenly the Lord you are seeking will come to his temple; the messenger of the covenant, whom you desire, will come," says the LORD Almighty.

Read 3:6-10:

⁶ "I the LORD do not change. So you, the descendants of Jacob, are not destroyed. ⁷ Ever since the time of your ancestors you have turned away from my decrees and have not kept them. Return to me, and I will return to you," says the LORD Almighty.
"But you ask, 'How are we to return?'
⁸ "Will a mere mortal rob God? Yet you rob me.
"But you ask, 'How are we robbing you?'
"In tithes and offerings. ⁹ You are under a curse—your whole nation—because you are robbing me. ¹⁰ Bring the whole tithe into the storehouse, that there may be food in my house. Test me in this," says the LORD Almighty, "and see if I will not throw open the floodgates of heaven and pour out so much blessing that there will not be room enough to store it.

There have been a slew of television evangelists who use these words to line their own pockets. Really study these verses. Look at verse 6. The Lord DOES NOT CHANGE. The

Jewish people, the descendants of Jacob, ARE NOT DESTROYED. And there's a promise here that the Lord makes: Return to me, and I WILL RETURN to you. Keep reading and notice the conversation that God invents between man and Himself. Are we robbing God? If we tithe and offer above and beyond our tithes, will He bless us? YES!

A little something extra: Remember the chiastic structure in Esther? Let's look at the chiastic structure in Malachi:

  A Superscription (1:1): Yahweh has a message for Israel.
    B First Disputation (1:2-5): God distinguishes between the good and the wicked. The proof of His love is His sparing the righteous and condemning the wicked.
      C Second Disputation (1:6—2:9): Condemnation of improper, begrudging offerings, promise of reversal of blessing, and the greatness of Yahweh's name among the nations.
        D Third Disputation (2:10-16): The Lord is witness to marital fidelity, and Judah is unfaithful.
        D' Fourth Disputation (2:17—3:6): The Lord is witness to marital fidelity, and Judah is unfaithful.
      C' Fifth Disputation (3:7-12): Condemnation of improper, begrudging offerings, promise of reversal of blessing, and the greatness of Yahweh's name among the nations.
    B' Sixth Disputation (3:13—4:3): God distinguishes between the good and the wicked. The proof of His love is His sparing the righteous and condemning the wicked.
  A' Summary challenge (4:4-6): Yahweh has a message for Israel.[1]

In our third pey book, 2nd Peter, we'll see if the pattern continues.

[1] Stuart, Douglas. "Malachi." In *The Minor Prophets: An Exegetical and Expositional Commentary*, 3:1245-1396. 3 vols. Edited by Thomas Edward McComiskey. Grand Rapids: Baker Books, 1992, 1993, and 1998.(p. 1250)

פ ף

Pey + 2nd Peter
In our third pey book Peter writes to the Christians giving a direct warning against false teachers, specifically the teachings of the Gnostics and antinomians. The Gnostics believed that in addition to believing in Christ, you must also receive the gnosis or esoteric knowledge. Antinomians believed that since salvation was by grace alone the requirements of the moral law were irrelevant and thus they could do whatever they wanted. Their lifestyle resulted in decadence and immoral behavior. (I think a lot of people today live like antinomians.)

After Peter gives a nice salutation he tells his readers to make sure their calling and election are secure. Let's read 1: 3 – 11:

³ His divine power has given us everything we need for a godly life through our knowledge of him who called us by his own glory and goodness. ⁴ Through these he has given us his very great and precious promises, so that through them you may participate in the divine nature, having escaped the corruption in the world caused by evil desires.
⁵ For this very reason, make every effort to add to your faith goodness; and to goodness, knowledge; ⁶ and to knowledge, self-control; and to self-control, perseverance; and to perseverance, godliness; ⁷ and to godliness, mutual affection; and to mutual affection, love. ⁸ For if you possess these qualities in increasing measure, they will keep you from being ineffective and unproductive in your knowledge of our Lord Jesus Christ. ⁹ But whoever does not have them is nearsighted and blind, forgetting that they have been cleansed from their past sins.
¹⁰ Therefore, my brothers and sisters, make every effort to confirm your calling and election. For if you do these things, you will never stumble, ¹¹ and you will receive a rich welcome into the eternal kingdom of our Lord and Savior Jesus Christ.

Read verse 3 again. God has already given us **everything** we need – what great potential we have! (We don't need to pray for strength or leading, we already have the strength and God is always leading us.) What are the promises in verse 4? Well, I'm not going to even try to list them. There are over 750 promises in the New Testament. A few of my favorites are found in Peter's letters:
1. Promise of salvation and preservation -- 1 Peter 1:3-7
2. Promise of answered prayers -- 1 Peter 3:7-12
3. Promise of victory over cares and the devil -- 1 Peter 5:6-11
4. Promise of living eternally in a new heaven and a new earth -- 2 Peter 3:10-13

Here are verses 5 – 7 in Young's Literal Translation. I've slipped in the Greek definitions in parentheses: "And this same also -- all diligence having brought in besides, superadd in your faith the worthiness (virtue, good quality, excellence of any kind, goodness with actions, virtuous deeds), and in the worthiness the knowledge (practical knowledge, discretion, prudence), and in the knowledge the temperance (self-control: to control our passions rather than being controlled by them), and in the temperance the endurance (patience, perseverance or constancy under suffering in faith and duty; cheerful or hopeful endurance), and in the endurance the piety (godliness, holiness; reverence only as directed toward God and denoting the spontaneous feeling of the heart – to be godly is to live reverently, loyally, and obediently toward God), and in the piety the brotherly kindness (brotherly love out of a common spiritual love – used only of the love of Christians one to another), and in the brotherly kindness the love (affectionate regard, goodwill, benevolence – the Greek word here is agape)".

Chapter 2 gives us Peter's warnings about false teachers. Read 2:1 – 3:

¹ But there were also false prophets among the people, just as there will be false teachers among you. They will secretly introduce destructive heresies, even denying the sovereign Lord who bought them—bringing swift destruction on themselves. ² Many will follow their depraved conduct and will bring the way of truth into disrepute. ³ In their greed these teachers will exploit you with fabricated stories. Their condemnation has long been hanging over them, and their destruction has not been sleeping.

Verse 1 mentions false prophets and false teachers. These words in Greek are pseudoprophetai and pseudodidaskaloi. The false teachers will introduce heresies, that is, deviation from the truth as well as sacrilege and heretical doctrine. Furthermore Peter says they will "deny" the Sovereign Lord who bought them. Deny is a strong word and must have had a very emotional meaning to Peter who denied Christ three times. Verse 2 tells us these false teachers' ways are "shameful", but it's even stronger than that. The Greek word implies damnable destruction, exclusion from the Messiah's kingdom. (Yikes!) Verse 3 says they will exploit with stories they have made up. Older translations have "feigned words." The Greek is "plastos" from which we get the word plastic, so these stories are molded, like plastic, any way they want to fool people.

Read 2: 4 – 10a:

⁴ For if God did not spare angels when they sinned, but sent them to hell, putting them in chains of darkness to be held for judgment; ⁵ if he did not spare the ancient world when he brought the flood on its ungodly people, but protected Noah, a preacher of righteousness, and seven others; ⁶ if he condemned the cities of Sodom and Gomorrah by burning them to ashes, and made them an example of what is going to happen to the ungodly; ⁷ and if he rescued Lot, a righteous man, who was distressed by the depraved conduct of the lawless ⁸ (for that righteous man, living among them day after day, was tormented in his righteous soul by the lawless deeds he saw and heard)— ⁹ if this is so, then the Lord knows how to rescue the godly from trials and to hold the unrighteous for punishment on the day of judgment. ¹⁰ This is especially true of those who follow the corrupt desire of the flesh and despise authority.

Peter gives three examples of apostates (traitors, deserters, defectors) from the past. Who are they? They are angels, sinners in Noah's day, and the people of Sodom and

Gomorrah. You see in verse 9 that God rescued godly men while punishing the unrighteous and holding them for judgment.

Of course, we want to be able to recognize false teachers so Peter tells us what their conduct will be like. Read 2: 10b – 19:

10 Bold and arrogant, they are not afraid to heap abuse on celestial beings; **11** yet even angels, although they are stronger and more powerful, do not heap abuse on such beings when bringing judgment on them from the Lord. **12** But these people blaspheme in matters they do not understand. They are like unreasoning animals, creatures of instinct, born only to be caught and destroyed, and like animals they too will perish.
13 They will be paid back with harm for the harm they have done. Their idea of pleasure is to carouse in broad daylight. They are blots and blemishes, reveling in their pleasures while they feast with you. **14** With eyes full of adultery, they never stop sinning; they seduce the unstable; they are experts in greed—an accursed brood! **15** They have left the straight way and wandered off to follow the way of Balaam son of Bezer, who loved the wages of wickedness. **16** But he was rebuked for his wrongdoing by a donkey—an animal without speech—who spoke with a human voice and restrained the prophet's madness.
17 These people are springs without water and mists driven by a storm. Blackest darkness is reserved for them. **18** For they mouth empty, boastful words and, by appealing to the lustful desires of the flesh, they entice people who are just escaping from those who live in error. **19** They promise them freedom, while they themselves are slaves of depravity—for "people are slaves to whatever has mastered them."

First they are bold, arrogant, slanderous. They blaspheme (swear, use foul language). They are like animals. They have eyes full of adultery. I guess that means they are sexually liberated. Notice that they never stop sinning, they seduce the unstable and they are experts in greed. They are not on the straight and narrow. Reread this paragraph right now and think about who fits the bill in modern day.

Now read 3: 1 – 2:

1 Dear friends, this is now my second letter to you. I have written both of them as reminders to stimulate you to wholesome thinking. **2** I want you to recall the words spoken in the past by the holy prophets and the command given by our Lord and Savior through your apostles.

Peter reveals his reason for writing: to stir up the readers to "wholesome thinking" or "pure minds" as the KJV says, which according to the Greek is the best translation, although translations that say "wholesome thinking" and "undistracted attention" may help you understand better.

Read 3: 3 – 6:

3 Above all, you must understand that in the last days scoffers will come, scoffing and following their own evil desires. **4** They will say, "Where is this 'coming' he promised? Ever since our ancestors died, everything goes on as it has since the beginning of creation." **5** But they deliberately forget that long ago by God's word the heavens came into being and the earth was formed out of water and by water. **⁶** By these waters also the world of that time was deluged and destroyed.

What do the scoffers, the skeptics, say? They say that things have gone on the same since the beginning. But Peter refutes that claim with proof that it hasn't: he cites creation itself and Noah's flood. Now continue with 7 – 10:

⁷ By the same word the present heavens and earth are reserved for fire, being kept for the day of judgment and destruction of the ungodly.
⁸ But do not forget this one thing, dear friends: With the Lord a day is like a thousand years, and a thousand years are like a day. **⁹** The Lord is not slow in keeping his promise, as some understand slowness. Instead he is patient with you, not wanting anyone to perish, but everyone to come to repentance.
¹⁰ But the day of the Lord will come like a thief. The heavens will disappear with a roar; the elements will be destroyed by fire, and the earth and everything done in it will be laid bare.

What's in store for the world? Judgment and destruction! What's the purpose of Peter saying a day is like 1000 years and 1000 years are like a day? He's saying that God is faithful in His promises. God is patient. God wants no one to perish. And that God's sense of time and ours are different.

Now let's see how we should live, knowing that God will at some sudden time come. Read 11 – 17:

¹¹ Since everything will be destroyed in this way, what kind of people ought you to be? You ought to live holy and godly lives **¹²** as you look forward to the day of God and speed its coming. That day will bring about the destruction of the heavens by fire, and the elements will melt in the heat. **¹³** But in keeping with his promise we are looking forward to a new heaven and a new earth, where righteousness dwells.
¹⁴ So then, dear friends, since you are looking forward to this, make every effort to be found spotless, blameless and at peace with him. **¹⁵** Bear in mind that our Lord's patience means salvation, just as our dear brother Paul also wrote you with the wisdom that God gave him. **¹⁶** He writes the same way in all his letters, speaking in them of these matters. His letters contain some things that are hard to understand, which ignorant and unstable people distort, as they do the other Scriptures, to their own destruction.
¹⁷ Therefore, dear friends, since you have been forewarned, be on your guard so that you may not be carried away by the error of the lawless and fall from your secure position.

How should we live? We should live holy and godly lives. We should look forward, eagerly awaiting the coming. We should be spotless, blameless, at peace with God, on guard. We don't want to fall away. We want to grow in grace and in knowledge.

A little something extra: Remember that we found chiastic structures in the other two pey p books, Esther and Malachi. I wondered if anyone had looked for such a thing in 2nd Peter. What I found is next.

In his *Notes on 2nd Peter*, Dr. Thomas L. Constable indicates a "somewhat chiastic structure" in chapter 3, verses 3 – 10:

A Last days – scoffers will come (3: 3)
   B Scoffers say everything continues as it has (3: 4)
   B' Peter refutes with reference to creation and flood as proof against things continuing unchanged (3:5-7)
A' Last days – end time events (3:8-10)

If you want to learn more about chiastic structure throughout the whole Bible check out http://www.bibleexplained.com/bible-chi.html

Chapter 18 Tzaddi

Aleph	1. Genesis	23. Isaiah	45. Romans
Bet	2. Exodus	24. Jeremiah	46. 1st Corinthians
Gimel	3. Leviticus	25. Lamentations	47. 2nd Corinthians
Dalet	4. Numbers	26. Ezekiel	48. Galatians
Hey	5. Deuteronomy	27. Daniel	49. Ephesians
Vav	6. Joshua	28. Hosea	50. Philippians
Zayin	7. Judges	29. Joel	51. Colossians
Het	8. Ruth	30. Amos	52. 1st Thessalonians
Tet	9. 1st Samuel	31. Obadiah	53. 2nd Thessalonians
Yod	10. 2nd Samuel	32. Jonah	54. 1st Timothy
Kaph	11. 1st Kings	33. Micah	55. 2nd Timothy
Lamed	12. 2nd Kings	34. Nahum	56. Titus
Mem	13. 1st Chronicles	35. Habakkuk	57. Philemon
Nun	14. 2nd Chronicles	36. Zephaniah	58. Hebrews
Samek	15. Ezra	37. Haggai	59. James
Ayin	16. Nehemiah	38. Zechariah	60. 1st Peter
Pey	17. Esther	39. Malachi	61. 2nd Peter
Tzaddi	*18. Job*	*40. Matthew*	*62. 1st John*
Quph	19. Psalms	41. Mark	63. 2nd John
Resh	20. Proverbs	42. Luke	64. 3rd John
Shin	21. Ecclesiastes	43. John	65. Jude
Tav	22. Song of Songs	44. Acts	66. Revelation

צ

Tzaddi + Job

The 18th Hebrew letter is tzaddi. Its literal meaning is fishhook, but in Scripture it is the basis for words having to do with **righteous** or righteousness: tzaddik. (Melchisedek comes from melech and tzaddik – king of righteousness.) Let's check some alphabetic verses first to see if righteous or righteousness appears as the first word (in Hebrew).

Psalm 119:137:

[137] You are **righteous**, LORD, and your laws are right.

Psalm 119:142:

[142] Your **righteousness** is everlasting and your law is true.

Psalm 34:17:

[17] The **righteous** cry out, and the LORD hears them; he delivers them from all their troubles.

Psalm 37:17:

[17] for the power of the wicked will be broken, but the LORD upholds the **righteous**.

Psalm 145:17:

[17] The LORD is **righteous** in all his ways and faithful in all he does.

Lamentations 1:18:

[18] "The LORD is **righteous**,
   yet I rebelled against his command.
Listen, all you peoples;
   look on my suffering.
My young men and young women
   have gone into exile.

Job is one of the few books in the Hebrew Bible that isn't named for the first words of the text. This book is called "Iyyowb" in Hebrew which means "hated one" or "persecuted one." Most scholars think that this book was written by Moses. It is the first of our 5 poetical books of wisdom. The purpose of the book is to show God's wisdom, the wisdom of His ways, His benevolence and also to answer the age-old question: why do bad things happen to good people? The preceding 17 books barely mentioned righteousness, but Job has 22 occurrences of the word. This will obviously be a theme here. Tzaddik means righteous, from the 18th letter Tzaddi.

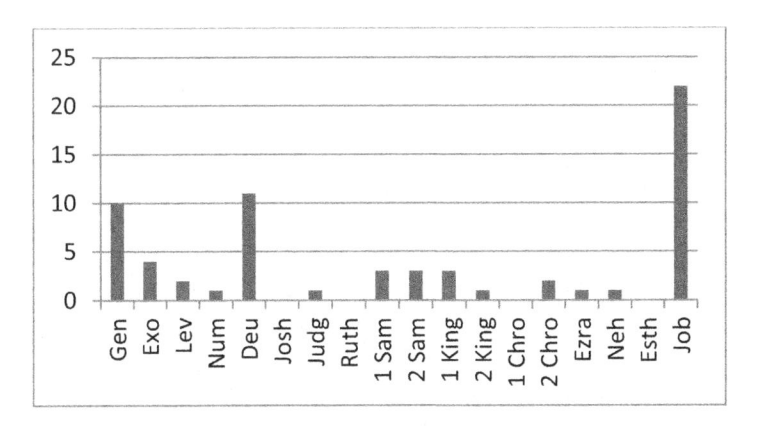

Let's start with chapter 1, verses 1 through 19:

¹ In the land of Uz there lived a man whose name was Job. This man was blameless and upright; he feared God and shunned evil. ² He had seven sons and three daughters, ³ and he owned seven thousand sheep, three thousand camels, five hundred yoke of oxen and five hundred donkeys, and had a large number of servants. He was the greatest man among all the people of the East.
⁴ His sons used to hold feasts in their homes on their birthdays, and they would invite their three sisters to eat and drink with them. ⁵ When a period of feasting had run its course, Job would make arrangements for them to be purified. Early in the morning he would sacrifice a burnt offering for each of them, thinking, "Perhaps my children have sinned and cursed God in their hearts." This was Job's regular custom.
⁶ One day the angels came to present themselves before the LORD, and Satan also came with them. ⁷ The LORD said to Satan, "Where have you come from?"
Satan answered the LORD, "From roaming throughout the earth, going back and forth on it."
⁸ Then the LORD said to Satan, "Have you considered my servant Job? There is no one on earth like him; he is blameless and upright, a man who fears God and shuns evil."
⁹ "Does Job fear God for nothing?" Satan replied. ¹⁰ "Have you not put a hedge around him and his household and everything he has? You have blessed the work of his hands, so that his flocks and herds are spread throughout the land. ¹¹ But now stretch out your hand and strike everything he has, and he will surely curse you to your face."
¹² The LORD said to Satan, "Very well, then, everything he has is in your power, but on the man himself do not lay a finger."
Then Satan went out from the presence of the LORD.
¹³ One day when Job's sons and daughters were feasting and drinking wine at the oldest brother's house, ¹⁴ a messenger came to Job and said, "The oxen were plowing and the donkeys were grazing nearby, ¹⁵ and the Sabeans attacked and made off with them. They put the servants to the sword, and I am the only one who has escaped to tell you!"

16 While he was still speaking, another messenger came and said, "The fire of God fell from the heavens and burned up the sheep and the servants, and I am the only one who has escaped to tell you!"

17 While he was still speaking, another messenger came and said, "The Chaldeans formed three raiding parties and swept down on your camels and made off with them. They put the servants to the sword, and I am the only one who has escaped to tell you!"

18 While he was still speaking, yet another messenger came and said, "Your sons and daughters were feasting and drinking wine at the oldest brother's house, **19** when suddenly a mighty wind swept in from the desert and struck the four corners of the house. It collapsed on them and they are dead, and I am the only one who has escaped to tell you!"

Job lives in Uz which is another word play as Uz means "take counsel" and if you're already familiar with the story of Job you know that he takes counsel from his friends after suffering family tragedy, financial losses and health problems. The description of Job depicts a righteous man. He was blameless and upright, feared God and shunned evil. The word shunned here is the translation of the Hebrew word "suwr" and is a verb that means to turn away, to go away, to desert, to quit, to keep far from, to stop, to take away, to remove. Job shows us how to be righteous: just shun evil.

Job is wealthy, look what he does in verses 4 and 5. He is pious and devout and vigilant keeping his family right with the Lord. He makes the appropriate sacrifices for his children, just in case.

Reread verses 6 – 11. What is Satan's contention? He thinks that Job is God-fearing because things are good, but he will certainly reject God if things go bad. He probably believes that because it seems so true even today. People are happy with God if things are good, but how many people do you know who get mad at God and quit going to church when they suffer a loss like the death of a child?

In verses 12 – 19 Job gets the worst possible news. Notice how quickly the tragedies follow one another. He must have been absolutely devastated. What does he do?

Read verses 20-22:

20 At this, Job got up and tore his robe and shaved his head. Then he fell to the ground in worship **21** and said:

"Naked I came from my mother's womb,
and naked I will depart.
The LORD gave and the LORD has taken away;
may the name of the LORD be praised."

22 In all this, Job did not sin by charging God with wrongdoing.

Wow! Learn from this. He praised God! He did not blame God!

Chapter 2 presents Job's second test and this time Satan afflicts him with sores and even his wife tells him to curse God and die, but Job says in verse 10 "You are talking like a foolish woman. Shall we accept good from God, and not trouble?" So Job holds onto his righteousness and maybe we see a little self-righteousness, too. It's important to also note that it is Satan who causes Job's troubles, not the Lord, though He allows it. Next Job's three friends come and sit with him silently for a week before Job speaks. In chapter 3 Job curses the day he was born and does it to the tune of 26 verses in poetic form. Then his friends speak. First it's Eliphaz whose name means "God is strong", followed by Bildad, "son of contention" and finally Zophar, "chatterer". To sum up, this is what they say:

1) Suffering is the result of sin so Job must have sinned.

2) The greater the suffering, the greater the sin must have been so Job must have been a big sinner.

3) Job should repent of his sins for God to restore his happiness. They warn him not to justify himself or he will just delay things.

4) They acknowledge that oftentimes the sinful prosper, but it's temporary and justice will eventually come through.

Job's answers to his friends are as follows:

1) He believes that a righteous man can be afflicted obviously because of his circumstances. He thinks his friends are wrong to accuse him of sin. He doesn't understand the why, but he accepts God's will. He believes he will eventually be able to justify himself and to complain as well.

2) Later Job takes back some of his statements and tends to agree that God generally afflicts the wicked and blesses the righteous. He does, however, insist that there are exceptions, his case in point.

3) He believes that it is our job to worship and adore God even when suffering undeservedly and we should not judge those who complain against God.

Throughout the book some important questions are asked: Why was I born? How can man be just with God? If a man dies will he live again? Let's look at some of what Job learns. Read chapter 14: 14 – 17:

> [14] If someone dies, will they live again?
> All the days of my hard service
> I will wait for my renewal to come.
> [15] You will call and I will answer you;
> you will long for the creature your hands have made.
> [16] Surely then you will count my steps
> but not keep track of my sin.
> [17] My offenses will be sealed up in a bag;
> you will cover over my sin.

What a great hope Job has! He trusted that the Lord would long for him, His creation, and that He would not keep track of Job's sins, sealing them up and covering them. Now read more about the certainty that Job felt (vs. 25 – 27):

> [25] I know that my redeemer lives,
> and that in the end he will stand on the earth.
> [26] And after my skin has been destroyed,
> yet in my flesh I will see God;

²⁷ I myself will see him
 with my own eyes—I, and not another.
 How my heart yearns within me!

    I know that my Redeemer lives. I am just as certain as Job. Notice that he says the redeemer will stand on earth. I believe that. Notice that even after the skin has been destroyed, Job expects to be back in the flesh to see God. I have that same knowledge.

    Continuing on, a new character speaks up. It is Elihu, which means "God of him" and he has some important statements to make. First we'll start with chapter 33, verses 3 and 4:

³ My words come from an upright heart;
 my lips sincerely speak what I know.
⁴ The Spirit of God has made me;
 the breath of the Almighty gives me life.

    Elihu's credentials are self-evident. He goes on in the rest of the chapter to explain that God may speak through dreams and visions to turn man away from evil and to preserve his soul.

    But, in actuality, we deserve every bad thing that happens to us and worse. In 34: 10 – 15 Elihu says:

¹⁰ "So listen to me, you men of understanding.
 Far be it from God to do evil,
 from the Almighty to do wrong.
¹¹ He repays everyone for what they have done;
 he brings on them what their conduct deserves.
¹² It is unthinkable that God would do wrong,
 that the Almighty would pervert justice.
¹³ Who appointed him over the earth?
 Who put him in charge of the whole world?
¹⁴ If it were his intention
 and he withdrew his spirit and breath,
¹⁵ all humanity would perish together
 and mankind would return to the dust.

    Reread those last two verses. What do they say to you?

    Elihu says in 36:26 that God is great and beyond our understanding. What an understatement.

    In Job's speeches, Job said that he wanted to meet God and that he wanted God to act as a judge. He believed that God would then declare that Job was innocent. However, Job did think that God caused his woes and he even spoke about God as if he were a cruel enemy and unfair.

Finally the Lord answers in chapters 38 – 41. He does not explain Job's troubles. Instead, He teaches. He gives a list of His mighty works such as laying out the earth's foundation, the seas, the clouds, the gates of death, the rain, the snow, the stars, all animal life and so on. Then he speaks to Job out of the storm and asks if Job is as mighty as God and says that if he were then he could save himself. Read 40: 9 – 14:

⁹ Do you have an arm like God's,
and can your voice thunder like his?
¹⁰ Then adorn yourself with glory and splendor,
and clothe yourself in honor and majesty.
¹¹ Unleash the fury of your wrath,
look at all who are proud and bring them low,
¹² look at all who are proud and humble them,
crush the wicked where they stand.
¹³ Bury them all in the dust together;
shroud their faces in the grave.
¹⁴ Then I myself will admit to you
that your own right hand can save you.

The Lord really lays it out pretty plainly: we cannot save ourselves.

In the last chapter Job is contrite; he has learned his lesson and repents, whereupon the Lord blesses him more than He had before.

Of the 30 verses in this book that use the tzaddi word righteous or righteousness my favorite is 33:26:

²⁶ then that person can pray to God and find favor with him, they will see God's face and shout for joy; he will restore them to full well-being.

Wait a minute, where's the word "righteousness"? The NIV translation uses "well-being". The actual literal word is "righteousness". Sometimes you have to do some comparisons of translations or check the original. Here is the same verse in the King James version:

²⁶He shall pray unto God, and he will be favourable unto him: and he shall see his face with joy: for he will render unto man his **righteousness**.

צ Tzaddi + Matthew

Our second tzaddi book is Matthew. The occurrences of the words "righteous" and "righteousness" should be greater than in the other gospels since Matthew is a tzaddi book. Here's a chart that shows the amazing truth:

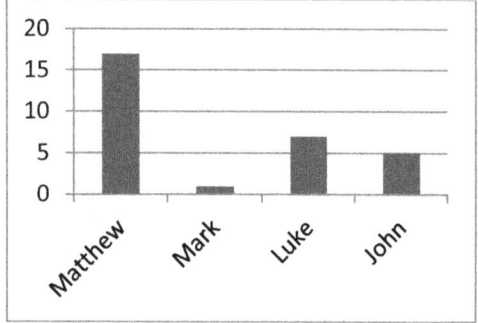

Matthew's name means "gift of Jehovah" which is interesting since we know that he was a tax collector. There is some evidence that he wrote this book originally in Hebrew and maybe in both Hebrew and Greek. There are 23 parables in Matthew, 11 of which do not appear in the other gospels. Of the twenty miracles recorded, three are unique to this account.

There's a lot to cover in Matthew. We're going to start with an overview which I have on a nice little power point presentation. Since you can't see that here I'll summarize: In Matthew you'll find the genealogy of Jesus, His birth, the story of the wise men being guided by the star, and the escape into Egypt. Then Matthew jumps thirty years ahead to John the Baptist preparing the way, Jesus' baptism and the calling of the disciples. There's the sermon on the mount and Jesus' ministry, including many healings and miracles, many parables and much teaching. Matthew records the triumphant entry into Jerusalem, Judas' betrayal, Peter's denial, the arrest, crucifixion, burial and resurrection.

Now we'll look at our tzaddi word "righteousness."

First compare the beatitudes as presented in Matthew with the equivalent verses in Luke. Matthew 5:6 says:

⁶ Blessed are those who hunger **and thirst for righteousness**, for they will be filled

Whereas Luke 6:21 says:

²¹ Blessed are you who hunger now, for you will be satisfied.

Compare the other parallel passages one after another and notice how the word "righteous" is evident in our tzaddi book but absent from Luke.

Matthew 5:10
10 Blessed are those who are persecuted because of **righteousness**, for theirs is the kingdom of heaven.
Luke 6:22
22 Blessed are you when people hate you,
when they exclude you and insult you
and reject your name as evil,
because of the Son of Man.

Matthew 6:33 **33** But seek first his kingdom and his **righteousness**, and all these things will be given to you as well.
Luke 12:31 **31** But seek his kingdom, and these things will be given to you as well.

Matthew 10:40, 41 **40** "Anyone who welcomes you welcomes me, and anyone who welcomes me welcomes the one who sent me. **41** Whoever welcomes a prophet as a prophet will receive a prophet's reward, and whoever welcomes a **righteous** person as a **righteous** person will receive a **righteous** person's reward.
Luke 9:48 **48** Then he said to them, "Whoever welcomes this little child in my name welcomes me; and whoever welcomes me welcomes the one who sent me. For it is the one who is least among you all who is the greatest."

Matthew 13:17 **17** For truly I tell you, many prophets and **righteous** people longed to see what you see but did not see it, and to hear what you hear but did not hear it.
Luke 10:24 **24** For I tell you that many prophets and kings wanted to see what you see but did not see it, and to hear what you hear but did not hear it."

Matthew 23:35 **35** And so upon you will come all the **righteous** blood that has been shed on earth, from the blood of **righteous** Abel to the blood of Zechariah son of Berekiah, whom you murdered between the temple and the altar.
Luke 11:50, 51 **50** Therefore this generation will be held responsible for the blood of all the prophets that has been shed since the beginning of the world, **51** from the blood of Abel to the blood of Zechariah, who was killed between the altar and the sanctuary. Yes, I tell you, this generation will be held responsible for it all.

Matthew 23:29 **29** "Woe to you, teachers of the law and Pharisees, you hypocrites! You build tombs for the prophets and decorate the graves of the **righteous**.
Luke 11:47 **47** "Woe to you, because you build tombs for the prophets, and it was your ancestors who killed them.

Let's stay in chapter 23 and really examine it. This is the last public speech that Jesus gives. It is Wednesday, two days before the crucifixion. In my Bible this chapter is headed the "Seven Woes" and it starts with a big slam of the current teachers of the law and the Pharisees. Read 23: 1 – 12:

¹ Then Jesus said to the crowds and to his disciples: ² "The teachers of the law and the Pharisees sit in Moses' seat. ³ So you must be careful to do everything they tell you. But do not do what they do, for they do not practice what they preach. ⁴ They tie up heavy, cumbersome loads and put them on other people's shoulders, but they themselves are not willing to lift a finger to move them.

⁵ "Everything they do is done for people to see: They make their phylacteries wide and the tassels on their garments long; ⁶ they love the place of honor at banquets and the most important seats in the synagogues; ⁷ they love to be greeted with respect in the marketplaces and to be called 'Rabbi' by others.

⁸ "But you are not to be called 'Rabbi,' for you have one Teacher, and you are all brothers. ⁹ And do not call anyone on earth 'father,' for you have one Father, and he is in heaven. ¹⁰ Nor are you to be called instructors, for you have one Instructor, the Messiah. ¹¹ The greatest among you will be your servant. ¹² For those who exalt themselves will be humbled, and those who humble themselves will be exalted.

This was Jesus' last public speech and He denounces the false leaders. He says in verse 2 that the Pharisees sit in Moses' seat which gives them great authority. The Greek word here is kathedra which means bench and is the basis of our word cathedral. In verse 3 he says to obey them and to do what they preach, which is the Law, but don't do what they do, because they don't practice what they preach. Let's jump down to the woes in verses 13 – 36:

¹³ "Woe to you, teachers of the law and Pharisees, you hypocrites! You shut the door of the kingdom of heaven in people's faces. You yourselves do not enter, nor will you let those enter who are trying to. [¹⁴] Woe to you, teachers of the law and Pharisees, you hypocrites! You devour widows' houses and for a show make lengthy prayers. Therefore you will be punished more severely.

(Some manuscripts do not have verse 14.) So, what's the first woe? What are the Pharisees doing wrong? They are shutting up the kingdom of heaven. If they had opened the kingdom, they would have recognized Jesus as the Messiah.

¹⁵ "Woe to you, teachers of the law and Pharisees, you hypocrites! You travel over land and sea to win a single convert, and when you have succeeded, you make them twice as much a child of hell as you are.

It sounds like the Pharisees were zealous in winning converts, but being ardent and passionate is eternally fatal if you are passionate about the wrong thing. Compare them to the Jehovah's Witnesses and the Mormons.

¹⁶ "Woe to you, blind guides! You say, 'If anyone swears by the temple, it means nothing; but anyone who swears by the gold of the temple is bound by that oath.' ¹⁷ You blind fools! Which is greater: the gold, or the temple that makes the gold sacred? ¹⁸ You also say, 'If anyone swears by the altar, it means nothing; but anyone who swears by the gift on the altar is bound by that oath.' ¹⁹ You blind men! Which is greater: the gift, or the altar that makes

the gift sacred? **20** Therefore, anyone who swears by the altar swears by it and by everything on it. **21** And anyone who swears by the temple swears by it and by the one who dwells in it. **22** And anyone who swears by heaven swears by God's throne and by the one who sits on it.

The Pharisees made false and deceptive oaths. You can kind of equate this with making a promise with your fingers crossed. But Jesus says that every oath is binding.

23 "Woe to you, teachers of the law and Pharisees, you hypocrites! You give a tenth of your spices—mint, dill and cumin. But you have neglected the more important matters of the law—justice, mercy and faithfulness. You should have practiced the latter, without neglecting the former. **24** You blind guides! You strain out a gnat but swallow a camel.

The Pharisees were obsessed over trivialities, but ignored the weightier matters that were much more important. Jesus gives a ridiculous and humorous comparison about straining out gnats and swallowing camels. (To be kosher they had to drain the blood and since a gnat was too small to be drained of its blood, it had to be strained or picked out of the food carefully.)

25 "Woe to you, teachers of the law and Pharisees, you hypocrites! You clean the outside of the cup and dish, but inside they are full of greed and self-indulgence. **26** Blind Pharisee! First clean the inside of the cup and dish, and then the outside also will be clean.

The Pharisees were concerned with their outward appearance, but their cleansing was superficial; they needed to be clean on the inside.

27 "Woe to you, teachers of the law and Pharisees, you hypocrites! You are like whitewashed tombs, which look beautiful on the outside but on the inside are full of the bones of the dead and everything unclean. **28** In the same way, on the outside you appear to people as righteous but on the inside you are full of hypocrisy and wickedness.

This sounds just like the last woe, so it must be important that Jesus again accuses them of being concerned with the outside appearance of righteousness, when they were not righteous on the inside.

29 "Woe to you, teachers of the law and Pharisees, you hypocrites! You build tombs for the prophets and decorate the graves of the righteous. **30** And you say, 'If we had lived in the days of our ancestors, we would not have taken part with them in shedding the blood of the prophets.' **31** So you testify against yourselves that you are the descendants of those who murdered the prophets. **32** Go ahead, then, and complete what your ancestors started!

In the last woe Jesus rebukes them for being the descendants of those who murdered the prophets of old. Though they claim they would not have taken part, it is obvious from their current rejection of Him that they are not guiltless.

Jesus does end His denunciation with a show of His great love. His words are harsh; He loves them and is warning them. From verses 37 – 39 I can imagine that Jesus is probably weeping (we know from Luke 19:41 that He wept as He looked at Jerusalem).

37 "Jerusalem, Jerusalem, you who kill the prophets and stone those sent to you, how often I have longed to gather your children together, as a hen gathers her chicks under her wings, and you were not willing. **38** Look, your house is left to you desolate. **39** For I tell you, you will not see me again until you say, 'Blessed is he who comes in the name of the Lord.'"

צ Tzaddi + 1st John

Our third tzaddi book is 1st John. This was written by the Apostle John around A.D. 90 and he is instructing believers about the heresies that were being spread among them. Since our key tzaddi word is **righteous** or righteousness I was interested to see if this book had a link that might appear supernatural. Here's a chart showing the occurrences of these words in all three of John's letters (1st John, 2nd John, 3rd John).

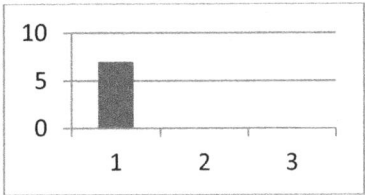

As you can see there are 7 occurrences in 1st John and none at all in 2nd and 3rd John. Furthermore, in the Gospel of John, which is 7 and a half times longer than this letter (!), there are fewer occurrences (same with Revelation, which John penned). I think God has established pretty clearly that this little book is right where it's supposed to be in the Bible.

Now, why did John write this letter? First he says he wrote it so our joy may be full (1 John 1:4), so that we may not sin (1 John 2:1), so that we may not be deceived (1 John 2:26) and so that we may know that we have eternal life (1 John 5:13). At that time, about 30 years past the crucifixion and resurrection, the Gnostics were spreading their false teachings. They denied the deity of Jesus. They believed that the spirit was good but the flesh was evil, hence Jesus could not be human and divine. They believed that Jesus was a godly teacher and that it was through His teachings that man was to evolve intellectually into a higher state of self-awareness, and that would be man's salvation. John refutes this in chapter 4: 1 – 3:

> ¹ Dear friends, do not believe every spirit, but test the spirits to see whether they are from God, because many false prophets have gone out into the world. ² This is how you can recognize the Spirit of God: Every spirit that acknowledges that Jesus Christ has come in the flesh is from God, ³ but every spirit that does not acknowledge Jesus is not from God. This is the spirit of the antichrist, which you have heard is coming and even now is already in the world.

Now you can see why John stresses that Jesus came in the flesh. The Gnostics were teaching that He could not have been God incarnate. Now look at chapter 5: 6 – 8:

> ⁶ This is the one who came by water and blood—Jesus Christ. He did not come by water only, but by water and blood. And it is the Spirit who testifies, because the Spirit is the truth.

7 For there are three that testify: **8** the Spirit, the water and the blood; and the three are in agreement.

There's a lot of discussion among Biblical scholars as to just what is meant by the water and the blood. Knowing, however, that he was repudiating the Gnostic influence it seems obvious to me that the water is an emblem of his baptism as a human man and the blood stands for his atoning death as the Son of God. Tying the two together argues against the Gnostics' false teaching that God could not take on the evil flesh.

Now let's look at this little book as a whole. Chapters 1 and 2 present God as Light, 3 and 4 present God as Love, and the last chapter shows God as Life. Light, Love, Life.

Read 1 John 1: 5 – 7 and 2: 8 – 10 **Light** (I took a yellow highlighter to this section – yes, in my Bible.)

5 This is the message we have heard from him and declare to you: God is **light**; in him there is no darkness at all. **6** If we claim to have fellowship with him and yet walk in the darkness, we lie and do not live out the truth. **7** But if we walk in the **light**, as he is in the **light**, we have fellowship with one another, and the blood of Jesus, his Son, purifies us from all sin.

8 Yet I am writing you a new command; its truth is seen in him and in you, because the darkness is passing and the true **light** is already shining.
9 Anyone who claims to be in the **light** but hates a brother or sister is still in the darkness. **10** Anyone who loves their brother and sister lives in the **light**, and there is nothing in them to make them stumble.

Read 1 John 3: 1, 11, 14, 16 – 18, 23, and 4: 7 – 12, 16 – 21. **Love**

1 See what great **love** the Father has lavished on us, that we should be called children of God! And that is what we are! The reason the world does not know us is that it did not know him.
11 For this is the message you heard from the beginning: We should **love** one another.
14 We know that we have passed from death to life, because we **love** each other. Anyone who does not **love** remains in death.
16 This is how we know what **love** is: Jesus Christ laid down his life for us. And we ought to lay down our lives for our brothers and sisters. **17** If anyone has material possessions and sees a brother or sister in need but has no pity on them, how can the **love** of God be in that person? **18** Dear children, let us not **love** with words or speech but with actions and in truth.
23 And this is his command: to believe in the name of his Son, Jesus Christ, and to **love** one another as he commanded us.
7 Dear friends, let us **love** one another, for **love** comes from God. Everyone who **loves** has been born of God and knows God. **8** Whoever does not **love** does not know God, because God is **love**. **9** This is how God showed his **love** among us: He sent his one and only Son into the world that we might live through him. **10** This is **love**: not that we **loved** God, but that he **loved** us and sent his Son as an atoning sacrifice for our sins. **11** Dear friends, since God so

loved us, we also ought to **love** one another. ¹² No one has ever seen God; but if we **love** one another, God lives in us and his **love** is made complete in us.

¹⁶ And so we know and rely on the **love** God has for us.

God is **love**. Whoever lives in **love** lives in God, and God in them. ¹⁷ This is how **love** is made complete among us so that we will have confidence on the day of judgment: In this world we are like Jesus. ¹⁸ There is no fear in **love**. But perfect **love** drives out fear, because fear has to do with punishment. The one who fears is not made perfect in **love**.

¹⁹ We **love** because he first **loved** us. ²⁰ Whoever claims to **love** God yet hates a brother or sister is a liar. For whoever does not **love** their brother and sister, whom they have seen, cannot **love** God, whom they have not seen. ²¹ And he has given us this command: Anyone who **loves** God must also **love** their brother and sister.

Read 1 John 5: 11 – 13, 20 **Life**

¹¹ And this is the testimony: God has given us eternal **life**, and this **life** is in his Son. ¹² Whoever has the Son has **life**; whoever does not have the Son of God does not have **life**. ¹³ I write these things to you who believe in the name of the Son of God so that you may know that you have eternal **life**.

²⁰ We know also that the Son of God has come and has given us understanding, so that we may know him who is true. And we are in him who is true by being in his Son Jesus Christ. He is the true God and eternal **life**.

Now let's look at how John ends his letter. It is very abrupt, but to the point. "Dear children, keep yourselves from idols." Idols at that time were the graven images of pagan gods. Do we have those today? If we keep ourselves from idols (anything that keeps us from putting God first) we are keeping ourselves **righteous**.

To conclude: in the book of Job we had the Wisdom of God's **Righteousness**, in Matthew the Gospel of God's **Righteousness** and in 1st John the Practice of God's **Righteousness**.

Chapter 19 Quph

Aleph	1. Genesis	23. Isaiah	45. Romans
Bet	2. Exodus	24. Jeremiah	46. 1st Corinthians
Gimel	3. Leviticus	25. Lamentations	47. 2nd Corinthians
Dalet	4. Numbers	26. Ezekiel	48. Galatians
Hey	5. Deuteronomy	27. Daniel	49. Ephesians
Vav	6. Joshua	28. Hosea	50. Philippians
Zayin	7. Judges	29. Joel	51. Colossians
Het	8. Ruth	30. Amos	52. 1st Thessalonians
Tet	9. 1st Samuel	31. Obadiah	53. 2nd Thessalonians
Yod	10. 2nd Samuel	32. Jonah	54. 1st Timothy
Kaph	11. 1st Kings	33. Micah	55. 2nd Timothy
Lamed	12. 2nd Kings	34. Nahum	56. Titus
Mem	13. 1st Chronicles	35. Habakkuk	57. Philemon
Nun	14. 2nd Chronicles	36. Zephaniah	58. Hebrews
Samek	15. Ezra	37. Haggai	59. James
Ayin	16. Nehemiah	38. Zechariah	60. 1st Peter
Pey	17. Esther	39. Malachi	61. 2nd Peter
Tzaddi	18. Job	40. Matthew	62. 1st John
Quph	**19. *Psalms***	**41. *Mark***	**63. *2nd John***
Resh	20. Proverbs	42. Luke	64. 3rd John
Shin	21. Ecclesiastes	43. John	65. Jude
Tav	22. Song of Songs	44. Acts	66. Revelation

ק

Quph + Psalms

The 19th Hebrew letter is pronounced quph (koof). It's a lot like our letter Q. Its symbolic meaning is the eye of a needle and in both the Hebrew and the English letters you should be able to visualize the round opening of the needle and a thread going through. This is easier to see in this English font:

Q.

and in this ancient Hebrew pictograph:

ዋ.

The three quph books are Psalms, Mark and 2nd John.

The Psalms were written by various authors spanning a time period of almost 1000 years. Among the authors were Moses, David and Solomon, and also priests or Levites who were responsible for providing music for sanctuary worship during David's reign. Fifty of the psalms designate no specific person as author. The oldest psalm in the collection is probably Psalm 90, the prayer of Moses and the latest psalm is probably 137, a song of mourning written when the Israelites were being held captive. The book of Psalms is a compilation of prayers, poems, and hymns that focus on praising and adoring God. Some were used in worship services of ancient Israel. According to Talmudic tradition, psalms were sung by the Levites immediately after the daily pouring of the wine offering. The word Psalm comes from the Greek word psalmoi meaning pious songs. The Hebrew title is Tehilim which means "hymns of praise." There are several types of Psalms, among them are hymns of praise, instructional hymns, and funeral songs.

The New Testament illustrates virtually the whole history of salvation in the light of the Psalms.

Jesus is the Son of God: Psalm 2:7, 22:10:

[7] I will proclaim the LORD's decree: He said to me, "You are my son; today I have become your father.
[10] From birth I was cast on you; from my mother's womb you have been my God.

Jesus is the Shepherd: Psalm 23:

[1] The LORD is my shepherd, I lack nothing.
[2] He makes me lie down in green pastures, he leads me beside quiet waters,
[3] he refreshes my soul. He guides me along the right paths for his name's sake.
[4] Even though I walk through the darkest valley, I will fear no evil, for you are with me; your rod and your staff, they comfort me.
[5] You prepare a table before me in the presence of my enemies. You anoint my head with oil; my cup overflows.

⁶ Surely your goodness and love will follow me all the days of my life, and I will dwell in the house of the LORD forever.

Jesus spoke in parables: Psalm 78:2:

² I will open my mouth with a parable; I will utter hidden things, things from of old—

Jesus calmed the storm: Psalm 89:9:

⁹ You rule over the surging sea; when its waves mount up, you still them.

Jesus was rejected: Psalm 69:8, 20:

⁸ I am a foreigner to my own family, a stranger to my own mother's children;
²⁰ Scorn has broken my heart and has left me helpless;
I looked for sympathy, but there was none, for comforters, but I found none.

Jesus was conspired against: Psalm 31:13:

¹³ For I hear many whispering, "Terror on every side!"
They conspire against me and plot to take my life.

Jesus was betrayed by Judas: Psalm 41:9, 55: 12 – 14:

⁹ Even my close friend, someone I trusted, one who shared my bread, has turned against me.
¹² If an enemy were insulting me, I could endure it;
if a foe were rising against me, I could hide.
¹³ But it is you, a man like myself, my companion, my close friend,
¹⁴ with whom I once enjoyed sweet fellowship at the house of God, as we walked about among the worshipers.

Jesus was crucified: Psalm 22:1,2,7,8, Psalm 89:50-51, 69:21, Psalm 22:14-18, 129:3, Psalm 34:20:

¹ My God, my God, why have you forsaken me?
Why are you so far from saving me,
so far from my cries of anguish?
² My God, I cry out by day, but you do not answer,
by night, but I find no rest.
⁷ All who see me mock me;
they hurl insults, shaking their heads.
⁸ "He trusts in the LORD," they say,
"let the LORD rescue him.

Let him deliver him,
   since he delights in him."
⁵⁰ Remember, Lord, how your servant has been mocked, how I bear in my heart the taunts of all the nations,
⁵¹ the taunts with which your enemies, LORD, have mocked,
   with which they have mocked every step of your anointed one.
²¹ They put gall in my food
   and gave me vinegar for my thirst.
¹⁴ I am poured out like water, and all my bones are out of joint. My heart has turned to wax; it has melted within me.
¹⁵ My mouth is dried up like a potsherd, and my tongue sticks to the roof of my mouth; you lay me in the dust of death.
¹⁶ Dogs surround me, a pack of villains encircles me; they pierce my hands and my feet.
¹⁷ All my bones are on display; people stare and gloat over me.
¹⁸ They divide my clothes among them and cast lots for my garment.
³ Plowmen have plowed my back and made their furrows long.
²⁰ he protects all his bones, not one of them will be broken.

Jesus conquered death: Psalm 16:10, Psalm 68: 18, Psalm 118: 20, Psalm 110:1, Psalm 80:17:

¹⁰ because you will not abandon me to the realm of the dead, nor will you let your faithful one see decay.
¹⁸ When you ascended on high, you took many captives;
²² The stone the builders rejected has become the cornerstone
¹ The LORD says to my lord: "Sit at my right hand until I make your enemies a footstool for your feet."
¹⁷ Let your hand rest on the man at your right hand, the son of man you have raised up for yourself.

Jesus is the King of Righteousness: Psalm 110:4:

⁴ The LORD has sworn and will not change his mind: "You are a priest forever, in the order of Melchizedek."

Jesus will judge the nations: Psalm 89: 3 – 5:

³ You said, "I have made a covenant with my chosen one, I have sworn to David my servant,
⁴ 'I will establish your line forever and make your throne firm through all generations.'"
⁵ The heavens praise your wonders, LORD, your faithfulness too, in the assembly of the holy ones.

His reign is eternal: Psalm 89: 35 – 37:

³⁵ Once for all, I have sworn by my holiness— and I will not lie to David—

³⁶ that his line will continue forever and his throne endure before me like the sun;
³⁷ it will be established forever like the moon, the faithful witness in the sky."

He will rule the Earth: Psalm 72: 8, 11:

⁸ May he rule from sea to sea and from the River to the ends of the earth.
¹¹ May all kings bow down to him and all nations serve him.

He will judge the Earth: Psalm 98:9, 50:4:

⁹ let them sing before the LORD, for he comes to judge the earth. He will judge the world in righteousness and the peoples with equity.
⁴ He summons the heavens above, and the earth, that he may judge his people

It's pretty clear that we can look to the Psalms for prophecies of Christ.
In our second quph book, Mark, Jesus says in 14:49

⁴⁹ Every day I was with you, teaching in the temple courts, and you did not arrest me. But the Scriptures must be fulfilled."

Luke quotes Jesus more specifically in 24:44:

⁴⁴ He said to them, "This is what I told you while I was still with you: Everything must be fulfilled that is written about me in the Law of Moses, the Prophets and the Psalms."

The New Testament as a whole has 224 separate passages from 103 different psalms. Some passages appear in multiple places making a total of 280 psalm quotations in the New Testament.

We have been looking at the acrostic verses in Psalms before studying each book of scripture because they are linked to each Hebrew letter and to each book of scripture in a supernaturally amazing relationship. To explain again, the acrostic (or alphabetic) verses are when the writer has used the letters of the Hebrew alphabet as the initial letters for a sequence of verses. Starting each verse or stanza with the next consecutive letter may have been an easier way of memorizing Scripture, but it is also an astounding proof that God has ordered the books of the Bible to fit with the key alphabetic words revealed in these special verses. Acrostics occur in Psalms 111 and 112, where each letter begins a line; in Psalms 25, 34, and 145, where each letter begins a verse; and in Psalm 37, where each letter begins every other whole verse with 4 exceptions where the letter starts 1 or 3 verses for a total of 40 verses. Psalm 119 is the most elaborate manifestation of the acrostic method where, in each section of eight verses, the same opening letter is used, and the twenty-two sections of the psalm move through the Hebrew alphabet, letter after letter. There are 176 verses, 8 verses for each of the 22 Hebrew letters. The first 8 verses each start with the Hebrew letter Aleph, the next 8 with Bet and so on through the alphabet (alephbet). We have lost the amazing beauty of the psalm in translation.

The quph verses in Psalm 34, Psalm 145 and Lamentations 3 all start with qarab (call) just like Psalm 119: 150 and 151. Other quph words from the acrostics are quwm (arise), qowl (voice), qarab (draw near), qal (swift), qadowsh (holy), qeren (horn), and qavah (wait). At first I thought these were random words, but when read in any order there seems to be a little story here. We're going to see the quph word qal (swift) play a role in our next 2 quph books, Mark and 2nd John.

ק

Quph + Mark

Our second quph book is the Gospel of Mark, the shortest Gospel. Mark belonged to a family who lived in Jerusalem where he became a Christian. He worked with both Paul and Peter. His gospel is unique because it emphasizes Jesus' actions more than His teachings, moving quickly from one episode to another. Thus we get our connection to the quph word qal (swift). Mark does not begin with a genealogy as Matthew did, because he is writing for the Gentiles who would not care about His lineage. He starts with John the Baptist preparing the way, then Jesus' baptism and the calling of the first disciples. Then Mark gives us healings and parables and miracles. We follow Our Lord's journeys through Galilee, the surrounding areas, and then to Judea at a rapid pace. In fact, the swiftness is revealed in the actually telling of the events. An example of this unique swiftness presents itself early on in chapter 1, verses 10 – 14 (this is from Young's Literal Translation so you can see the fast pace exactly as it was written):

[9]**And it came to pass** in those days, Jesus came from Nazareth of Galilee, **and** was baptized by John at the Jordan;

[10]**and immediately** coming up from the water, he saw the heavens dividing, **and** the Spirit as a dove coming down upon him;

[11]**and a voice came** out of the heavens, `Thou art My Son -- the Beloved, in whom I did delight.'

[12]**And immediately** doth the Spirit put him forth to the wilderness,

[13]**and he was there** in the wilderness forty days, being tempted by the Adversary, **and** he was with the beasts, **and** the messengers were ministering to him.

Whew! Notice the punctuation? Just two sentences. Now let's compare other nearly identical scenes recorded in Matthew, Mark and Luke and see how Mark uses a particularly "swift" word:

1) The Healing of the Demon-possessed man – the demon (Legion) sent into a herd of pigs:

Matthew 8:28: [28] When he arrived at the other side in the region of the Gadarenes, two demon-possessed men coming from the tombs met him.

Mark 5:6: [6] When he saw Jesus from a distance, he **ran** and fell on his knees in front of him.

Luke 8: 27: [27] When Jesus stepped ashore, he was met by a demon-possessed man from the town.

2) The Five Thousand Fed

Matthew 14:13: [13] When Jesus heard what had happened, he withdrew by boat privately to a solitary place. Hearing of this, the crowds followed him on foot from the towns.

Mark 6:33: **33** But many who saw them leaving recognized them and **ran** on foot from all the towns and got there ahead of them.

Luke 9:11: **11** but the crowds learned about it and followed him. He welcomed them and spoke to them about the kingdom of God, and healed those who needed healing.

3) Healings at Gennesaret

Matthew 14: 34-36: **34** When they had crossed over, they landed at Gennesaret. **35** And when the men of that place recognized Jesus, they sent word to all the surrounding country. People brought all their sick to him **36** and begged him to let the sick just touch the edge of his cloak, and all who touched it were healed.

Mark 6:54-56: **54** As soon as they got out of the boat, people recognized Jesus. **55** They **ran** throughout that whole region and carried the sick on mats to wherever they heard he was. **56** And wherever he went—into villages, towns or countryside—they placed the sick in the marketplaces. They begged him to let them touch even the edge of his cloak, and all who touched it were healed.

4) Before the Healing of a Boy with an Evil Spirit

Matthew 17:14: **14** When they came to the crowd, a man approached Jesus and knelt before him.

Mark 9:15: **15** As soon as all the people saw Jesus, they were overwhelmed with wonder and **ran** to greet him.

Luke 9:37: **37** The next day, when they came down from the mountain, a large crowd met him.

5) The Rich Young Man

Matthew 19:16: **16** Just then a man came up to Jesus and asked, "Teacher, what good thing must I do to get eternal life?"

Mark 10:17: **17** As Jesus started on his way, a man **ran** up to him and fell on his knees before him. "Good teacher," he asked, "what must I do to inherit eternal life?"

Luke 18:18: **18** A certain ruler asked him, "Good teacher, what must I do to inherit eternal life?"

In all of these examples Mark shows the speed and swiftness unique to this book lining up supernaturally with the Hebrew letter quph.

Mark is unique in that he kept a few Hebrew words and simply transliterated them into Greek. Naturally, these are words that begin with quph. In Mark 5:41 we find:

41 He took her by the hand and said to her, *"Talitha koum!"* (which means "Little girl, I say to you, get up!"). **42** Immediately the girl stood up and began to walk around (she was twelve years old). At this they were completely astonished. **43** He gave strict orders not to let anyone know about this, and told them to give her something to eat.

Some translations spell it cumi, but here in the NIV we have a closer approximation of the actual Hebrew word quwm (arise). Remember, it's one of the words from the acrostic verses. How marvelous that Mark would use it here.

Now read Mark 7:10-13:

10 For Moses said, 'Honor your father and mother,' and, 'Anyone who curses their father or mother is to be put to death.' **11** But you say that if anyone declares that what might have been used to help their father or mother is Corban (that is, devoted to God)— **12** then you no longer let them do anything for their father or mother. **13** Thus you nullify the word of God by your tradition that you have handed down. And you do many things like that."

What is this word "Corban?" Mark has transliterated another Hebrew word. Corban or qorban means offering. In Temple times they labeled vessels with the letter quph to mark that the contents were sacred. The root of the word qorban is from the verb which means "to come close" or "to bring." Rabbis explain that the sacrifices, the qorban, brought worshippers closer to God.

Now let's link our first quph book, Psalms, to Mark. In Psalms 89 and 107 the Psalmist declares that God rules the raging sea and calms the waves. In Mark 4:39 we find Jesus rebuking the wind and sea and bringing about a great calm.

39 He got up, rebuked the wind and said to the waves, "Quiet! Be still!" Then the wind died down and it was completely calm.

We can find the calming of the sea recorded in Matthew and Luke, too, however in Mark we are told Jesus' words as well and therefore we find another cool, or rather qol (voice), link to the letter quph.

ק

Quph + 2nd John

Our third quph book is 2nd John. This is an extremely small book, just 13 verses. That smallness definitely links to the letter quph which means eye of a needle – something truly small. Also keeping with the quph word **swift** we should expect to find something to do with running as in the book of Mark.

2nd John was most likely written by the Apostle John sometime between A.D. 85 and A.D. 95. He begins the letter with an identification of himself as "the elder". The Greek word generally means old, and John would be old at this time, but it also means leader and here it probably means leader over several churches in Ephesus. John continues by identifying that he is writing to a chosen or elect lady and her children. Most scholars interpret the Greek in one of two ways: either there was a specific lady with children or saying "the lady" is a secret way of writing to the church. The children therefore would be the members of the church. Either way he is writing to Christians.

The tiny book can be summarized as dealing with Truth and Love (vs. 1 – 3), Truth and How to Live (vs. 4 – 6), Truth and Error (vs. 7 – 11) and a Final Greeting (vs. 12 – 13).

First read verses 1 – 3 (truth and love):

¹ The elder,
  To the lady chosen by God and to her children, whom I love in the truth—and not I only, but also all who know the truth— ² because of the truth, which lives in us and will be with us forever:
  ³ Grace, mercy and peace from God the Father and from Jesus Christ, the Father's Son, will be with us in truth and love.

First of all we have already identified the elder as John and the lady and her children as Christians, now notice that he says he loves them "in the truth" that means he truly loves other Christians and so do all who know the truth. Look, he next says that the TRUTH is in us and will be with us forever.

In verse 3 he mentions three things that will be with us in truth and love. What are they? Now notice the order because that's important. Grace first, then mercy, followed by peace. That's the only order you can have. Think about it – grace is first because in it is the revelation of salvation through Christ, the Incarnate Word. Mercy is God's kindness and goodwill toward us who are miserable and afflicted, and He shows His desire to redeem us. Then, having accepted Christ, we are secure in God's love and that brings peace. Grace before mercy before peace.

Now read verses 4 - 6 (truth and how to live):

⁴ It has given me great joy to find some of your children walking in the truth, just as the Father commanded us. ⁵ And now, dear lady, I am not writing you a new command but one we have had from the beginning. I ask that we love one another. ⁶ And this is love: that we

walk in obedience to his commands. As you have heard from the beginning, his command is that you walk in love.

    Verse 4 sounds like John might be saying that only some of the people in the church to which he's writing are walking in the truth, but in the original and literal translations it is clear that what he means is that, of the people he has met from there, those people were walking in the truth. He writes then that he is reiterating a command they have had from the beginning and he asks that they love one another. Would it surprise you to know that the word "love" appears almost exactly the same number of times in both the Old and New Testaments? (Approximately 275 times in each testament) Verse 6 is the key verse of this little letter as John defines love that is commanded: walk in obedience to God's commands. Think about that. Walk in obedience to God's commands. By using the verb walk he is saying that we need to take action and put our love of God into practice. The second half of the verse reemphasizes it – walk in love.
    Look at verses 7 – 11 (truth and error):

7 I say this because many deceivers, who do not acknowledge Jesus Christ as coming in the flesh, have gone out into the world. Any such person is the deceiver and the antichrist. **8** Watch out that you do not lose what we have worked for, but that you may be rewarded fully. **9** Anyone who runs ahead and does not continue in the teaching of Christ does not have God; whoever continues in the teaching has both the Father and the Son. **10** If anyone comes to you and does not bring this teaching, do not take them into your house or welcome them. **11** Anyone who welcomes them shares in their wicked work.

    Now we've gotten to the crux of the problem, the reason why John wrote this epistle. There were deceivers, false teachers, who were preaching that Jesus did not come in human flesh. I guess all the warnings given in the previous epistle weren't enough and there were still antichrists among them. Now look again at verse 9. Earlier John directed them to "walk in love", but in verse 9 we see that some have "run ahead" and are not continuing in Christ's teachings. Here we have a direct connection with our quph word qal which means "swift." I told you we should expect to find it. Remember how there were several verses in Mark that included the word "ran" when parallel verses in the other Gospels did not? Now, here, in this teeny tiny book we have this term included. Actually, the Greek is literally translated here as "transgressing," though Greek scholars present the argument that this text means "goes beyond the limits of Christian doctrine." Look at how strict John is about how we are to treat those who "run ahead" deceiving: do not take him into your house or welcome him! What will happen if you do? See verse 11 above.
    Final greetings are in the last two verses:

12 I have much to write to you, but I do not want to use paper and ink. Instead, I hope to visit you and talk with you face to face, so that our joy may be complete.
13 The children of your sister, who is chosen by God, send their greetings.

John mentions paper and ink. The Jews wrote on many things such as leaves, pomegranate rinds, animal skins and tablets. Tablets were interesting as they were made of thin pieces of wood strung together and then covered with papyrus or wax. Papyrus was a smooth reed with a large stalk containing pith. The pith was cut into strips, assembled in crosswise layers that were pasted together and then pressed tightly together under pressure. The ink was made from soot or vegetable or mineral matter. They sometimes colored them red or gold, but here we know he used black because the word for ink here is "melanov" which means "that which is black".

Why doesn't he want to use paper and ink? Because he hopes to visit and talk face to face.

2nd John ends with greetings from "your chosen sister". It is curious that this is the only book in the whole Bible that is addressed to a woman and John does so in the opening and the closing. It's quite possible that by using these phrases he is being secretive in case the letter falls into the wrong hands.

In Mark 10: 25 Jesus says that it's easier for a camel to go through the eye of a needle than for a rich man to enter heaven. Later He says that with God all things are possible. In light of learning about these Hebrew letters I wonder if He might have been straight forwardly talking about the letter gimel that represents a camel and this letter quph that represents the eye of a needle and they just missed it. What do you think?

Chapter 20 Resh

Aleph	1. Genesis	23. Isaiah	45. Romans		
Bet	2. Exodus	24. Jeremiah	46. 1st Corinthians		
Gimel	3. Leviticus	25. Lamentations	47. 2nd Corinthians		
Dalet	4. Numbers	26. Ezekiel	48. Galatians		
Hey	5. Deuteronomy	27. Daniel	49. Ephesians		
Vav	6. Joshua	28. Hosea	50. Philippians		
Zayin	7. Judges	29. Joel	51. Colossians		
Het	8. Ruth	30. Amos	52. 1st Thessalonians		
Tet	9. 1st Samuel	31. Obadiah	53. 2nd Thessalonians		
Yod	10. 2nd Samuel	32. Jonah	54. 1st Timothy		
Kaph	11. 1st Kings	33. Micah	55. 2nd Timothy		
Lamed	12. 2nd Kings	34. Nahum	56. Titus		
Mem	13. 1st Chronicles	35. Habakkuk	57. Philemon		
Nun	14. 2nd Chronicles	36. Zephaniah	58. Hebrews		
Samek	15. Ezra	37. Haggai	59. James		
Ayin	16. Nehemiah	38. Zechariah	60. 1st Peter		
Pey	17. Esther	39. Malachi	61. 2nd Peter		
Tzaddi	18. Job	40. Matthew	62. 1st John		
Quph	19. Psalms	41. Mark	63. 2nd John		
Resh	*20. Proverbs*	*42. Luke*	*64. 3rd John*		
Shin	21. Ecclesiastes	43. John	65. Jude		
Tav	22. Song of Songs	44. Acts	66. Revelation		

ר

Resh + Proverbs
The name of the 20th Hebrew letter is a variation of the common Hebrew word for **head**. You may have heard of the Jewish New Year called Rosh Hashanah, meaning "head of the year." (The first of Tishrei, 5782, is September 7, 2021.) If we look for the word head in our biggest acrostic Psalm, 119, we find it in verse 160:

¹⁶⁰Thy word is true from the beginning *(rosh – beginning, **head**):* and every one of thy righteous judgments endureth for ever. (KJV)

In Psalm 111: 10 we read:

¹⁰ The fear of the LORD is the beginning *(reshith – beginning, principal part, **head**)* of wisdom;
  all who follow his precepts have good understanding. To him belongs eternal praise.

Other key resh words that appear as the first word in alphabetic verses are mercy, wickedness and look upon (consider, see). I'm excited to see how the Lord has worked these words into the corresponding resh books of Proverbs, Luke and 3rd John.

Proverbs in the Hebrew bible is mishleh which, of course, is the first word in this book. It comes from the word mashal which conveys a sense of superiority in thought as well as being the root word for governing or ruling. I read the first line in this book in Hebrew and discovered that I had already learned every word here so I didn't need the translation. The first two words say "mishleh shlomo" or "the best part of Solomon." What was the best part of Solomon? His wisdom, his superiority in thought. The book got its English name from the Latin *proverbium*, "a common saying," from the parts *pro* "forth" and *verbum* "word" – putting words forth – I should have figured that out on my own. We've come to understand proverbs as concise, to the point sayings that hold the wisdom of Solomon. The word wisdom, in fact, appears 53 times in this book, more than twice as many times as any of the other books considered wisdom books.

Proverbs has six main sections: Solomon's wise lessons (chapters 1 – 9), Solomon's wise words (chapters 10 – 22), 30 wise lessons (chapters 22 – 24), more wise words of Solomon (chapters 25 - 29), the puzzles of Agur and Lemuel (chapters 30 – 31) and a poem about a perfect wife (chapter 31).

Let's start at the beginning and read the first 7 verses of chapter 1. I'll use the KJV because it's closer to the Hebrew:

¹The proverbs of Solomon the son of David, king of Israel;
²To know wisdom and instruction; to perceive the words of understanding;
³To receive the instruction of wisdom, justice, and judgment, and equity;
⁴To give subtilty to the simple, to the young man knowledge and discretion.

⁵A wise man will hear, and will increase learning; and a man of understanding shall attain unto wise counsels:
⁶To understand a proverb, and the interpretation; the words of the wise, and their dark sayings.
⁷The fear of the LORD is the beginning of knowledge: but fools despise wisdom and instruction.

Read that last verse again. Did you notice that this sounds a lot like the alphabetic verse from Psalm 111: 10? Wow, God was pretty obvious this time as he linked up this book with that resh verse. Now, let's look at the reasons we should read these proverbs: 1) to know wisdom and instruction (primarily through the father or a father figure teacher, usually orally, but it can be by the rod); 2) to perceive words of understanding (that understanding is knowledge of the Holy One); 3) to receive instruction in four areas: wisdom, justice (righteousness), judgment (verdict) and equity (uprightness); 4) to give subtlety to the simple (that is, teaching prudence/wisdom to the simple); 5) giving knowledge and discretion (advisement) to the young.

Now let's look at the very first warning, read verses 8 and 9 (Young's Literal Translation):

⁸Hear, my son, the instruction of thy father, And leave not the law of thy mother,
⁹For a graceful wreath [are] they to thy head, And chains to thy neck.

Well, it didn't take long for the resh word **head** to show up, did it?
Let's look at the benefits of wisdom according to the book of Proverbs.
Read 2: 12 – 15:

¹² Wisdom will save you from the ways of wicked men,
from men whose words are perverse,
¹³ who have left the straight paths
to walk in dark ways,
¹⁴ who delight in doing wrong
and rejoice in the perverseness of evil,
¹⁵ whose paths are crooked
and who are devious in their ways.

Ooooh. A lot of strong words there. I definitely want to be saved from the "ways of wicked men"; nobody's going to scam me; I'm not going to get pulled into some stupid prank or dangerous activity – teenagers take note.
Read 3: 1 – 2:

¹ My son, do not forget my teaching,
but keep my commands in your heart,
² for they will prolong your life many years
and bring you peace and prosperity.

Did you catch the blessing that comes with remembering the Lord's teaching and command? Long life. Peace. Prosperity.
Read 3: 5 – 6:

5 Trust in the LORD with all your heart
and lean not on your own understanding;
6 in all your ways submit to him,
and he will make your paths straight.

We don't like to submit to anyone, but let's submit to the Lord. Trust Him, don't trust yourself.
Read 4: 7:

7 The beginning of wisdom is this: Get wisdom.
Though it cost all you have, get understanding.

This is so simple yet complex at the same time. The beginning of wisdom is that you need to understand that you don't have it and it's a good thing to go and get it. As soon as you realize that you need to get wisdom you're at the beginning of wisdom. Keep it up.

This next verse I claimed as my "life verse" long before I started teaching. Proverbs 4: 13:

13 Hold on to instruction, do not let it go;
guard it well, for it is your life.

Everybody should have a "life verse." For me, I spent my whole career and beyond dedicated to teaching so I did "hold on to instruction." It was (and still is) my life. It was extra easy for me to remember where to find this verse because 4:13 is 4/13, my birthday. Isn't God marvelous?
Read 6: 16 – 19:

16 There are six things the LORD hates,
seven that are detestable to him:
17 haughty eyes,
a lying tongue,
hands that shed innocent blood,
18 a heart that devises wicked schemes,
feet that are quick to rush into evil,
19 a false witness who pours out lies
and a person who stirs up conflict in the community.

Come on, you have to read that more than once. List the 7 things God hates. Having haughty eyes implies a haughty or proud demeanor. Don't be proud. Don't lie. Don't murder. Don't think up evil plans. Don't follow your friends into evil goings-on. Don't be a false witness (no more lying, if you didn't get number 2). Don't stir up problems.

Read 9: 10:

10 The fear of the LORD is the beginning of wisdom,
and knowledge of the Holy One is understanding.

Again, "fear" of the Lord means you need to revere, honor, and be in awe of Him. Don't be foolish, be wise. The beginning of wisdom is to worship, respect and venerate the Lord.

Read 25: 6 – 7:

6 Do not exalt yourself in the king's presence,
and do not claim a place among his great men;
7 it is better for him to say to you, "Come up here,"
than for him to humiliate you before his nobles.

Do you recognize this situation? Here is Jesus' parable of humility at the table:

7 When he noticed how the guests picked the places of honor at the table, he told them this parable: **8** "When someone invites you to a wedding feast, do not take the place of honor, for a person more distinguished than you may have been invited. **9** If so, the host who invited both of you will come and say to you, 'Give this person your seat.' Then, humiliated, you will have to take the least important place. **10** But when you are invited, take the lowest place, so that when your host comes, he will say to you, 'Friend, move up to a better place.' Then you will be honored in the presence of all the other guests. **11** For all those who exalt themselves will be humbled, and those who humble themselves will be exalted."

How wonderful that Jesus connected this story, found only in Luke's gospel, chapter 14, to Proverbs as both are resh books.

The last 22 verses of the last chapter in Proverbs are acrostic verses, following the Hebrew letters in order. It's kind of like God is putting his seal on this book by ending it with his alphabet. Interestingly, this section is about the perfect or noble wife. Read chapter 31: 10 – 31 and see what you should look for in a wife (if you're a man) or how you should behave (if you're a woman). Here's what I got out of it:

1) I am very valuable if I have a noble character and my husband will have confidence in me.
2) I should try not to harm anyone or anything.
3) I should be a hard (and eager) worker and capably manage our household.
3) I should be generous.
4) I don't have to shovel the snow. (Really, my husband even pointed that out to me. Verse 21.)
5) I should keep up a cheerful attitude.

6) I should speak with wisdom and keep faithful instruction on my tongue (trying to do that here, folks).
7) I'm not going to keep my looks so I should concentrate on fearing the Lord.

There are so many wise sayings in this wonderful book that you should try to read from Proverbs every day.

ר

Resh + Luke

Our second resh book is Luke. Luke is our third gospel account of the life of Christ. Luke writes from a perspective different from the others because he was not an apostle, however, as a Greco-Syrian physician who traveled with St. Paul and spoke with many eyewitnesses, his accounts are accepted and authenticated. Luke was a well-educated man as evidenced by his command of the Greek language. His Latin name hints that he was probably not Jewish. Scholars believe his Gospel was written between 70 and 80 A.D.

Right away I'm going to link Luke to Proverbs, our first resh book. In my research I found instances where writers referred to Luke as the "Proverbial Gospel" so I did my own chart to see if I could corroborate this claim. I found 41 parables in all in Matthew, Mark and Luke. John doesn't have a single parable though it does contain allegories. The chart on the next page shows that there are 41 different parables, 23 in Matthew, only 9 in Mark, and the most, 29, in Luke with 17 of those being unique to this Gospel.

First I want to show you how the word parable relates to the word proverb. In Luke 4:23 we find this:

²³ Jesus said to them, "Surely you will quote this proverb to me: 'Physician, heal yourself!' And you will tell me, 'Do here in your hometown what we have heard that you did in Capernaum.'"

It's interesting first of all that Luke, the physician, uses this quotation from Jesus. Second, the word here in Greek for proverb is parabolé from which we get the word parable. You could say that all of these parables are like proverbs in that they are wise sayings. Furthermore, we find Luke describing Jesus' early life in the following two verses (Luke 2: 40, 52):

⁴⁰ And the child grew and became strong; he was filled with **wisdom**, and the grace of God was on him.
⁵² And Jesus grew in **wisdom** and stature, and in favor with God and man.

Now read these three nearly identical passages from Matthew 10: 19, 20, Mark 13: 11, 12 and Luke 21:12-15:

¹⁹ But when they arrest you, do not worry about what to say or how to say it. At that time you will be given what to say, ²⁰ for it will not be you speaking, but the Spirit of your Father speaking through you.
¹¹ Whenever you are arrested and brought to trial, do not worry beforehand about what to say. Just say whatever is given you at the time, for it is not you speaking, but the Holy Spirit.
¹² "But before all this, they will seize you and persecute you. They will hand you over to synagogues and put you in prison, and you will be brought before kings and governors, and

all on account of my name. **13** And so you will bear testimony to me. **14** But make up your mind not to worry beforehand how you will defend yourselves. **15** For I will give you words and **wisdom** that none of your adversaries will be able to resist or contradict.

Only in Luke do we find the promise of wisdom added to the story. How would Luke know that by including this he would be making a perfect link to the Old Testament book? But wait, there's more. In Matthew 23: 34 Jesus says:

34 Therefore I am sending you prophets and sages and teachers. Some of them you will kill and crucify; others you will flog in your synagogues and pursue from town to town.

But in Luke 11: 49 Jesus' words from the same speech are recorded like this:

49 Because of this, God in his **wisdom** said, 'I will send them prophets and apostles, some of whom they will kill and others they will persecute.'

Thus, Luke, or rather God, has interlocked this book with the book of Proverbs through the word wisdom.

I wondered if there were other words that would show up in greater numbers in the three resh books if I did a search. Of course they would have to be words that started with this Hebrew letter. In *The Bible Wheel* by Richard Amiel McGough words such as physician (ropheh), to heal (rapha), friend (reyah), and racham (mercy, compassion and with different vowel points womb) are given as key words that link to these three books. I chose "friend" and did a search. On the next page is my chart of what I found:

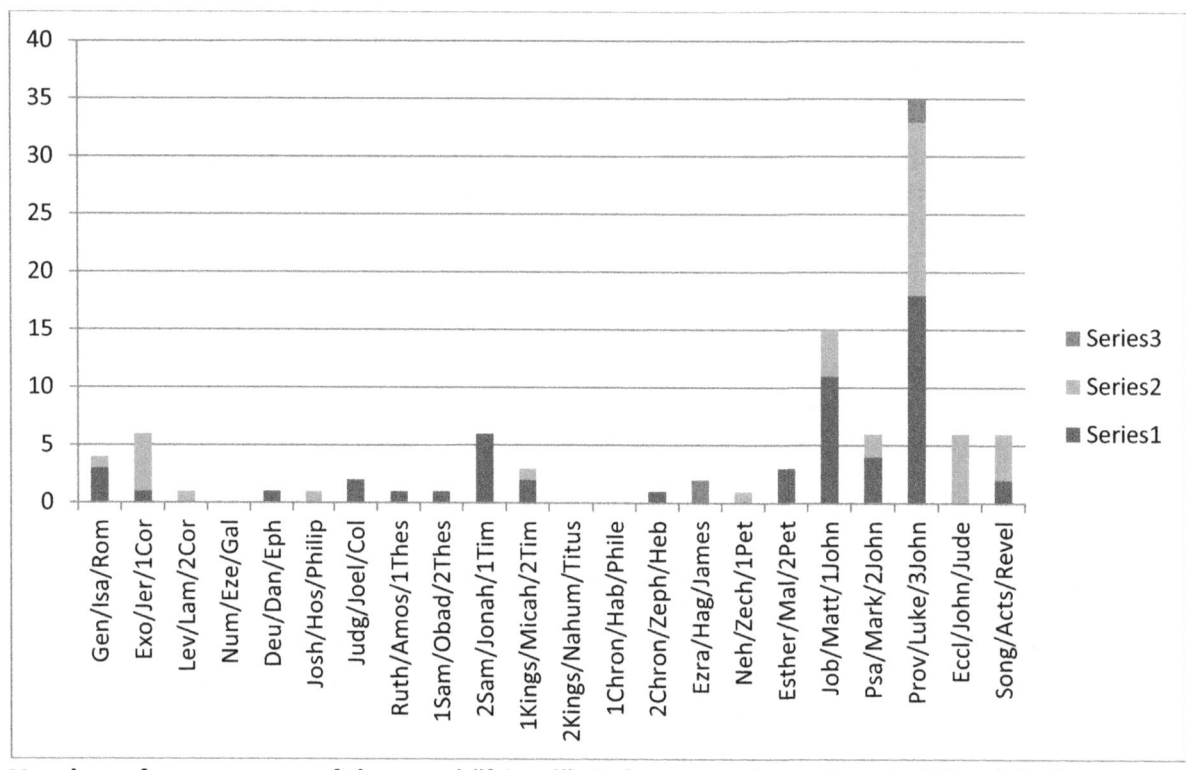

Number of occurrences of the word "friend", Hebrew reyah or, Greek philos φιλoξ

I think it's pretty amazing that these three resh books have a higher number of occurrences of the word friend than any other book in their series, i.e., of the first 22 books in the Bible Proverbs wins, of the second 22 books Luke wins and in the third 22 books teeny, tiny 3rd John ties with James – a book that is almost 8 times longer – so I think 3rd John wins.

I checked Luke for the other resh words – physician, heal, mercy and womb – and those words occurred more in Luke than any other New Testament book. I thought it was particularly interesting that mercy and womb would be written with the same Hebrew letters. Is there some deeper connection there? As I searched out answers I found that womb exemplifies a woman's attributes of warmth, a nurturing spirit, love and mercy toward her child as well as protection. When we come across the words mercy or compassion in reference to God we can infer that He has those same "womb" characteristics as a mother. English is much less descriptive than Hebrew and again we lose so much in translation.

Now, we can't cover all there is in Luke, but I thought we would look at Mary's hymn of praise, called the Magnificat in Luke 1:45-55 (with Greek definitions inserted). I suggest you read it in your own Bible first because all my insertions may be confusing upon first glance:

⁴² In a loud voice she exclaimed: "Blessed (ευλογημενη eulogeo – speak well of, invoke a benediction upon that God will use the Holy Spirit to affect her heart and life, humanity implied) are you among women, and blessed (υλογημενος eulogeo – speak well of, to praise and thank him, Godhood implied) is the child you will bear!

⁴⁵ Blessed (μακαρια makarios – extremely blessed, fortunate, well off) is she who has believed that the Lord would fulfill (τελειωσις teleios – completely) his promises (literally, things spoken to her by the Lord, hence promise is implied) to her!"

⁴⁶ And Mary said:

"My soul (ψυχη psuche – breath, by implication spirit) glorifies the Lord
⁴⁷ and my spirit (πνευμα pneuma – breath, the rational soul) rejoices in God my Savior (σωτηρι soter – deliverer, used of God and Christ) (Mary is revealing that she knows she is a sinner), see note 1
⁴⁸ for he has been mindful
of the humble state of his servant (by using the word servant she is showing her unworthiness and humility). see note 2
From now on all generations will call me blessed (μακαρια makarios – blessed, note this is a different blessed than vs.45, in reality this phrase means "they shall bless me"),
⁴⁹ for the Mighty One has done great things (μεγαλεια megaleios – magnificent things, wonderful works, great miracle) for me—
holy (αγιον hagios – sacred, including the notion of respect and veneration) is his name. see note 3
⁵⁰ His mercy (ελεος eleos – mercy, compassion, active pity) extends to those who fear (φοβουμενοις root: phobeo – to be in awe, revere, honor, to stand in awe of God, worship and adore Him) him,
from generation to generation. see note 4
⁵¹ He has performed mighty deeds with his arm;
he has scattered those who are proud in their inmost thoughts. see note 5
⁵² He has brought down rulers from their thrones
but has lifted up the humble.
⁵³ He has filled the hungry with good things see note 6
but has sent the rich away empty. see note 7
⁵⁴ He has helped his servant Israel,
remembering to be merciful
⁵⁵ to Abraham and his descendants forever,
just as he promised our ancestors."

Following are the 7 notes inserted as superscript numbers above. They all refer to Old Testament Scripture that Mary was obviously quite familiar with.

[1] Isaiah 45:21; [2] Psalm 138:6; [3] Psalm 111:9; [4] Exodus 20:6 and Psalm 103:17; [5] Genesis 11:8; [6] Psalm 107:9; [7] 1st Samuel 2:1-10.

This prayer is often called the Magnificat from the first words in Latin "magnifying" God's name. There are 19 references to God in this song as Mary magnifies Him. She tells 8 things he has done starting in verse 50. What are they? 1) extended mercy to those who fear him; 2: performed mighty deeds: 3) scattered those who are proud; 4) brought down rulers; 5) lifted up the humble; 6) filled the hungry; 7) sent away the rich; 8) helped His servant Israel.

    She certainly magnifies the Lord, doesn't she? Shouldn't you?

Resh + 3rd John

Our third resh book is 3rd John. This is the third of John's letters and the only letter to be addressed to a specific person. Before you read the entire letter through let me set up a story. Let's say there are one or two churches in a certain area and three of the best known leaders are Gaius, Diotrephes and Demetrius. Gaius is faithful in sharing the truth and he is hospitable to other traveling missionaries who, though strangers to him, are out spreading the good news. Demetrius is also well spoken of, but the other guy, Diotrephes, is maybe a little too self-centered. He loves to be first and he has a bad habit of gossiping. In fact, he has gossiped spitefully about John and John's group. He even refused to pass on one or more of John's letters. He has not been hospitable like Gaius and has turned away the missionaries and not welcomed them. Apparently Diotrephes is not a false teacher, just an ego-centric, arrogant man. Now let's read 3rd John. It's so short that I'll print the entire letter below:

¹ The elder,
   To my dear friend Gaius, whom I love in the truth.
² Dear friend, I pray that you may enjoy good health and that all may go well with you, even as your soul is getting along well. ³ It gave me great joy when some believers came and testified about your faithfulness to the truth, telling how you continue to walk in it. ⁴ I have no greater joy than to hear that my children are walking in the truth.
⁵ Dear friend, you are faithful in what you are doing for the brothers and sisters, even though they are strangers to you. ⁶ They have told the church about your love. Please send them on their way in a manner that honors God. ⁷ It was for the sake of the Name that they went out, receiving no help from the pagans. ⁸ We ought therefore to show hospitality to such people so that we may work together for the truth.
⁹ I wrote to the church, but Diotrephes, who loves to be first, will not welcome us. ¹⁰ So when I come, I will call attention to what he is doing, spreading malicious nonsense about us. Not satisfied with that, he even refuses to welcome other believers. He also stops those who want to do so and puts them out of the church.
¹¹ Dear friend, do not imitate what is evil but what is good. Anyone who does what is good is from God. Anyone who does what is evil has not seen God. ¹² Demetrius is well spoken of by everyone—and even by the truth itself. We also speak well of him, and you know that our testimony is true.
¹³ I have much to write you, but I do not want to do so with pen and ink. ¹⁴ I hope to see you soon, and we will talk face to face.
   Peace to you. The friends here send their greetings. Greet the friends there by name.

Notice how John calls Gaius his dear friend four times in this short epistle. In the original Greek the word is agapetos, which means beloved. This term conveys such great affection for him that we can assume that John thought very highly of him. What else stands out?

I thought it interesting that this letter begins as well with John saying he will pray for Gaius's health. As stated before in researching the book of Luke, the words health, heal and physician show up more in that book than any other New Testament book. In fact, when looking at the last 22 books of the Bible the word health show's up only in 3rd John, the matching resh book.

To tie it all together look at these verses from the 16th chapter of Proverbs, the 2nd resh book:

²² Prudence is a fountain of life to the prudent,
but folly brings punishment to fools.
²³ The hearts of the wise make their mouths prudent,
and their lips promote instruction.
²⁴ Gracious words are a honeycomb,
sweet to the soul and healing to the bones.

This sounds like it could have been written as a commentary on 3rd John. Surely Diotrophes will get some kind of punishment for his foolishness while Gaius, John and Demetrius, with wise hearts, speak gracious words and receive "healing to the bones."

Cool stuff I learned from the 3 resh books:
1) If you list the 66 books of the Bible in three columns Proverbs, Luke and 3rd John all line up.
2) They also line up with the 20th Hebrew letter, resh. The symbolic meaning of resh is "head." (Ever heard of Rosh Hashana? The Jewish New Year or "Head of the Year")
3) The letter resh starts the Hebrew word for friend which occurs more than twice as often in these 3 books combined than any other 3 books.
4) The Greek word for proverb is parabole from which we get parable. There are more parables in Luke than in any of the other Gospels. (John has none.)
5) Proverbs are words of wisdom. When Luke tells the same story as Matthew and Mark, Luke makes a reference to wisdom. (Luke 21:12-15, Matt. 10:19-20, Mark 13:11-12) (Luke 11:49, Matt. 23:34)
6) Luke describes Jesus (2:40, 52): And the child grew and became strong; he was filled with *wisdom*, and the grace of God was on him. And Jesus grew in *wisdom* and stature, and in favor with God and man.
7) Other Hebrew words that start with resh are physician, heal, mercy and womb which all occur more in Luke than any other New Testament book.
8) Mercy and Womb are written with the exact same Hebrew letters. Womb exemplifies a woman's attributes of warmth, a nurturing spirit, love and mercy toward her child as well as protection. When we come across the words mercy (compassion) in reference to God we can infer that He has those same "womb" characteristics as a mother. (English is so much less descriptive than Hebrew and we lose so much in translation.)
9) To connect Proverbs and Luke to the tiny letter of 3rd John we can look beyond the #3 above – that the word friend occurs many times – and see a connection with the word "health". This word appears more in Proverbs than any Old Testament book. Luke was

written by a physician. 3rd John opens with John saying he will pray for Gaius's health (the only reference to health in all 22 epistles).

I love God's word more every day.

Chapter 21 Shin

Aleph	1. Genesis	23. Isaiah	45. Romans
Bet	2. Exodus	24. Jeremiah	46. 1st Corinthians
Gimel	3. Leviticus	25. Lamentations	47. 2nd Corinthians
Dalet	4. Numbers	26. Ezekiel	48. Galatians
Hey	5. Deuteronomy	27. Daniel	49. Ephesians
Vav	6. Joshua	28. Hosea	50. Philippians
Zayin	7. Judges	29. Joel	51. Colossians
Het	8. Ruth	30. Amos	52. 1st Thessalonians
Tet	9. 1st Samuel	31. Obadiah	53. 2nd Thessalonians
Yod	10. 2nd Samuel	32. Jonah	54. 1st Timothy
Kaph	11. 1st Kings	33. Micah	55. 2nd Timothy
Lamed	12. 2nd Kings	34. Nahum	56. Titus
Mem	13. 1st Chronicles	35. Habakkuk	57. Philemon
Nun	14. 2nd Chronicles	36. Zephaniah	58. Hebrews
Samek	15. Ezra	37. Haggai	59. James
Ayin	16. Nehemiah	38. Zechariah	60. 1st Peter
Pey	17. Esther	39. Malachi	61. 2nd Peter
Tzaddi	18. Job	40. Matthew	62. 1st John
Quph	19. Psalms	41. Mark	63. 2nd John
Resh	20. Proverbs	42. Luke	64. 3rd John
Shin	***21. Ecclesiastes***	***43. John***	***65. Jude***
Tav	22. Song of Songs	44. Acts	66. Revelation

Shin + Ecclesiastes

Shin is the 21st Hebrew letter and symbolically means **tooth** since the word for tooth is "shen." Its ancient script form looked more like the jagged teeth of a grinning pumpkin. At first I thought that this was a strange word to be linked to a Hebrew letter, but as I did a search I was astonished to find "tooth" or "teeth" appearing 51 times in the Old and New Testaments combined. Teeth appear as symbols of things that bite or crush or consume.

Let's look first to the alphabetic "codes." Here is verse 10 of Psalm 112 where the last three Hebrew letters start each line, shin is the middle one:

> **10** The wicked will see and be vexed,
> they will gnash their teeth and waste away;
> the longings of the wicked will come to nothing.

It would be so nice if it translated as beautifully in English as it is in the original. Then you would see these lines starting with r, s, and t. The flow is amazing. An examination of the 8 shin verses in Psalm 119 gives us a few more words that start with this letter such as prince, peace, rejoice and hope. That is just too interesting not to repeat: prince . . . peace . . . rejoice . . . hope.

Our first shin book is Ecclesiastes. We don't know who wrote this, but tradition assigns authorship to Solomon. The word Ecclesiastes comes from the Greek word Ekklesiastes which means "speaker of a called out assembly". The Hebrew Bible calls this book Qoheleth from the word in verse 1, chapter 1, that many translations have as "preacher":

> **1** The words of the Teacher, son of David, king in Jerusalem:

or as you see here "teacher", but the original means "assembler" or "collector" of wisdom. Who was a collector of wisdom and son of David? Solomon seems to be the obvious answer. After his scandalous backsliding he made public what he learned from his experiences. Whereas in Proverbs he reveals God's wisdom, in Ecclesiastes he despairs over the complexity of life, the failure of natural wisdom and the futility of looking for truth and happiness apart from God. The major theme of the book is that without God's blessing nothing satisfies, not wisdom, power, pleasure or riches. In fact, without God those things bring disillusionment and disappointment. Solomon says it right away. Read verse 2:

> **2** "Meaningless! Meaningless!"
> says the Teacher.
> "Utterly meaningless!
> Everything is meaningless."

Many translations use the word "vanity" instead of "meaningless". Other interpretations are "worthlessness" or "emptiness." The Hebrew Bible translates this word with the word "futility." To me that really adds a feeling of helplessness. Read on and feel the futility:

> 3 What do people gain from all their labors
>   at which they toil under the sun?
> 4 Generations come and generations go,
>   but the earth remains forever.
> 5 The sun rises and the sun sets,
>   and hurries back to where it rises.
> 6 The wind blows to the south
>   and turns to the north;
> round and round it goes,
>   ever returning on its course.
> 7 All streams flow into the sea,
>   yet the sea is never full.
> To the place the streams come from,
>   there they return again.
> 8 All things are wearisome,
>   more than one can say.
> The eye never has enough of seeing,
>   nor the ear its fill of hearing.
> 9 What has been will be again,
>   what has been done will be done again;
>   there is nothing new under the sun.
> 10 Is there anything of which one can say,
>   "Look! This is something new"?
> It was here already, long ago;
>   it was here before our time.
> 11 No one remembers the former generations,
>   and even those yet to come
> will not be remembered
>   by those who follow them.
>
> 12 I, the Teacher, was king over Israel in Jerusalem. 13 I applied my mind to study and to explore by wisdom all that is done under the heavens. What a heavy burden God has laid on mankind! 14 I have seen all the things that are done under the sun; all of them are meaningless, a chasing after the wind.
>
> 15 What is crooked cannot be straightened;
>   what is lacking cannot be counted.
>
> 16 I said to myself, "Look, I have increased in wisdom more than anyone who has ruled over Jerusalem before me; I have experienced much of wisdom and knowledge." 17 Then I applied myself to the understanding of wisdom, and also of madness and folly, but I learned that this, too, is a chasing after the wind.
>
> 18 For with much wisdom comes much sorrow;
>   the more knowledge, the more grief.

Woe is me! And doesn't Solomon write eloquently? "A chasing after the wind" is such a supreme metaphor. Some translations have "a chase after wind" and old KJV bibles have "vexation of spirit." The Hebrew Bible translates it as "pursuit of wind" and footnotes that the word comes from the verb "to shepherd". Can you imagine trying to shepherd the wind? Pretty futile. The phrase is used 9 times in Ecclesiastes. Chapters 1 and 2 examine the vanity, or meaninglessness, of human pleasure and wisdom. Solomon tries to apply his wisdom to the problem of finding happiness. If you read chapter 2 you find that he tries laughter, wine, building projects, and enjoying his wealth through slaves and singers and a harem. He sums it all up in verses 10 and 11:

¹⁰ I denied myself nothing my eyes desired;
I refused my heart no pleasure.
My heart took delight in all my labor,
and this was the reward for all my toil.
¹¹ Yet when I surveyed all that my hands had done
and what I had toiled to achieve,
everything was meaningless, a chasing after the wind;
nothing was gained under the sun.

Everything was meaningless, he says. The result of his quest was great disappointment. Next he examines wisdom and then work and still comes to the same conclusion – it's all meaningless – again: a chasing after the wind.

The next three chapters look at earthly happiness, its difficulties and means of advancement. Read 3: 1-8:

¹ There is a time for everything,
and a season for every activity under the heavens:
   ² a time to be born and a time to die,
a time to plant and a time to uproot,
³ a time to kill and a time to heal,
a time to tear down and a time to build,
⁴ a time to weep and a time to laugh,
a time to mourn and a time to dance,
⁵ a time to scatter stones and a time to gather them,
a time to embrace and a time to refrain from embracing,
⁶ a time to search and a time to give up,
a time to keep and a time to throw away,
⁷ a time to tear and a time to mend,
a time to be silent and a time to speak,
⁸ a time to love and a time to hate,
a time for war and a time for peace.

Pete Seeger adapted these verses into the lyrics for the song Turn, Turn, Turn, sung by The Byrds. The general impression doesn't seem so meaningless. Keep reading:

9 What do workers gain from their toil? **10** I have seen the burden God has laid on the human race. **11** He has made everything beautiful in its time. He has also set eternity in the human heart; yet no one can fathom what God has done from beginning to end. **12** I know that there is nothing better for people than to be happy and to do good while they live. **13** That each of them may eat and drink, and find satisfaction in all their toil—this is the gift of God. **14** I know that everything God does will endure forever; nothing can be added to it and nothing taken from it. God does it so that people will fear him.

So Solomon argues that there is nothing better than to be happy and to do good. It seems easy to find happiness: eat, drink, find satisfaction in work. Then Solomon gets solemn again and by the time you get to the end of the chapter, where he reiterates the happiness formula, he has measured once more the futility:

19 Surely the fate of human beings is like that of the animals; the same fate awaits them both: As one dies, so dies the other. All have the same breath; humans have no advantage over animals. Everything is meaningless. **20** All go to the same place; all come from dust, and to dust all return. **21** Who knows if the human spirit rises upward and if the spirit of the animal goes down into the earth?"
22 So I saw that there is nothing better for a person than to enjoy their work, because that is their lot. For who can bring them to see what will happen after them?

You can't change things, so "don't worry, be happy". I guess Solomon was the first to figure that out. In the next few chapters he looks at all the impediments to happiness: oppression, envy, riches, and evil.
True (and practical) wisdom is explored in chapters 6 through 8:15. Read and ponder a few of the verses from chapter 7:

1 A good name is better than fine perfume,
and the day of death better than the day of birth.
5 It is better to heed the rebuke of a wise person
than to listen to the song of fools.
7 Extortion turns a wise person into a fool,
and a bribe corrupts the heart.
14 When times are good, be happy;
but when times are bad, consider this:
God has made the one
as well as the other.

From 8:16 to 10:20 we find the relation of true wisdom to man's life. Consider first 8:16, 17:

16 When I applied my mind to know wisdom and to observe the labor that is done on earth—people getting no sleep day or night— **17** then I saw all that God has done. No one can comprehend what goes on under the sun. Despite all their efforts to search it out, no one can discover its meaning. Even if the wise claim they know, they cannot really comprehend it.

We are humans with finite minds. Of course we can't comprehend it all. Solomon continues in 9:11:

> ¹¹ I have seen something else under the sun:
>   The race is not to the swift
> or the battle to the strong,
> nor does food come to the wise
>   or wealth to the brilliant
>   or favor to the learned;
> but time and chance happen to them all.

Time and chance – that's an interesting translation. The original Hebrew has "the time of mischance comes to us all" meaning that we all die. "Mischance" was a euphemism for death. Yet wise old Solomon wasn't completely sold on hopelessness. His conclusion finishes out the book. Read 12: 13, 14:

> ¹³ Now all has been heard;
> here is the conclusion of the matter:
> Fear God and keep his commandments,
>   for this is the duty of all mankind.
> ¹⁴ For God will bring every deed into judgment,
>   including every hidden thing,
>   whether it is good or evil.

Whew! That will sober you up. Ecclesiastes is often called the most pessimistic book in the Bible. Why did God allow such a biting (shin=tooth) discourse on meaninglessness, futility and pessimism to sit in this 21st spot? Hmm, could it be so it would stand as a contrasting view to the hopeful optimism of the next shin book, the New Testament gospel of John?

Ecclesiastes is the original source for phrases like "the sun also rises" and "there's nothing new under the sun". In fact, the word sun (shemesh), a shin key word, is found more in this book than any other. There are 32 verses in Ecclesiastes that contain one or more instances of this word. Every chapter in Ecclesiastes contains at least one and as many as five verses with the word "sun." Interestingly enough our next two shin books have zero references to the sun, but they are full of the light of the Son.

ש

Shin + John

First let's look at the book of John and examine the alphabetic links later. Written by the beloved apostle John around A.D. 90 this book is sharply different from Matthew, Mark and Luke. First of all it was written much later and most of the church already possessed copies of the other Gospels. These Christians wanted deeper truths and there wasn't anyone better to write them than someone from the Master's inner circle. John was the one who leaned on Jesus at the last supper, the one who didn't flee from Christ's judgment, the one who stood at the cross and received Jesus' request to care for Mary.

Matthew, Mark and Luke are called the synoptic gospels because they include many of the same stories in the same order, thus they are synoptic (one view, of the same eye), but John doesn't follow that pattern. In fact, we don't even find the parables that are so prevalent in the other gospels. In John the themes are deeper, such as the pre-existence of Christ, His incarnation, the work of the Holy Spirit and Jesus' relation to the Father.

The book of John can be divided into several major parts. It begins with the pre-existence of Jesus. Let's look at chapter 1, verses 1 – 5:

> [1] In the beginning was the Word, and the Word was with God, and the Word was God. [2] He was with God in the beginning. [3] Through him all things were made; without him nothing was made that has been made. [4] In him was life, and that life was the light of all mankind. [5] The light shines in the darkness, and the darkness has not overcome it.

What did this start with? "In the beginning was the Word." "In the beginning" is an allusion to Genesis 1:1. Now the interesting thing here is that 1st century Christians with a Jewish background would get this right away but the Gentile Christians would focus on the next phrase "was the Word". The Greek word used in the original is "logos," Both Hebrews and Greeks responded to using "the Word" as a reference to deity. In the Old Testament God spoke and things happened. There are thousands of references to his word, his voice, what he said. As for the Greeks, their philosophers had long called God's mind the Logos, the word.

This whole first verse is quoted so often that you may not have considered the depth of this complex sentence. There are three clauses. "In the beginning was the Word" claims the **eternal** quality of and **existence of Jesus**. The second clause, "and the Word was with God", shows **Jesus' communion with God**, the Father. The third clause, "and the Word was God", reveals **Jesus' divinity**. This is a point that cannot be denied. **Jesus is God**. Anyone who denies that is a false teacher, an antichrist. When people say, oh, He was a great teacher or a good prophet, they deny his divinity and are blaspheming. Do you believe that Jesus was and is God?

Verse 2 restates the first clause in case John's readers didn't get it – He, Jesus, was **with God** in the beginning. Verse 3 states the same fact first as a positive and then as a negative so you won't miss it – Jesus created **everything**, there's **nothing** he didn't create. This again alludes to his **eternal existence**. Verse 4 says that in him was life.

This word, zoe, is used here in the sense of existence in an absolute sense and without end. That makes the rest of the passage scream with hope for us: that life is in us and shines, but those in the dark do not understand.

"The light shines in the darkness." This is the start of multiple passages referring to the light. Remember in our 1st shin book, Ecclesiastes, we found more instances of the word sun than in any other Bible book. There is not one sun in John.

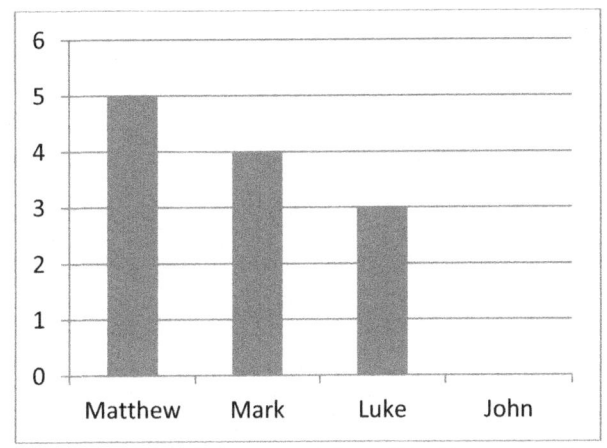

Occurrences of the word "sun" in the gospels.

There is no reason for such an absence other than to show God's precision in His design of the Bible. It's almost as though John is linked to Ecclesiastes by this singular contrast. However, despite the absence of the sun look how the **light** shines in John.

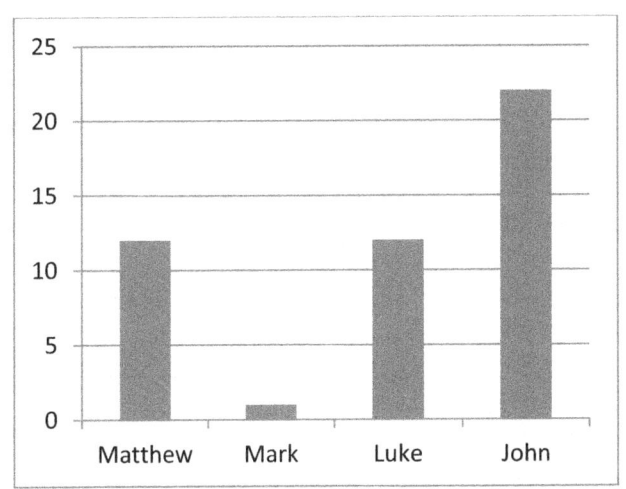

Occurrences of the word "light" in the gospels. The following are from the KJV:

John 1:4: In him was life; and the life was the **light** of men.
John 1:5: And the **light** shineth in darkness; and the darkness comprehended it not.

John 1:7: The same came for a witness, to bear witness of the **Light**, that all men through him might believe.

John 1:8: He was not that **Light**, but was sent to bear witness of that Light.

John 1:9: That was the true **Light**, which lighteth every man that cometh into the world.

John 3:19: And this is the condemnation, that **light** is come into the world, and men loved darkness rather than **light**, because their deeds were evil.

John 3:20: For every one that doeth evil hateth the **light**, neither cometh to the **light**, lest his deeds should be reproved.

John 3:21: But he that doeth truth cometh to the **light**, that his deeds may be made manifest, that they are wrought in God.

John 5:35: He was a burning and a shining **light**: and ye were willing for a season to rejoice in his light.

John 8:12: Then spake Jesus again unto them, saying, I am the **light** of the world: he that followeth me shall not walk in darkness, but shall have the **light** of life.

John 9:5: As long as I am in the world, I am the **light** of the world.

John 11:9: Jesus answered, Are there not twelve hours in the day? If any man walk in the day, he stumbleth not, because he seeth the **light** of this world.

John 11:10: But if a man walk in the night, he stumbleth, because there is no **light** in him.

John 12:35: Then Jesus said unto them, Yet a little while is the **light** with you. Walk while ye have the **light**, lest darkness come upon you: for he that walketh in darkness knoweth not whither he goeth.

John 12:36: While ye have **light**, believe in the **light**, that ye may be the children of **light**. These things spake Jesus, and departed, and did hide himself from them.

John 12:46: I am come a **light** into the world, that whosoever believeth on me should not abide in darkness.

As I studied this book I found several outlines by various commentators. They tended to divide the book up into 5 or 6 parts: 1st the opening or foreword in chapter 1 with the theme of the pre-existence of Christ, 2nd the beginning of his ministry, the "big reveal," so to speak, up through chapter 6. Then the 3rd section is the next year of his ministry and how his claims were rejected (through chapter 12). I noticed that the verses with the word **light** stopped abruptly then (see above). The next section contains Holy Week, the passion, the crucifixion, burial and resurrection. The last section (chapters 20 – 22) is of the 40 days following His resurrection.

Back in verse 1 of chapter 1 we found that Jesus was eternal, was with God and was God. Let's look at his claims found in John that **He is God**:

John 3:16; 6:32-35, 6:39-40; 8:16; 8: 23-24; 8: 58; 10:9; 10:30; 11:25-27; 12:44-45; 14:6,7. You can look them up for yourself or read them at the end of this section.

I'm going to return to the alphabetic psalms at this point to examine some of the shin words and their amazing prevalence in the book of John. In Psalm 119 some of the shin words are rejoice (sus), peace (shalom), hope (sabar) and keep watch (shamar). There are an extremely high number of these words in John chapter 14. Let's look at a couple of remarkable pairings:

Alphabetic Psalm 145: 20:

20 The LORD **watches over** all who **love** him,
but all the wicked he will destroy.

Alphabetic Psalm 119:167 (KJV):

167 My soul hath **kept** thy testimonies; and I **love** them exceedingly.

Now compare to John 14:23 (KJV):

23 Jesus answered and said unto him, If a man **love** me, he will **keep** my words: and my Father will love him, and we will come unto him, and make our abode with him.

And John 14:15:

15 "If you **love** me, **keep** my commands.

In his book, *The Bible Wheel,* Richard Amiel McGough writes several pages on the amazing density of this special word shamar, to keep. You can buy and/or download for free his wonderful book from www.biblewheel.com.

As stated above, **Jesus is God**. He said he was God so either He was deliberately lying . . . or He was a lunatic . . . or He was and is Lord. Here are those verses in case you didn't look them up for yourself:

John 3:16 For God so loved the world that he gave his one and only Son, that whoever believes in him shall not perish but have eternal life.

John 6:32-35 Jesus said to them, "Very truly I tell you, it is not Moses who has given you the bread from heaven, but it is my Father who gives you the true bread from heaven. **33** For the bread of God is the bread that comes down from heaven and gives life to the world."
34 "Sir," they said, "always give us this bread."
35 Then Jesus declared, "I am the bread of life. Whoever comes to me will never go hungry, and whoever believes in me will never be thirsty.

John 6:39-40 And this is the will of him who sent me, that I shall lose none of all those he has given me, but raise them up at the last day. **40** For my Father's will is that everyone who looks to the Son and believes in him shall have eternal life, and I will raise them up at the last day."

John 8:16 But if I do judge, my decisions are true, because I am not alone. I stand with the Father, who sent me.

John 8: 23-24 But he continued, "You are from below; I am from above. You are of this world; I am not of this world. **24** I told you that you would die in your sins; if you do not believe that I am he, you will indeed die in your sins."

John 8:58 "Very truly I tell you," Jesus answered, "before Abraham was born, I am!"

John 10:9 I am the gate; whoever enters through me will be saved. They will come in and go out, and find pasture.

John 10:30 I and the Father are one.

John 11: 25-27 Jesus said to her, "I am the resurrection and the life. The one who believes in me will live, even though they die; ²⁶ and whoever lives by believing in me will never die. Do you believe this?"
²⁷ "Yes, Lord," she replied, "I believe that you are the Messiah, the Son of God, who is to come into the world."

John 12: 44-45 Then Jesus cried out, "Whoever believes in me does not believe in me only, but in the one who sent me. ⁴⁵ The one who looks at me is seeing the one who sent me.

John 14: 6-7 Jesus answered, "I am the way and the truth and the life. No one comes to the Father except through me. ⁷ If you really know me, you will know my Father as well. From now on, you do know him and have seen him."

Jesus brings Light and Life. The blind man in John chapter 9 is in for the surprise of his life. Watch how he gets physical sight and how he gains another sense, too – spiritual sight. If you don't know the story read it now or the summary below:

Jesus and his disciples come across the blind man, Jesus heals him, the Pharisees are in an uproar because He healed on the Sabbath, there's an investigation and the Pharisees kick the formerly blind man out of synagogue, and the story ends with Jesus revealing His divinity to the man who then gains spiritual sight. That's the story in a nutshell.

Now, you be the blind guy:

You've heard the scriptures read, you know the prophecies, you hang around the temple all the time begging and listening. You hear some men talking about you. They're asking their leader if you or your parents are responsible for your blindness. The leader says neither you nor your parents are responsible; he says that you're blind so the work of God can be displayed in your life. You're more alert. You hear them get closer and the leader puts something on your face over those rounds things that are called eyes, but have no function for you. He tells you to wash it off in the Pool of Siloam. You have some faith so you do.

What is this?! Is this sight?! This is unbelievable! You cannot contain your excitement. You find your way home and your neighbors think you're an imposter. You tell them what happened. They ask how this could be. You say it was "the man."

The Pharisees are mad at "the man" and send for you. You tell them your story. It's so simple: he put mud on your eyes, you washed, and now you see. Some are wondering how a sinner could do this miraculous thing. You are beginning to put it together, remembering the prophecies. He is not a sinner, he is "a prophet," you tell them.

They do not believe any of your story. They send for your parents. You know your parents will be kicked out of the synagogue, ruined, if they even hint that this "man," this "prophet," could be the Messiah. Luckily for them they say that you're of age, you can testify for yourself.

A second time the Pharisees ask you and you reply "I was blind but now I see!" But how? What did he do? They still want to know and you've already answered. You're getting more than a little frustrated with their unbelief. In fact, you're impatient and you're going to get a bit sarcastic with them. You say, "I have told you already and you did not listen. Why do you want to hear it again? Do you want to become his disciples, too?"

You've gone too far. They hurl insults at you, but you, in your anger, stand up for the "man", the "prophet", and claim he must be from God. Your inner eyes are beginning to see and as they throw you out of the synagogue you start to know in your heart who healed you.

And then He finds you and He asks you if you believe in the Son of Man. You ask who He is and the "man," the "prophet" this Jesus, tells you that **He** is the Son of Man.

"Lord," you say, "I believe."

You have been blind, but now you see. At first you thought Jesus was just a man or just a prophet, but now you know He is Lord.

There is another side to this story. Look at the Pharisees in this account. Remaining blind in your unbelief is tragic. We saw how the blind man received both physical and spiritual sight and became a believer in Jesus Christ, the Messiah. The Pharisees, however, remained spiritually blind and hence doomed.

They come into the story at the point where the (formerly) blind man is brought before them. Now they've been following things all along in regards to this Jesus person and have already closed their minds. In fact, they have decided that anyone who acknowledges that Jesus is the Messiah would be "put out" of the synagogue. That meant financial ruin. They also intended the "putting out" to result in spiritual ruin as well, but claiming Jesus as the Christ has just the opposite outcome.

The Pharisees are divided after they question the (formerly) blind man. Some think that Jesus couldn't be the Messiah because he performed this miracle on the Sabbath. Others wonder how a sinner could perform a miracle. Isn't it interesting that neither side disputes the miracle? Obviously they aren't blind to the miracle; they seem to accept that as a fact even though they question the poor guy several times. But they are themselves blind. Why don't they acknowledge their own scriptures? Isaiah 29:18, 35:4, 5 and 42:7 all predict that the coming Savior would open the eyes of the blind – something that had never, ever been done before Jesus did it.

Not only are they blind, refusing to admit the truth, but they are liars, too. What? Religious people are liars? Yes, after the (formerly) blind man gets a little snippy with them as they persist in their repetitive questions (John 9: 26, 27) the Pharisees claim they are disciples of Moses and don't even know where Jesus comes from. Liars! They knew all about Jesus and just a few verses before we found out that they would expel anyone who declared that Jesus was the Messiah. And as for claiming to be disciples of Moses, these same Pharisees (in chapter 8) had just been arguing with Jesus, saying that they were children of Abraham. They had such an argument with Jesus that they picked up stones to stone him, but Jesus slipped away. Yet now they say they don't even know where Jesus comes from. Apparently they were deaf as well as blind.

The (formerly) blind man goes beyond snippy now to bold and sarcastic. He says, "Now that is remarkable! You don't know where he comes from, yet he opened my eyes. We know that God does not listen to sinners. He listens to the godly man who does His will. Nobody has ever heard of opening the eyes of a man born blind. If this man were not from God, he could do nothing." Wow, what an argument he throws back at them. His deductive reasoning is logical, the premises sound and irrefutable. Do they refute him? No, they can't so they throw him out.

A few Pharisees are around when Jesus seeks out the blind man and reveals Himself as Lord. The Pharisees ask, "Are we blind, too?" and Jesus answers, "If you were blind, you would not be guilty of sin; but now that you claim you can see, your guilt remains." And thus they receive judgment (condemnation) by their unbelief. They are doomed. Are you? Open your eyes, open your spiritual eyes.

ש

Shin + Jude
Our third shin s book is Jude. Jude identifies himself in the opening of the letter as the servant of Jesus Christ and brother of James. This James is the Lord's half brother, hence Jude also is Jesus' half brother.

Right away we're going to see a link to the shin word shamar which means to keep, to guard or to watch. Read Jude 1 – 2:

> ¹ Jude, a servant of Jesus Christ and a brother of James,
> To those who have been called, who are loved in God the Father and **kept** for Jesus Christ:
> ² **Mercy, peace** and **love** be yours in abundance.

"Kept" for Jesus. Some translations have "preserved." The Greek word is tereo, "guarded" and matches the Hebrew shin word. Notice that Jude gives not his human, earthly relationship with Jesus, but rather his spiritual one – that he is a servant of Jesus Christ. Not just Jesus, but Jesus Christ – the Greek word for Messiah. By adding that he is the brother of James he clarifies his identity. He is writing to those who have been "called". This word implies that he is writing to those who have been invited to the kingdom of heaven and who have obeyed this call, that is, Christians/saints. He sends them mercy, peace and love. Mercy (eleos) – compassion, active pity. Peace (eirene) – to join together that which has been separated. Love (agape) – specifically the love of God.

Read verses 3 and 4:

> ³ Dear friends, although I was very eager to write to you about the salvation we share, I felt compelled to write and urge you to contend for the faith that was once for all entrusted to God's holy people. ⁴ For certain individuals whose condemnation was written about long ago have secretly slipped in among you. They are ungodly people, who pervert the grace of our God into a license for immorality and deny Jesus Christ our only Sovereign and Lord.

We learn here that Jude originally wanted to write about salvation, but changed his theme when he found out that certain men (spies, traitors) had slipped in amongst them. These godless men were false prophets and we know from 2nd Peter as well that they perverted the word. The word Jude uses here for godless is "asebes" which means these men were choosing to live as if God did not exist and they had no regard for Him. How did they get into the church? Look around. Are they in our churches today?

In verses 5, 6 and 7 Jude gives some warnings:

> ⁵ Though you already know all this, I want to remind you that the Lord at one time delivered his people out of Egypt, but later destroyed those who did not believe. ⁶ And the angels who did not keep their positions of authority but abandoned their proper dwelling— these he has kept in darkness, bound with everlasting chains for judgment on the great Day. ⁷ In a similar way, Sodom and Gomorrah and the surrounding towns gave themselves up to

sexual immorality and perversion. They serve as an example of those who suffer the punishment of eternal fire.

Some Israelites, some angels, the people of Sodom and Gomorrah – all examples of what God did to those who deserved punishment. What were their sins? Unbelief. Pride. Immorality.

Now, when this letter was read in the church it was sent to, you can be pretty sure that those "godless" men were there, too, hearing the letter being read. Jude makes a statement about them, calling them dreamers (vs. 8-10):

8 In the very same way, on the strength of their dreams these ungodly people pollute their own bodies, reject authority and heap abuse on celestial beings. **9** But even the archangel Michael, when he was disputing with the devil about the body of Moses, did not himself dare to condemn him for slander but said, "The Lord rebuke you!" **10** Yet these people slander whatever they do not understand, and the very things they do understand by instinct—as irrational animals do—will destroy them.

What were the three things that these infiltrators do? They pollute their own bodies probably by defiling their flesh through sexual immorality; they reject authority by denying the Lordship of Christ; they heap abuse on celestial beings. Woe to them – verse 11:

11 Woe to them! They have taken the way of Cain; they have rushed for profit into Balaam's error; they have been destroyed in Korah's rebellion.

There are three things to explain in this tiny verse, three wicked things. Cain, Balaam and Korah were three infamous Old Testament characters. Cain (Genesis 4) killed his brother Abel, Balaam (Deuteronomy 23:4) accepted money in exchange for pronouncing a curse on Israel, and Korah (Numbers 16) rose up against Moses and Aaron, rejecting their God-given authority. So Jude is saying that these false teachers in the church are making those same mistakes. Those who read or heard his letter in those days would have gotten the references immediately. He further maligns them with metaphors in verses 12 and 13 that are beautiful and awful at the same time:

12 These people are blemishes at your love feasts, eating with you without the slightest qualm—shepherds who feed only themselves. They are clouds without rain, blown along by the wind; autumn trees, without fruit and uprooted—twice dead. **13** They are wild waves of the sea, foaming up their shame; wandering stars, for whom blackest darkness has been reserved forever.

I said awful and beautiful at the same time because, as an English major, I can really appreciate the descriptive devices used here. Notice that these word pictures include different regions of the physical world. These men are blemishes at the love feasts. The actual literal Greek here is that they are "craggy rocks" which implies that they are like rocks beneath the surface of the sea – very dangerous. They feed only themselves – very selfish. Being like clouds without rain means they promise good things but don't deliver. Fruitless, uprooted trees are twice dead and thoroughly useless. As wild waves they foam up their own shame. As wandering stars they are destined to eternal darkness. (Whew! Back in the classroom with that verse!)

Now before we read the next couple of verses let me explain a little about the apocryphal book of Enoch since Enoch is mentioned here in Jude. This book was lost for many centuries, from about 200 A.D. until 1773 A.D. The book contains a narrative of the fall of the angels, Enoch's tour of heaven and earth, and the mysteries he sees. There are also parables concerning the kingdom of God, the Messiah and the Messianic future as well as visions and exhortations to Methuselah and his descendants. With that little background let's read verses 14-16.

14 Enoch, the seventh from Adam, prophesied about them: "See, the Lord is coming with thousands upon thousands of his holy ones **15** to judge everyone, and to convict all of them of all the ungodly acts they have committed in their ungodliness, and of all the defiant words ungodly sinners have spoken against him." **16** These people are grumblers and faultfinders; they follow their own evil desires; they boast about themselves and flatter others for their own advantage.

Verse 15 uses the word ungodly (some translations have impious) 3 times. The KJV manages to use ungodly 4 times. What do you think Jude is trying to emphasize? Now do a self-awareness check and make sure you don't fit any of the traits in verse 16. Ask yourself: Am I a grumbler? Do I find fault? Do I follow my own evil desires? Do I boast about myself? Do I flatter others for my own advantage? (There are days when I answer yes to one or all of these. Forgive me, Father, and help me.)

Jude's tone changes as we read on:

17 But, dear friends, remember what the apostles of our Lord Jesus Christ foretold. **18** They said to you, "In the last times there will be scoffers who will follow their own ungodly desires." **19** These are the people who divide you, who follow mere natural instincts and do not have the Spirit.
20 But you, dear friends, by building yourselves up in your most holy faith and praying in the Holy Spirit, **21** keep yourselves in God's love as you wait for the mercy of our Lord Jesus Christ to bring you to eternal life.
22 Be merciful to those who doubt; **23** save others by snatching them from the fire; to others show mercy, mixed with fear—hating even the clothing stained by corrupted flesh.

Ponder these words, read them again, they are meant for you. Jude concludes thus:
24 To him who is able to keep you from stumbling and to present you before his glorious presence without fault and with great joy— **25** to the only God our Savior be glory, majesty, power and authority, through Jesus Christ our Lord, before all ages, now and forevermore! Amen.

This is a beautiful doxology and focuses on our Lord. Contemplate the words glory, majesty, power and authority. This ending also provides an alphabetic link back to our second shin book, John. An important shin word was shamar meaning to keep, to guard, to watch over. In Greek there are two words that mean to keep. Phulasso means to watch in the sense of keeping your eye on things for safety, like a shepherd. Tereo means to watch with the intent of retaining custody and keeping something in one's possession. Compare John 17:11b, 12, 15 (KJV):

Holy Father, **keep** through thine own name those whom thou hast given me, that they may be one, as we are.

[12]While I was with them in the world, I **kept** them in thy name: those that thou gavest me I have **kept**, and none of them is lost, but the son of perdition; that the scripture might be fulfilled.

[15]I pray not that thou shouldest take them out of the world, but that thou shouldest **keep** them from the evil.

and Jude 21, 24:

[21] **keep** yourselves in God's love as you wait for the mercy of our Lord Jesus Christ to bring you to eternal life.

[24] To him who is able to **keep** you from stumbling and to present you before his glorious presence without fault and with great joy

Amazing, isn't it?

Chapter 22 Tav

Aleph	1. Genesis	23. Isaiah	45. Romans
Bet	2. Exodus	24. Jeremiah	46. 1st Corinthians
Gimel	3. Leviticus	25. Lamentations	47. 2nd Corinthians
Dalet	4. Numbers	26. Ezekiel	48. Galatians
Hey	5. Deuteronomy	27. Daniel	49. Ephesians
Vav	6. Joshua	28. Hosea	50. Philippians
Zayin	7. Judges	29. Joel	51. Colossians
Het	8. Ruth	30. Amos	52. 1st Thessalonians
Tet	9. 1st Samuel	31. Obadiah	53. 2nd Thessalonians
Yod	10. 2nd Samuel	32. Jonah	54. 1st Timothy
Kaph	11. 1st Kings	33. Micah	55. 2nd Timothy
Lamed	12. 2nd Kings	34. Nahum	56. Titus
Mem	13. 1st Chronicles	35. Habakkuk	57. Philemon
Nun	14. 2nd Chronicles	36. Zephaniah	58. Hebrews
Samek	15. Ezra	37. Haggai	59. James
Ayin	16. Nehemiah	38. Zechariah	60. 1st Peter
Pey	17. Esther	39. Malachi	61. 2nd Peter
Tzaddi	18. Job	40. Matthew	62. 1st John
Quph	19. Psalms	41. Mark	63. 2nd John
Resh	20. Proverbs	42. Luke	64. 3rd John
Shin	21. Ecclesiastes	43. John	65. Jude
Tav	22. *Song of Songs*	*44. Acts*	*66. Revelation*

ת

Tav + Song of Songs

The 22nd Hebrew letter, the last one, is Tav. Its symbolic meaning is mark, sign or **cross**. Tav represents the ideas of consummation, completion, covenant and sealing. In Rabbinic tradition this letter is called the "Seal of Creation" and the "Seal of Truth". It is nothing short of wondrous that our Lord would complete this holy alphabet with a letter that means **cross**.

There are several key words that begin with this letter, such as perfection (tahm), completed (tamam), to crucify (talah) and resurrection (t'chiyah). This gives me chills.

Our first tav book is Song of Songs (in older versions – Song of Solomon), written by King Solomon. In Hebrew this book is called Shir Ha-Shirim; by naming this Song of Songs its superiority to other songs (or psalms) is recognized much like saying "king of kings" or "holy of holies". This song is really a poem about love. The main speakers are a man and the woman whom he loves. At the start of the poem the couple is not yet engaged. The woman is not sure about the man. She twice sends him away. She does not seem to want to share his life, but in the end she learns to trust him and they marry. Well, that's one interpretation. It was, perhaps, originally written as an ancient musical play. Here's another way to view it: The dark skinned maiden, the Shulamite, loves a shepherd boy but the king sees her beauty and takes her off to the castle to be one of his wives. The shepherd had cared about her heart and soul, but the king is lustful. She must choose between the riches (lustful sex) of the king and the true love (and sensual caring sex) of the shepherd. She chooses . . . read it for yourself. If you find this book a bit hard to read because of how the verses switch from friends speaking to the lover speaking to the beloved speaking and so on, then I highly recommend that you visit the following website and read this marvelous version which has the book rewritten as a theatrical style play script:

http://www.westarkchurchofchrist.org/library/songofsongs.htm.

Jews interpret this lovely story as God's love for Israel and Christians see it as the expression of pure marital love as ordained by God and pictured here as the bridegroom, Christ, and the bride, the Church. Either way, we are covenanted with God Himself. We may sometimes feel out of touch with Jesus, as the girl in the story, but He has not left us. He is near even when we don't feel His presence.

One thing I really like about Song of Songs is that the verses clearly affirm the goodness and sanctity of sex in marriage. The key tav word 'tahm' is seen in verse 6 of chapter 8 – "a seal over your heart, like a seal on your arm". We'll see a striking concentration of this word when we get to the third tav book.

Now for the really cool stuff: Song of Songs is the 22nd book, matching up as a tav book with the 44th book, Acts, and the 66th book, Revelation. How did God weave these three books together? Beautifully. Read Song of Songs 5:2:

> ² I slept but my heart was awake.
>   Listen! My beloved is knocking:
> "Open to me, my sister, my darling,
>   my dove, my flawless one.
> My head is drenched with dew,
>   my hair with the dampness of the night."

Now compare that to Revelation 3:20:

> ²⁰ Here I am! I stand at the door and knock. If anyone hears my voice and opens the door, I will come in and eat with that person, and they with me.

Knocking at the door! I did a search and there is not another verse in the entire Old Testament that has the word knock. Study these two verses. Do you see the connection?

Song of Songs is all about love and marriage; Revelation is filled with songs and metaphors for marriage. I'll leave those amazing verses for the chapter on Revelation.

Let me sum up the major connections of these three books in this way: in accordance with the key tav word for consummation, Song of Songs shows the consummation of a divine marriage, Acts shows the consummation of the Jewish age when the bride of Christ (the Church) is born, and Revelation reveals how all of history will be consummated as Christ receives His bride. Consummation. Marriage. These three books are aligned perfectly with the exact Hebrew letter that denotes consummation. Awesome.

ת

Tav + Acts

Tav is the last of the 22 Hebrew letters. Its symbolic meaning is mark, sign or **cross**. We saw in the first tav ת book, Song of Songs, that there is a strong correlation between these books and this letter having to do with consummation and marriage. The number one major theme of the book of the Acts of the Apostles is the receiving of the Holy Spirit followed by the profession of Christ to the Jews at Pentecost and then to the Gentiles. This was the beginning of the Christian church which is, in all respects, the beginning of the Bride of Christ.

In Acts the first nine chapters recount the rise of the early church with Peter being the prominent character; the rest of the book follows with the conversion and ministry of the Apostle Paul. It is written by the physician, Luke, who spent much time alongside Saint Paul, traveling and witnessing. In his previous book Luke wrote about all that Jesus began to do and to teach until the ascension. That book was written to a certain Theophilus, a man who was probably wealthy enough to help Luke get his information published, and Acts is also addressed to this same Theophilus. His name, by the way, means "lover of God" or "loved by God". With that in mind I like to think that these books were written personally to me.

The thesis verse of Acts is found in chapter 1, verse 8, when Jesus says the following:

⁸ But you will receive power when the Holy Spirit comes on you; and you will be my witnesses in Jerusalem, and in all Judea and Samaria, and to the ends of the earth."

You can divide this book and align it with this statement since first we find the apostles witnessing in Jerusalem (through Acts 8:3), going into Judea and Samaria (Acts 8:4 – 13:3) and to the ends of the earth (Acts 13:4 – 28:31) spreading the good news and building the church.

Let's check the acrostic verses for clues as to what we want to focus on in Acts.
Psalm 119: 175:

¹⁷⁵ Let me live that I may praise you,
and may your laws sustain me.

Let me live. Literally the Hebrew says "Let my soul live." That kind of gives us a longer range plan, doesn't it? The Hebrew word for "live" is the root for "resurrection."
Lamentations 4:22:

²² Your punishment will end, Daughter Zion;
he will not prolong your exile.
But he will punish your sin, Daughter Edom,
and expose your wickedness.

Punishment will end. The Hebrew word here is "tamam" meaning "completed." Psalm 25:21:

21 May integrity and uprightness protect me,
because my hope, LORD, is in you.

Integrity is the word used here to translate the Hebrew tav word "tom" which also means perfection, completion and moral purity. Taken together from these alphabetic verses we get the theme of living forever, all things being completed, finished.

Let's read from Acts the part where the Holy Spirit descends upon them. Jesus had told his disciples not to leave Jerusalem until they were "baptized with the Holy Spirit" (Acts 1:4-5). So they (about 120 people) were gathered together waiting. Acts 2:1-13:

1 When the day of Pentecost came, they were all together in one place. **2** Suddenly a sound like the blowing of a violent wind came from heaven and filled the whole house where they were sitting. **3** They saw what seemed to be tongues of fire that separated and came to rest on each of them. **4** All of them were filled with the Holy Spirit and began to speak in other tongues as the Spirit enabled them.
5 Now there were staying in Jerusalem God-fearing Jews from every nation under heaven. **6** When they heard this sound, a crowd came together in bewilderment, because each one heard their own language being spoken. **7** Utterly amazed, they asked: "Aren't all these who are speaking Galileans? **8** Then how is it that each of us hears them in our native language? **9** Parthians, Medes and Elamites; residents of Mesopotamia, Judea and Cappadocia, Pontus and Asia, **10** Phrygia and Pamphylia, Egypt and the parts of Libya near Cyrene; visitors from Rome **11** (both Jews and converts to Judaism); Cretans and Arabs—we hear them declaring the wonders of God in our own tongues!" **12** Amazed and perplexed, they asked one another, "What does this mean?"
13 Some, however, made fun of them and said, "They have had too much wine."

Ha! That last part makes me laugh only because it seems ludicrous. After all, why would you think someone was drunk if he was speaking in several different foreign languages? Notice what happens first – a loud sound. This sound is indescribable. The only way Luke can explain it is to say the sound was <u>like</u> the blowing of a violent wind. And it filled the house. Try to imagine a very loud sound suddenly filling the room where you are right now.

Next come the tongues of fire. Are they really fire? I don't know. Luke says they saw "what seemed to be" tongues of fire. This was something unique and inexplicable. These strange things separated and came to rest on each of them. They heard something, they saw something and then next they felt something. What was it? The Holy Spirit filled them and they began to speak in other languages. Real languages. The Greek word here is "glossa" which means language (an English related word is glossary). This was the time of Pentecost and there were God-fearing Jews from other nations there who heard them in their own native language! They were amazed! Confounded! Now, did you notice what the Christians were saying in all of these different foreign languages? Were they preaching about Jesus? Not yet. At first they were "declaring the wonders of God". Then Peter stands front and center and speaks to the crowd. Read the rest of chapter 2 for yourself and see how Peter makes his argument. I'll summarize it here: First Peter quotes the prophet Joel (2:28-32) about God pouring out the Spirit. They have just witnessed that. Second he reminds them of the great works, signs, wonders and miracles that Jesus undisputedly performed and he also describes His death and resurrection. Third, he quotes the Old Testament scriptures again (Psalm 16:8-11) where David foretold the Messiah's kingship after resurrection. Fourth, he offers himself and the entire group as 120 witnesses to the fact that God raised Jesus to life. At that point the listeners were "cut to the heart" and asked what they should do. Did you read the account? Do you know how many believed and were saved that day? Three thousand!

    I love when God uses numbers in wonderful ways. That day **3000 were saved**. What day was it? It was Pentecost. The Feast of Pentecost was the day the Holy Spirit was poured out onto the disciples! The very first Pentecost (about 1500 years before) was 7 weeks after the death of the Passover lambs. On that day Moses received the Law on the stone tablets and when he returned to camp **3000 men died** because of their sin. **3000!** It certainly looks to me like the book of Acts is showing us our tav key word's meaning of "completion," for surely at this point the Jewish Age is completed.

    Remember how in the first tav book, Song of Songs, a king received his bride and their marriage was consummated? It was an allegory (parable, story) of the loving union of Christ and His Church. In Acts we witness the birth of that bride, the Church. In Song of Songs the bride had a "seal" (remember the symbolic meaning of tav is mark, sign or cross) on her arm. In Acts we see the Church being sealed (marked) by the Holy Spirit. We'll see a third sealing, lots of seals in fact, when we get to the last tav book, Revelation.

    There is much to learn from the book of Acts. I did a Bible study on it that took 13 months so I know that there is a lot of material here. I recommend studying this marvelous little book of early Christian history as delving into each and every verse is like opening a bottomless treasure chest.

ת

Tav + Revelation

The final book of Scripture is Revelation. We've gone from aleph to tav and now we are at the completion of the Holy Word. It is more than appropriate that this Hebrew letter, t, represents the ideas of consummation, completion, covenant and sealing. The alphabetic verses that correspond to this letter emphasize various words that start with this letter such as perfection (tahm), completed (tamam), crucify (talah) and praise (tehillah). Resurrection (t'chiyah) and resurrection of the dead (t'chiyath-hammethim) are tav words. My favorite tav phrase is "the hope of Israel" (tiqvah Yisrael).

Revelation was written by the Apostle John when he was banished to the island of Patmos. The revelation covers things past, things present and things future. It is a mysterious and puzzling book that I have been studying for over forty years. It is not as impossible to understand as some people would have you believe. It is rich in symbolism and imagery and fits perfectly into its spot as the 66th book, connecting amazingly with the 44th and 22nd books that match it.

There is a wonderful thing that this book has that no other book of Holy Scripture has. Read Revelation 1:3:

> ³ Blessed is the one who reads aloud the words of this prophecy, and blessed are those who hear it and take to heart what is written in it, because the time is near.

Just for reading the book of Revelation or hearing it read YOU WILL RECEIVE A BLESSING. I encourage you to read this book (aloud) and then to do a little research on your own into the interpretations and symbolism. There are lots of websites and books available to help you interpret the mysteries here. I have made my own outlines, charts and graphs, but my purpose in writing this book is to reveal the connective fabric of the 66 books to the 22 Hebrew letters and so I will keep on that theme.

With that in mind let's look first at the marriage metaphors since they are so obvious in Revelation and relate so perfectly with the first tav book.

Revelation 19:7; 21:2; and 22:17:

> ⁷ Let us rejoice and be glad
> and give him glory!
> For the wedding of the Lamb has come,
> and his bride has made herself ready.
> ² I saw the Holy City, the new Jerusalem, coming down out of heaven from God, prepared as a bride beautifully dressed for her husband.
> ¹⁷ The Spirit and the bride say, "Come!" And let the one who hears say, "Come!" Let the one who is thirsty come; and let the one who wishes take the free gift of the water of life.

We saw in Song of Songs, the first tav book, a picture of the marriage between Christ and His bride, the Church. The bride was sealed at Pentecost by the Holy Spirit in Acts, the second tav book. Now in Revelation, the third tav book, Christ receives His bride. How beautifully woven are the Holy Scriptures!

Read this tav alphabetic verse, Lamentations 3:44:

44 You have covered yourself with a cloud
so that no prayer can get through.

I actually found the above verse *after* I learned of the "Christ coming in the clouds" connection between Acts and Revelation. I figured that God must have put a clue in the acrostics and a quick search for "cloud" revealed the above verse. Now look at Acts 1: 9-11:

9 After he said this, he was taken up before their very eyes, and a cloud hid him from their sight.
10 They were looking intently up into the sky as he was going, when suddenly two men dressed in white stood beside them. **11** "Men of Galilee," they said, "why do you stand here looking into the sky? This same Jesus, who has been taken from you into heaven, will come back in the same way you have seen him go into heaven."

Compare that to Revelation 1:7:

7 "Look, he is coming with the clouds,"
and "every eye will see him,
even those who pierced him";
and all peoples on earth "will mourn because of him."
So shall it be! Amen.

Does it not amaze you that these two verses are juxtaposed exactly in the first chapters of these two tav t books? And if Revelation has such a perfect counterpart in Acts, will there be something equally harmonizing (pun intended) in Song of Songs? Of course! I highlighted a few words so you can't possibly miss it. Revelation 5:9; 14:3; and 15:2b – 3:

9 And they sang **a new song**, saying:
"You are worthy to take the scroll
and to open its **seals**,
because you were slain,
and with your blood you purchased for God
persons from every tribe and language and people and nation.
3 And they **sang a new song** before the throne and before the four living creatures and the elders. No one could learn the **song** except the 144,000 who had been redeemed from the earth.
2 They held harps given them by God **3** and **sang the song** of God's servant Moses and of the Lamb:
"Great and marvelous are your deeds,
Lord God Almighty.

Just and true are your ways,
   King of the nations.

From Song of Songs to "a new song" in Revelation. And did you notice the "seals"? There are exactly 22 (!) verses in Revelation that contain this word. In Song of Songs (8:6) it says:

⁶ Place me like a seal over your heart,
like a seal on your arm;

And in Acts the Church is sealed by the Holy Spirit. Praise God!

Final Thoughts

God isn't operating a religious buffet! You don't get to pick and choose what you want. You cannot say you believe some of the Scripture, but find some things intolerant, narrow-minded or simply unbelievable. You stand in front of Him ALL THE TIME as a guilty sinner needing a Savior. God doesn't negotiate a deal. He has already made the deal: If you repent of your sins, turn to the Lord and accept that Christ died for you and paid for those sins already, then you are saved. God is merciful. He extends His grace to each of us. Just believe. If you cling to your own righteousness or think that you can "get into Heaven" by being "good," forget it. You can never be "good enough."

Jesus said He was God. That means He was either a liar or a lunatic or He was God. Anybody who says He was a great prophet but not God hasn't thought about it very much and is probably just parroting what they've heard at home (a Muslim home, Jewish home, Buddhist home, etc.). A great prophet who asserts that He is God should be disregarded unless, of course, He is God. Everyone **must** decide if Jesus is God or not.

BOOKS by Debra Chapoton

Young adult to Adult:

EDGE OF ESCAPE Innocent adoration escalates to stalking and abduction in this psychological thriller. SOMMERFALLE is the German version of EDGE OF ESCAPE

THE GUARDIAN'S DIARY Jedidiah, a 17-year-old champion skateboarder with a defect he's been hiding all of his life, must risk exposure to rescue a girl that's gone missing.

SHELTERED Ben, a high school junior, has found a unique way to help homeless teens, but he must first bring the group together to fight against supernatural forces.

A SOUL'S KISS When a tragic accident leaves Jessica comatose, her spirit escapes her body. Navigating a supernatural realm is tough, but being half dead has its advantages. Like getting into people's thoughts. Like taking over someone's body. Like experiencing romance on a whole new plane - literally.

EXODIA By 2093 American life is a strange mix of failing technologies, psychic predictions, and radiation induced abilities. Tattoos are mandatory to differentiate two classes, privileged and slave. Dalton Battista fears that his fading tattoo is a deadly omen. He's either the heir of the brutal tyrant of the new capital city, Exodia or he's its prophesied redeemer. (A retelling of the story of Moses)

OUT OF EXODIA In this sequel to EXODIA, Dalton Battista takes on his prophesied identity as Bram O'Shea. When this psychic teen leads a city of 21st century American survivalists out from under an oppressive regime, he puts the escape plan at risk by trusting the mysterious god-like David Ronel.

THE GIRL IN THE TIME MACHINE A desperate teen with a faulty time machine. What could go wrong? 17-year-old Laken is torn between revenge and righting a wrong. SciFi suspense.

THE TIME BENDER A stolen kiss could put the universe at risk. Selina doesn't think Marcum's spaceship is anything more than one heck of a science project … until he takes her to the moon and back.

THE TIME PACER Alex discovered he was half-alien right after he learned how to manipulate time. Now he has to fight the star cannibals, fly a space ship, work on his relationship with Selina, and stay clear of Coreg, full-blooded alien rival and possible galactic traitor. Once they reach their ancestral planet all three are plunged into a society where schooling is more than indoctrination

THE TIME STOPPER Young recruit Marcum learns battle-craft, infiltration and multiple languages at the Interstellar Combat Academy. He and his arch rival Coreg jeopardize their futures by exceeding the space travel limits and flying to Earth in search of a time-bender. They find Selina whose ability to slow the passage of time will be invaluable in fighting other aliens. But Marcum loses his heart to her and when Coreg takes her twenty light years away he remains on Earth in order to develop a far greater talent than time-bending. Now he's ready to return home and get the girl.

THE TIME ENDER Selina Langston is confused about recurring feelings for the wrong guy/alien. She's pretty sure Alex is her soulmate and Coreg should not be trusted at all. But Marcum … well, when he returns to Klaqin and rescues her she begins to see him in a different light.

TO DIE UPON A KISS Several teenagers' lives intertwine during one eventful week full of love, betrayal and murder in this futuristic, gender-swapped retelling of Shakespeare's *Othello*.

HERE WITHOUT A TRACE Hailey and Logan try to rescue a friend from a parallel world without getting trapped themselves, but as they slip in someone or something slips out.

Non-fiction:

HOW TO BLEND FAMILIES This guide gives step by step advice from experienced educators and also provides several fill-in worksheets to help you resolve family relationships, deal with discipline, navigate the financials, and create a balanced family with happy people.

BUILDING BIG PINE LODGE A journal of our experiences building a full log home

CROSSING THE SCRIPTURES A Bible Study supplement for studying each of the 66 books of the Old and New Testaments.

300 PLUS TEACHER HACKS and TIPS A guide for teachers at all levels of experience with hacks, tricks, and tips to help you get and give the most out of teaching.

HOW TO HELP YOUR CHILD SUCCEED IN SCHOOL A guide for parents to motivate, encourage and propel their kids to the head of the class. Includes proven strategies and tips from teachers.

BRAIN POWER PUZZLES Volume 1

Stretch yourself by solving anagrams, word searches, cryptograms, mazes, math puzzles, Sudoku, crosswords, daisy puzzles, boggle boards, pictograms, riddles, and more in these entertaining puzzles books.

BRAIN POWER PUZZLES Volume 2 – 10 More puzzles Volume 5 for Spanish students, Volume 8 BIBLE edition and Volume 10 Christmas edition

Children's books:

THE SECRET IN THE HIDDEN CAVE 12-year-old Missy Stark and her new friend Kevin Jackson discover dangerous secrets when they explore the old lodge, the woods, the cemetery, and the dark caves beneath the lake. They must solve the riddles and follow the clues to save the old lodge from destruction.

MYSTERY'S GRAVE After Missy and Kevin solved THE SECRET IN THE HIDDEN CAVE, they thought the rest of the summer at Big Pine Lodge would be normal. But there are plenty of surprises awaiting them in the woods, the caves, the stables, the attic and the cemetery. Two new families arrive and one family isn't human.

BULLIES AND BEARS In their latest adventure at Big Pine Lodge, Missy and Kevin discover more secrets in the caves, the attic, the cemetery and the settlers' ruins. They have to stay one step ahead of four teenage bullies, too, as well as three hungry bears. This summer's escapades become more and more challenging for these two twelve-year-olds. How will they make it through another week?

A TICK IN TIME 12-year-old Tommy MacArthur plunges into another dimension thanks to a magical grandfather clock. Now he must find his way through a strange land, avoid the danger lurking around every corner, and get back home. When he succeeds he dares his new friend Noelle to return with him, but who and what follows them back means more trouble and more adventure.

BIGFOOT DAY, NINJA NIGHT When 12-year-old Anna skips the school fair to explore the woods with Callie, Sydney, Austin, and Natalie, they find evidence of Bigfoot. No way! It looks like his tracks are following them. But that's not the worst part. And neither is stumbling upon Bigfoot's shelter. The worst part is they get separated and now they can't find Callie or the path that leads back to the school.

In the second story Luke and his brother, Nick, go on a boys only camping trip, but things get weird and scary very quickly. Is there a ninja in the woods with them? Mysterious things happen as day turns into night.

THE TUNNEL SERIES 12-year-old Nick escapes from a reformatory but gets side-tracked traveling through multiple tunnels, each with a strange destination. He must find his way home despite barriers like invisibility. When he teams up with Samantha they begin to uncover the secret to all the tunnels.

Made in the USA
Coppell, TX
18 November 2020